TRANSACTIONS

OF THE

AMERICAN PHILOSOPHICAL SOCIETY

HELD AT PHILADELPHIA
FOR PROMOTING USEFUL KNOWLEDGE

NEW SERIES—VOLUME 55, PART 2
1965

THE ENGLISH PRESBYTERIANS AND THE STUART RESTORATION, 1648–1663

GEORGE R. ABERNATHY, JR.

*Associate Professor of History, University of North Carolina
at Charlotte*

THE AMERICAN PHILOSOPHICAL SOCIETY
INDEPENDENCE SQUARE
PHILADELPHIA

MAY, 1965

PUBLICATIONS

OF

The American Philosophical Society

The publications of the American Philosophical Society consist of PROCEEDINGS, TRANSACTIONS, MEMOIRS, and YEAR BOOK.

THE PROCEEDINGS contains papers which have been read before the Society in addition to other papers which have been accepted for publication by the Committee on Publications. In accordance with the present policy one volume is issued each year, consisting of six bimonthly numbers, and the price is $5.00 net per volume.

THE TRANSACTIONS, the oldest scholarly journal in America, was started in 1769 and is quarto size. In accordance with the present policy each annual volume is a collection of monographs, each issued as a part. The annual subscription price is $6.00 net per volume; for both the PROCEEDINGS and the TRANSACTIONS $10.00. Individual copies of the TRANSACTIONS are offered for sale. This issue is priced at $2.50.

Each volume of the MEMOIRS is published as a book. The titles cover the various fields of learning; most of the recent volumes have been historical. The price of each volume is determined by its size and character.

The YEAR BOOK is of considerable interest to scholars because of the reports on grants for research and to libraries for this reason and because of the section dealing with the acquisitions of the Library. In addition it contains the Charter and Laws, and lists of present and former members, and reports of committees and meetings. The YEAR BOOK is published about April 1 for the preceding calendar year. The price is $1.50.

An author desiring to submit a manuscript for publication should send it to the Editor, George W. Corner, American Philosophical Society, 104 South Fifth Street, Philadelphia, Pa., 19106.

TRANSACTIONS

OF THE

AMERICAN PHILOSOPHICAL SOCIETY

HELD AT PHILADELPHIA
FOR PROMOTING USEFUL KNOWLEDGE

NEW SERIES—VOLUME 55, PART 2
1965

THE ENGLISH PRESBYTERIANS AND THE STUART RESTORATION, 1648–1663

GEORGE R. ABERNATHY, JR.

*Associate Professor of History, University of North Carolina
at Charlotte*

THE AMERICAN PHILOSOPHICAL SOCIETY
INDEPENDENCE SQUARE
PHILADELPHIA

MAY, 1965

TO
MR. AND MRS. GEORGE ROSS ABERNATHY

PREFACE

Some years ago the late Professor Godfrey Davies suggested as a dissertation topic a study of English Presbyterian thought in the age of Oliver Cromwell and Charles II. Research on Presbyterian pamphleteers and the Stuart Restoration soon revealed poor documentation, numerous inaccuracies, omissions, and a mixture of fact and fiction in the standard accounts of the Presbyterian program from late 1648 to mid-1663. New and unused materials, or improperly used materials, pointed to new conclusions about the period of Cromwell and the Restoration and led to the present study, which examines English Presbyterian policy from Colonel Pride's Purge of the Long Parliament in December, 1648, until Charles II's acceptance of the Act of Uniformity of 1662. Emphasis is placed on the period from May, 1659, when the Cromwellian order collapsed, to April, 1663, when Charles II abandoned his plan for relaxation of the Act of Uniformity. An attempt is made to trace the evolution of Presbyterian thought and action, to evaluate the influence of the Presbyterians on the Stuart Restoration, and to explain the failure of the Presbyterians to obtain adoption of their program.

English Presbyterianism varied so much from individual to individual that it defies precise and universal definition. It differed from Laudian Anglicanism in that it leaned more toward Calvinistic theology and less toward the prelatical government which the Church of England had inherited from Rome. In a sense it was the residuum of an older Puritanism, from which the Independents of various kinds had departed for more radical courses. In 1640 the position of the English Presbyterians fell, with some exceptions, between that of the Laudian Anglicans and that of the Scottish Presbyterians. Through the influence of the Scottish divines and as a condition of Scottish military assistance, the Presbyterian members of Long Parliament and the Westminster Assembly of Divines adopted a modified Scottish doctrine and government, concerning which the English Presbyterians were divided from the first.

Further study of English Presbyterianism will, I think, reveal that most of the English Presbyterians were actually closer to the majority of the Anglicans than to the Scottish Presbyterians and that there was not much more unity among the English Presbyterians prior to 1648 than there was in 1660. I am also convinced that earlier students of political thought have exaggerated the demand for popular and parliamentary sovereignty voiced by English Presbyterians prior to 1649 and that they have thereby confused the history of a period that offers natural confusion in abundance. Historians of the period have, I think, tended to overestimate the number of true Presbyterians, both clerical and lay, and also to forget the circumstances under which they advanced their thoughts and projects.

To Professor Frank Holloway of Sam Houston State College I am indebted for my first real exposure to political theory, and to Professor Emeritus Milton R. Gutsch of the University of Texas for my introduction to Stuart history. Although I never had the privilege of knowing Professor Godfrey Davies personally, I bear a heavy debt to him and the fine tradition which he kept alive, and also to Mr. R. C. Latham and the late Professor R. H. Tawney, whose seminars at the Institute of Historical Research, London, provided me with countless and treasured things.

Many persons have helped to point me toward the raw materials of this study. Special thanks are extended to Professor Caroline Robbins of Bryn Mawr College for permitting me to use certain materials in her possession and for referring me to others and also for making available on several occasions her insight and wealth of knowledge of the Stuart period. Dr. Geoffrey Nuttall, Trustee of Dr. Williams' Library, provided advice and information on the Baxter manuscripts. Appreciation is likewise due to numerous staff members of the Public Record Office, the British Museum, Dr. Williams' Library, the Bodleian Library, the University of Texas, and the Henry E. Huntington Library and Art Gallery.

Several persons have generously provided me with their knowledge on various points. Of these, I must mention Dr. Peter Collinson of King's College, London, Professor Paul Hardacre of Vanderbilt, Professor Richard Schlatter of Rutgers, Professor Thomas G. Barnes of the University of California at Berkeley, and Professor David Underdown of Virginia.

Especial appreciation is due Professor J. Harry Bennett, Jr., of the University of Texas for advice, encouragement, assistance, and friendship far in excess of my ability to repay. It was under his supervision that the original version of this work was executed and presented to the Graduate School of the University of Texas.

Portions of this work have appeared in *The Journal of Ecclesiastical History* (11: pp. 53–73) and *The Huntington Library Quarterly* (24: pp. 215–231), and I am grateful to the editors for permitting inclusion of that material in this volume. Financial assistance has been rendered at various times by the University of Texas, the Fulbright Program, the Henry E. Huntington Library and Art Gallery, and the American Philosophical Society.

GEORGE R. ABERNATHY, JR.

THE ENGLISH PRESBYTERIANS AND THE STUART RESTORATION, 1648–1663

GEORGE R. ABERNATHY, JR.

CONTENTS

INTRODUCTION

When Elizabeth I ascended the throne of England in 1558 there was but a faint whisper of Calvinism present in her realm. Whisper became general chatter on the return of the Marian exiles from Frankfort, Geneva, and elsewhere, and in a short time the English Calvinists were corresponding and conversing with the Scottish Calvinists beyond the Tweed. Within the first year of their return from exile the English Calvinists, usually styled Puritans, presented a serious challenge to those who were already engaged in restoring Edward VI's revision of his father's Church of England. After suffering defeat by a narrow margin in the convocation and by a larger margin in the parliament, the Elizabethan Puritans went several ways. Some went into total separation from the Established Church of England. Some adopted a policy of incomplete conformity. Some reluctantly conformed in full but continued to labor for further reform in the direction of primitive purity. Most, if not all, of the total separatists desired local or congregational polity. Among the partial and reluctant conformists were persons who leaned toward either the Congregational or Presbyterian position on theology, service, and polity. Until the time of Charles I and William Laud most of the Presbyterians normally found some door of the Church of England open to partial conformity or to furtive nonconformity. The differences between the Congregationalists and the Presbyterians were subtle at first and did not cause alarm for either group so long as each group solicited the assistance of the other in a seemingly common battle against surviving or reviving Romanism within the Church of England.

In the second decade of Elizabeth's reign some of the Calvinistic Puritans advocated officially and implemented unofficially a plan for church government along the Genevan lines. In accordance with the Scottish experience and the genius of John Knox, the English Presbyterians broadened the Geneva plan so as to make it fit a national, rather than a local, need. The theorist of the Elizabethan Presbyterians was Thomas Cartwright who, together with his associates, was silenced within a decade. By 1593 Elizabethan Presbyterianism had been driven into silence and general, though reluctant, conformity. In a milder form it reappeared before James I at the Hampton Court Conference where it was again denounced by the bishops and rejected by the king. For the better part of three decades the Puritans of all sorts had to content themselves with various evasive practices and with guarded criticism of the Church of England as reconstructed by Elizabeth and as administered by William Laud and Charles I.

Cartwright's scheme for church government was little mentioned between 1593 and 1641. By the end of 1641 the clamor for the Genevan type of church polity rose to new and greater heights than in the days of Elizabeth. Even before 1641 the Puritans, both lay and clerical, had been aroused from their near conformity to almost general nonconformity. A number of the protesters had suffered, were suffering, or were to suffer both financial and physical penalties at the hands of Charles I and Laud. With each such punishment the victim and his friends and associates became more embittered against the existing order in both church and state and rapidly moved to positions which they had not anticipated assuming. Among the religious protesters the Presbyterians were the most numerous and the most important, but unaided by the Congregationalists and others the Presbyterians could not have created the stir they did.

Also running in an uneven line from Elizabeth to Charles I was political dissent which came to be labeled Presbyterian by 1643 and Presbyterian and Independent by 1648. As shall be seen in due course, these political labels were hardly appropriate or descriptive, but tradition compels their continued use. It is certainly true that many having political and personal grievances against the governments of Elizabeth I, James I, and Charles I were supporters of those clergymen who accepted or leaned toward either Presbyterianism or some other school of nonconformity or separatism, but many more, for reasons of an exceedingly complex nature, shared nothing more than an outgroup relationship with the Presbyterians or religious

Independents, though events soon united distinct elements into temporary, artifical compounds, which separated as soon as the uniting force was removed.

Just as the protest against government in church and state reached dangerous proportions in England, Charles I and his advisers in church and state drove the Scottish Calvinists into a state of rebellion which, in turn, forced Charles to open the halls of parliament and convocation to dissenters from the established order in church and state. Then came news that Ireland was in a state of rebellion against foreign and Protestant rule. Control of the army proved to be the spark required to ignite the fires of revolution in England. By the middle of 1642 revolution by legislation and impeachment had turned into revolution by arms. In order to obtain armed assistance from the Scots, the English Presbyterians and others in and out of parliament sold their independence on religious policy to the Scots who came to London with their Covenant and with a detailed set of plans for the erection of a Genevan church of the Scottish type in England. Step by step the Long Parliament and the Westminster Assembly of Divines were persuaded to adopt a modified version of the Presbyterian Church of Scotland. By the end of 1648 the official church in England was Presbyterian and episcopacy of all allegiances was illegal.

During the same seven years the Long Parliament adopted a political and constitutional program which by tradition is labeled Presbyterian. The Presbyterian plan for both church and state called for the preservation of monarchy and other historic institutions. In practice and usually in theory the Presbyterian program called for less royal authority and more popular participation in the formulation and implementation of public policy. Just as the Presbyterians disagreed with the king and his party on the degree of popular participation so they disagreed with those called Independents on the value of monarchy and aristocracy and on the degree of popular participation. There was some difference of opinion and practice on socio-economic matters. At least there were few Presbyterians who were prepared to accompany the left wing of the Independents along the road that seemed to lead toward a leveling of purses and ranks. With a membership that was in its majority more conservative on socio-economic, political, and religious issues than the religious and political Independents, the Long Parliament and the Westminster Assembly of Divines incurred the displeasure of the Independents who counted among their number men of various socio-economic, political, and religious positions, though most were congregationalist on church polity and Calvinistic on most points of theology. The differences between the conservative and radical elements of the Parliamentary Party are easily traced back to the days of Elizabeth, but they caused little friction prior to 1643 and the Westminster Assembly

of Divines and the serious negotiations with Charles I for a compromise between the Parliamentary and Royalist programs for church and state.

The clash over religious policy became obvious when the Independents within the Westminster Assembly of Divines filed their minority opinion against the Scottish program. The political break between the Presbyterian and Independent factions became apparent to all as soon as the Long Parliament began discussing its plans for a negotiated settlement with Charles I. The Presbyterians perceived dangers on the horizon the day Coronet Joyce seized possession of Charles I. The dangers were fully realized the day Colonel Pride used the power of his sword to purge the Long Parliament of its more obvious Presbyterians. These two events were soon followed by Oliver Cromwell's open alliance with the Independents and by his preemption of authority. By practice, and perhaps by conviction, Oliver Cromwell leaned toward the Independent position on the state and toward the Congregational position on church polity and theology. The conservative or traditionalist strain in Cromwell's personality was at all times tempered by his inability to disband and silence the unpaid freemen who filled the ranks of the New Model Army and its successors and by his awareness of the growing influence and number of the Independent pulpits. With the army's triumph over civil authority, the execution of Charles I, and the rise of Oliver Cromwell, the Presbyterian dream of a vastly modified but national church and of a sharply moderated monarchy exploded into fragments which repeatedly eluded all attempts at repair.

What follows is an attempt to reach a better understanding of the dreams and activities of the lay and clerical Presbyterians from Colonel Pride's Purge in December, 1648, when the Presbyterians fell from power, until the middle of 1663 when the restored Charles II submitted to the wishes of the Cavalier Parliament.

I. THE PRESBYTERIAN CHURCH AND THE CROMWELLIAN STATE

From December, 1648, when Colonel Pride purged the Long Parliament of its more obvious Presbyterians, until the abdication of Richard Cromwell in May, 1659, the English Presbyterians, or those so-called, had to reckon with the absolute and effective rule of Oliver and Richard Cromwell. The Presbyterian clergy were increasingly upset by the fact that the religious Independents prevailed on Oliver Cromwell to withdraw all support from the partially established Presbyterian system and to grant almost universal toleration. The religious state was soon atomized. The Presbyterians, who insisted on order, unity, and discipline, were increasingly disturbed by what they saw. For nine years, 1650 to 1659, the leading Presbyterian ministers attempted to overcome the lack of discipline and organization which resulted from the Cromwellian religious policy. Some fought on for the Solemn League and Covenant; others worked for union of the major groups within a single system. Their efforts for unity and ecclesiastical discipline ended, except at the local level, in failure. The Presbyterian experiences during the Cromwellian period proved the futility of attempting any understanding with the religious Independents, but the activities of the moderate Anglicans gave some Presbyterians reason to hope for a future reconciliation with a modified Anglican establishment.

From the moment of its legal adoption in England, Presbyterianism was at all times at a numerical disadvantage, and some of its tenets never took root, even among the Presbyterian zealots. According to Richard Baxter of Kidderminster, Worcestershire, the institution of presbytery was such "a stranger" to England that most of those called Presbyterians were opposed to the

Jus Divinum of Lay Elders, and for the moderate Primitive Episcopacy, and for a narrow Congregational or Parochial Extent of ordinary Churches, and for an accommodation of all Parties, in order to Concord. . . .[1]

Baxter's statement seems correct in its essentials. In 1648 the Presbyterians in the Long Parliament were prepared to sacrifice Presbyterianism for Charles I.[2] Sir Edward Hyde, later Earl of Clarendon, reached the same conclusion as early as 1649 and never changed his thinking.[3]

However, at the time of Oliver Cromwell's *coup d'etat* of December, 1648, the Long Parliament had authorized the establishment of a Presbyterian system, and the implementing authorities had executed the laws in some parts of England. Eighteen districts erected some degree of classical presbytery, but only seven provinces (Essex, Lancashire, London, Shropshire, Somerset, Suffolk, and Surrey) ever established anything approaching a complete system. Lancashire and London were the only provinces to enforce the full Presbyterian system and discipline for any length of time. Many provinces were confronted with a situation similar to that in Somerset where the commissioners desired nine classes but reported that, "by reason of the scarcity of fitting ministers and elders to

constitute so many classes, we have been necessitated to reduce them for the present into 4." [4]

What was the numerical position of Presbyterianism in England? No estimate can be made of the number of Presbyterian laymen, but it is possible to estimate the number of Presbyterian clergy. The Presbyterian *Testimonies* of 1648 contained 900 clerical signatures; undoubtedly there were Presbyterian clergy who failed to subscribe. Hertford and Suffolk, for example, presented similar declarations in 1646, but did not do so in 1648.[5] An estimate of 1,000 to 1,200 Presbyterian clergy should be acceptably close to the mark. In any event, the clergy were not numerous enough to staff a national church or to gain an easy victory over either the Independents or the Anglicans. This fact influenced many to consider union with other groups. In London and Lancashire, where the Presbyterians were numerous, there was a reluctance to depart from the Solemn League and Covenant.

Inadequate numerical support accounted for part of the Presbyterian difficulties and the rapid decay of the partially established system. The Presbyterians gained many solid adherents during the course of the Westminster Assembly debates and continued to do so throughout the Interregnum, but they lost many supporters along the way. It is also extremely doubtful whether the support for the Presbyterian clergy reached deep into the ranks of the laity. Certain prominent nobility and gentry spoke warmly for the divine efficacy of presbyteries, but these conspicious individuals failed to become lay elders. The most conclusive of evidence indicates that these champions, both lay and clerical, were too few in number ever to maintain the Presbyterian system. W. A. Shaw, after an extensive examination of the surviving Presbyterian records, concluded that

the universal record of the decay of the parish eldership can only be read as a sure sign at once of the impotence of presbytery, and of the indifference, or dislike, of the great bulk of the laity.[6]

In London and Lancashire, where the Presbyterian clergy were numerous, the classical system survived until 1659, but in other areas the system was never established or collapsed soon after 1648.

Another important factor in the decay of the presbyteries was the loss of government support after 1648. Immediately following his *coup d'etat* Cromwell withdrew all government support from the presbyteries which had been established, and the Rump Parliament, with encouragement from the Independents, adopted

---

[1] Richard Baxter, *Reliquiae Baxterianae: Or, Mr. Richard Baxter's Narrative of the Most Memorable Passages of His Life and Times,* ed. Matthew Sylvester (London, 1696), Pt. II: p. 145; hereafter cited as *Reliquiae Baxterianae.* A modern edition of this work is among the more pressing needs of students of English dissent. The original editor saw fit to suppress certain passages, and to change others, in the manuscript left by Baxter, who had already "forgotten" to mention many events.

[2] William A. Shaw, *A History of the English Church during the Civil Wars and under the Commonwealth, 1640–1660* (2 v., London, 1900) 2: p. 73; hereafter cited as *History of the English Church.*

[3] Samuel R. Gardiner, "Draft by Sir Edward Hyde of a Declaration To Be Issued by Charles II in 1649," *English Historical Review* 8 (1893): pp. 304–305.

[4] Shaw, *History of the English Church* 2: p. 413; see 2, Appendix III (*b*), for a list of the classical organizations.

[5] Based on the *Testimonies* of 1648 as printed by A. G. Matthews, *Calamy Revised, Being a Revision of Edmund Calamy's Account of the Ministers and Others Ejected and Silenced, 1660–2* (Oxford, 1934), pp. 553–558; hereafter cited as *Calamy Revised.*

[6] Shaw, *History of the English Church* 2: p. 100.

a policy of toleration, which was maintained through-out the Cromwellian period. The Rump Parliament began a lengthy consideration of toleration not long after Pride's Purge and legislated in behalf of dissent on September 27, 1650.[7] For the next eighteen months the Rump practically ignored religious issues. On February 11, 1652, the Rump Parliament returned to the subject of religion. The occasion was the sub-mission of a report by the Committee for the Propa-gation of the Gospel.[8] This Committee, with one or two exceptions, was composed of Independents. Its report contained thirteen propositions which recom-mended conformity to certain fundamental principles of religion and a liberal degree of toleration on other points. The ejection of the Rump on April 20, 1653, left the religious problems unsolved, and the Presby-terian system still legally intact.[9]

Meanwhile, the Presbyterians, fearing an attack and disliking the Independents, publicly defended their system against Cromwell and the Independents. When the fatal attack failed to develop, the Presbyterians, or at least some of them, gave consideration to feeble overtures from Cromwell and some Independents for a union, accommodation, association, or comprehension scheme. The initial reaction of the Presbyterians to Cromwell's seizure of power took the form of *Testi-monies*, which were published in 1648 and 1649, in which they argued that "the Presbyteriall Government is that Government which is most agreeable to the minde of Jesus Christ, revealed in Scripture," and lamented England's backwardness to embrace and forwardness to oppose Presbyterian government. They also declared their continued allegiance to the Solemn League and Covenant and denounced general toleration.[10] Published defenses of Presbyterianism, or attacks on Independency, were especially numerous through 1650 but diminished until the political and religious disturbances of 1658 and 1659 stimulated a revival of pamphlet warfare.[11]

In the intervening years, beginning in 1650 and ending in 1659, a growing number of Presbyterians turned their attention to the hopes generated by some Independents and Anglicans for the establishment of a broad national church and limited rather than general toleration. When a national church eluded their grasp

some Presbyterians joined with Independents and Anglicans in forming local associations of a voluntary nature.

As early as 1647, John Dury, a Congregationalist of sorts who conformed after the Restoration, proposed a treaty between the Independents and the Presbyter-ians. Dury's proposal called for three or four of each party to work out an accommodation on the basis of "a reconcilement" or "forbearance of inoffensive differ-ences." Some months later the scheme was endorsed by Joseph Caryl, a Congregationalist.[12] Dury was probably behind Cromwell's invitation of January, 1649, to the leading Presbyterian clergy of London to a conference with him and his officers on religion. The London Presbyterians rejected and denounced Crom-well's invitation in January,[13] but on November 2, 1649, the London Provincial Assembly, after pointing out the dangers of separatism, appealed to the Inde-pendents to "study, for the time to come, all ways of Union and Accommodation," with a promise that the Presbyterians would undertake a similar study.[14] The tangible results, if any, of these early suggestions have failed to survive the ravages of time. It is al-together possible, however, that the report of the Committee for the Propagation of the Gospel in 1652 was, in part, an outgrowth of the earlier proposals.

By 1652 Richard Baxter of Kidderminster, a Presby-terian clergyman of moderate convictions, had assumed the leadership of those Presbyterians actively working for some understanding among the several religious factions. Baxter was the strongest and most active proponent of union, both before and after the Restor-ation, and was the author of the first concrete plan for consolidation. It should be pointed out, however, that Baxter borrowed heavily from men like John Dury and Richard Vines, with whom he carried on regular correspondence. W. A. Shaw and Frederick J. Po-wicke, Baxter's biographer, presented Baxter's efforts as though they concerned only his famous Worcester-shire Association.[15] Historians, including Shaw and Powicke, have been misled about Baxter's activities and aims by too much reliance on his autobiography which was edited in such a way as to place Baxter and the Presbyterians in the best possible light.

According to the autobiography, Baxter began his consultations with others about "a year and a half"

[7] *Commons Journals* 6: p. 470.

[8] *Ibid.* 7: p. 258.

[9] See Shaw, *History of the English Church* 2: pp. 74–97, for detailed coverage.

[10] Matthews, *Calamy Revised*, pp. 553–558.

[11] [London Provincial Assembly], *A Serious and Faithfull Representation of the Judgements of Ministers of the Gospel within the Province of London . . . .* (London, 1649); [London Provincial Assembly], *A Vindication of the Presbyteriall-Gov-ernment, and Ministry . . . .* (London, 1650); [London Provin-cial Assembly], *Jus Divinum Ministerii Evangelici . . . .* (Lon-don, 1654); [London Provincial Assembly], *Jus Divinum Regiminis Ecclesiastici . . . .* (London, 1654); and John Col-lings, *Vindiciae Ministerii Evangelici . . . .* (London, 1651), are representative of the Presbyterian defenses.

[12] John Dury, *A Peace-Maker without Partiality and Hypoc-risie. Or the Gospel-way to make up the present breaches of Brotherhood, and heale the divisions . . . .* (London, 1648), pp. 10 and 115.

[13] [London Provincial Assembly], *A Serious and Faithful Representation of the Judgements of Ministers of the Gospel within the Province of London . . . .*, p. 1.

[14] [London Provincial Assembly], *A Vindication of the Pres-byteriall-Government, and Ministry . . . .*, pp. 12–13.

[15] Shaw, *History of the English Church* 2: pp. 152–163; Frederick J. Powicke, *A Life of the Reverend Richard Baxter, 1615–1691* (London, 1924), pp. 163–167; hereafter cited as *Richard Baxter*.

prior to October, 1653.[16] The truth is that Baxter drafted his first plan for national union some time prior to July 21, 1650, when Robert Abbott wrote Baxter a letter of appreciation for being consulted about such a plan.[17] Baxter sent the basic outline of the plan to John Dury, who was then a member of the Committee for the Propagation of the Gospel and an adviser to Cromwell, on May 9, 1652. Baxter requested Dury "to expound to people in Power, that they will speedily choose (or else cause the several parties to choose) some few men (4 or 5) of each of the differing parties (Episcopal, Presbyterian, Independent & Erastian)" to discuss their differences and to prepare a commonly acceptable set of fundamental principles on religion, worship, and discipline. Baxter predicted that such an agreement "would heale all Politicall quarrells." It is worth noting that he specifically recommended that the Anglicans be represented by Archbishop James Usher, Bishop Joseph Hall, Bishop Ralph Brownrigge, and Bishop Thomas Morton, the Presbyterians by Stephen Marshall and Richard Vines, and the Independents by Joseph Symonds and William Greenhill.[18] Baxter's list represents a breadth seldom found in the religious negotiations of the period and indicates his latitudinarian position.

Reduced to its essentials, Baxter's plan called for the formation of regional associations not dissimilar to the Presbyterian assemblies of the Elizabethan period, the adoption of broad doctrinal principles and service books, and the establishment of a moderate amount of civil supervision. This scheme differed markedly from the county association proposal by the inclusion of centralized supervision in the first but not in the second.[19] Baxter's thinking was remarkably close to that of Archbishop Usher, and his scheme for national union much resembled Usher's for reducing episcopacy.[19a]

Baxter's proposal met with no immediate response and then with some disfavor. Dury, an advocate of union among all the Protestant churches of Europe, was in Sweden during part of 1652 and did not reply to Baxter's letter until October 29, 1652:

When you wrote yours, there was a Committee afoot for the propagating of the Gospel, & before my journey into Sweden I did joyne with others to offer some propositions to that Committee; now I find the same Committee is revived, & it is now seasonable to agitat something about this subject in a public way. . . .

Dury was in agreement with the general principles of Baxter's plan, which he submitted to the Committee, and thus to Cromwell, but Dury was reluctant to hold any unauthorized meetings of the London clergy. Cromwell, who was a member of the Committee, submitted something similar to Baxter's plan, but he wished to include "all such as are counted Godly" within the proposed national church. Dury agreed with Baxter that initial membership should be limited to the Episcopal, Presbyterian, Independent, and Erastian groups. Time was to prove that the Independents and the Presbyterians could not agree on the limits and powers of a state church.

An essential point on which Dury and Cromwell disagreed with Baxter was the manner in which the union should be effected. To Baxter's suggestion that the clergy should initiate and direct the project through representatives, Dury and Cromwell replied that "the directive power" should rest with the Rump Parliament.[20] Baxter refused to substitute a secular assembly for a clerical body,[21] and was never completely converted from his original position.

Having received some indication that further efforts would not be out of order, Baxter sought support for his plan from the inhabitants of Worcestershire and from two members of parliament, Colonel John Bridges and Thomas Foley. On December 22, 1652, Bridges and Foley presented the Rump Parliament with a petition, allegedly signed by more than six thousand, from Worcestershire. The petitioners requested the government to continue the "Able, Godly, Faithful Ministry," to insure that the ministry did not become ignorant, hungry, or beggarly, to provide a sufficient ministry, and to support the universities. Such demands were not the exclusive property of the Presbyterians, but they were included in most Presbyterian petitions and pamphlets. In their final section the petitioners paraphrased Baxter's proposals to John Dury:

because our sad divisions in matter of Religion, especially about Church-Government, have been such a hinderance to

[16] Baxter, *Reliquiae Baxterianae*, Pt. II: p. 165.

[17] Robert Abbott to Richard Baxter, July 21, 1650, Dr. Williams' Library, Baxter MSS, Letters V, No. 254; subsequent references to Baxter MSS will not contain Dr. Williams' Library in the note.

[18] Richard Baxter to John Dury, May 9, 1652, *ibid.*, VI, No. 4/2.

[19] Baxter, *Reliquiae Baxterianae*, Pt. II: pp. 194–197; a later and slightly different version was published by Baxter in *Humble Advice* . . . (London, 1655), which resulted from his sermon before parliament on December 24, 1654. In none of his works appear full dates and circumstances.

[19a] Usher's plan was first offered in 1641, when various reform schemes were being considered by the Long Parliament. Imperfect and unauthorized versions appeared in print between 1642 and 1656, when an authorized version was edited by Dr. Nicholas Bernard. The main principle of Usher's plan was the reduction of clerical power at every level to one of presidency or superintendency. A bishop would be assisted and advised at regular and frequent intervals by suffragans and by the parish clergy. A parish clergyman would be assisted and advised by the churchwardens and sidesmen. Shaw, *History of the English Church*

2: pp. 69–71; Baxter, *Reliquiae Baxterianae*, Pt. I: pp. 206, 238–240.

[20] John Dury to Richard Baxter, October 29, 1652, Baxter MSS, Letters VI, No. 3/6.

[21] Richard Baxter to John Dury, November 20, 1652, *ibid.*, VI, No. 4/1.

the propagation of the Gospel, [we request] that you will be pleased speedily to imploy your utmost wisdom and power for the healing of them: And to that end would call together some of the most godly, prudent, peaceable Divines of each party, that differs in points of Church-Government, and lay upon them your Commands and Adjuration, that they cease not amicable consulting and seeking God, till they have found out a meet way for accommodation and unity, and acquainted you therewith.

Anticipating the possibility of failure to discover terms for "accommodation and unity," the petitioners requested the government to consult with those divines who were "least addicted to parties" and on the basis of these consultations to "recommend at least to the people, so much of Church-Order and Government, as you finde to be clearly required by Jesus Christ, and vouchsafe it your publique Countenance and Encouragement, though you scruple on enforcement." [22] By this means Baxter placed his scheme before the Rump Parliament. When the petition drew fire from the enemy, Baxter dashed off a pamphlet in its defense.[23] Evidence of a direct connection between the Worcestershire petition of 1652 and the conference of 1654 does not seem to exist, but there is no reason to exclude the possibility that the parliament of 1654 borrowed from the petition or Baxter's scheme when it convened a meeting of ministers to consider religion.

In spite of the political appeal to the Rump Parliament and an occasional assist from some clergymen, support for Baxter's ideas was slow in appearing. Dury finally wrote Baxter in January, 1653, that he had purposely deferred action until he "should see what the course would be of the revived Committee for propagating the Gospel." The results had proved discouraging, for, as Dury reported,

after several debates amongst themselves wherein they are not come to any material conclusion what to do: so that for ought that I can learne they are in the darke as yet, what they should intend to doe, where they should beginne & how they should proceed.

Dury, probably speaking for his Congregational friends and Cromwell, still insisted that any plan for union or comprehension must have parliamentary approval:

so that they themselves should have a hand in making & contriving the termes of the agreement & in joining their assent thereunto for I think it not an agreement justly ratifiable by the Parliament, except the Godly Parliament-men deputed to the worke concurre judiciously with the other Godly in the termes of the Agreement; as for the inforcing of the Conclusions of the Assembly by the powers of the Magistrate upon dissenters; it never came in my thought that any such power should be given to [magistrates], or that any assembly should bee called upon whose

Conclusions all men should bee obliged to yeeld by force, if they should not do it willingly.[24]

Here was clearly expressed the difference between the Independents and most Presbyterians on the important question of coercive power of the civil government in the religious sphere, and this difference was to trouble every effort to unite the two parties.[25]

Growing tired of the delays in London and fearing that his plan for national union was doomed to failure, Baxter attempted to effect the same thing through the indirect means of county associations. In a letter of February 5, 1653, to Dury, Baxter presented his famous plan for county associations of a voluntary nature. In the previous September, more than two years after he had started to work on national union, Baxter held a meeting of Worcestershire ministers. At Baxter's suggestion, the ministers agreed to adopt his plan for union and cooperation among themselves. They further agreed to request Dury "to get 4 or 5 divines of each party" in London to form a voluntary association as an example for the entire nation. This was nothing more than an indirect and unofficial means of effecting the national union already proposed by Baxter. Baxter added a personal request to Dury that his letter and its enclosures be shown to Archbishop Usher in the interest of peace with "our brethren of the Episcopall judgment." [26] There is no evidence that the various groups in London ever gave serious consideration to Baxter's letter and the papers of the Worcestershire Association.

Dury had little success in prosecuting Baxter's two plans. He contacted Usher, and he attempted to rally lay support through Baxter's friend Colonel John Bridges.[27] Yet the months passed by with few encouraging developments. Finally, on April 9, 1653, Dury informed Baxter that he had difficulty getting the brethren "to meet so often, as was requisite to engage them in a joynt prosecution of our designe."

Dury, in preparation for a forthcoming trip to Sweden, placed the project and Baxter's papers in the hands of George Griffiths, Congregational minister of the Charterhouse in London. Dury's reasons for selecting Griffiths provide much insight into the problems which confronted the movement for union. Griffiths was described as

a young man of Excellent spirit, and good abilities, zealous for the arme of warre, no wayes engaged in any Party; and

[22] [Worcestershire], The Humble Petition of Many Thousands, Gentlemen, Freeholders, and Others, of the County of Worcester . . . (London, 1652).

[23] [Richard Baxter], The Worcester-Shire Petition . . . Defended . . . (London, 1653).

[24] John Dury to Richard Baxter, January 6, 1653, Baxter MSS, Letters VI, No. 3/1.

[25] See Richard Vines, Obedience to Magistrates, Both Supreme and Subordinate . . . (London, 1656), for a representative statement of the Presbyterian view on civil magistrates.

[26] Richard Baxter to John Dury, February 5, 1653, Baxter MSS, Letters VI, No. 6; the plan can be found in Baxter, Reliquiae Baxterianae, Pt. II: pp. 146–150, and in Baxter, Christian Concord . . . (London, 1653).

[27] John Dury to Richard Baxter, February 22, 1653, Baxter MSS, Letters VI, No. 3/2.

well accepted of by all the orthodoxee, and I chose him rather then any one of greater age because I am persuaded his zeale will carry him on to act more freely then perhaps some others that are counted leading men would doe. Secondly because I find that most of those that are counted leading men are commonly byassed, with some particular collaterall businesses, and affection: which clodge the freedome of their spirit in carrying on a worke of this kind; and thirdly Christs saying that new wine must be put into new Bottles; may give us some direction in this matter; to carry it on prudently; namely by making use of those that are not the savour of any prejudice, and therefore are fittest to carry on a new worke; for such as have drawn blood in the controversies of the times (though otherwise Godly men) I find are swayed with preengagements, and cannot take off their thoughts reddily from jalousies, and partiall designements in the manner of their proceeding about necessary duties.

Clearly, Dury found it difficult to persuade the leading members of the several parties to forget old animosities and commitments long enough to give serious consideration to any plan for peaceful union. Although Dury never openly accused the government of lukewarmness toward Baxter's proposals, he obviously had difficulty in securing anything more than nominal support from Cromwell and the leading politicans. All Dury had accomplished by April, 1653, was to acquaint some of the London ministers with the principles of Baxter's proposals.[28]

Slight progress was made during the summer of 1653. As late as October 27, 1653, Dury had to report that he had not been able to obtain a single meeting of all the London ministers, though

true it is that some have severall times engaged to meet about it, but they never all came together, & such as came not being willing to act without those that were absent the endevours have been ineffectual. . . .

Dury did feel, however, that some progress was being made, for he wrote that the

worke & thoughts of union amongst Brethren are not wholly laid aside: but many in a privat way are drawn forth in their affections to mind them; & some in public place of chief authoritie are setting them on upon the spirits of such as are counted the pillars of the parties dissenting; & I hope that God hath his hand in the worke; and that the orthodox who do joyne in the ordinances of Christ, & stand for a Gospell Ministerie will see it necessary for them to professe their unity in that whereunto they have attained to walke by one rule, & not to breake all Communion for their difference in lesser matters.[29]

The reference to "some in public place of chief authoritie" suggests that Cromwell and his circle were at last giving serious thought to the religious disunity which was disturbing civil affairs.

The persistence of Baxter and Dury finally bore fruit. In February, 1654, Dury informed Baxter

that he had just held a meeting of the London ministers for the purpose of considering accommodation among them. The ministers chose a committee of ten, five Presbyterians and five Independents, with Dury as chairman, to make a study of the problems involved in the proposal for unity.[30]

The last news of Dury's committee and of Baxter's proposals is contained in Dury's letter of April 2, 1654. About to depart for the continent again, Dury was highly hopeful of success. He told Baxter that "wee are at home in a farre way at composing differences amongst ourselves." The government was at last encouraging the ministers to reconcile their differences, and the committee of five Presbyterians and five Independents had "mett & set themselves in a course to proceed." [31]

One explanation, and it may be the only one, for the disappearance of Dury's committee is that Cromwell and the parliament of 1654 decided to bring the discussions under official sponsorship. Cromwell had dissolved the Rump Parliament in 1653 before it could abolish the tithe system. He had served on the Committee for the Propagation of the Gospel and had given some support to the unification efforts.[32] After a short experiment with the Barebones or Nominated Parliament of 1653, Cromwell called for an elected parliament in 1654.

The parliament of 1654, apparently with Cromwell's consent, immediately undertook an examination of those articles of the Instrument of Government dealing with religion. This led to an attempt to restore peace and unity and to a merger of Dury's committee and Baxter's plans with those of the government. Following debates in a grand committee from October 26 to November 1, a subcommittee was appointed to consult with Cromwell about the fundamentals of religion. This was an obvious step toward a national establishment and one which Baxter had long advocated. Each member of the subcommittee named a minister to assist in drafting a report for the grand committee's consideration.[33] According to the Venetian minister, Lorenzo Paulucci, the parliament's purpose was "to make some regulations . . . reducing the numerous sects . . . to a single one." [34] Only one Anglican was invited to serve, however,. Lord Broghill, a Presbyterian member of the subcommittee and

---

[28] John Dury to Richard Baxter, April 9, 1653, *ibid.*, VI, No. 3/3.

[29] John Dury to Richard Baxter, October 27, 1653, *ibid.*, VI, No. 3/4.

[30] John Dury to Richard Baxter, February 22, 1654, *ibid.*, V, No. 294.

[31] John Dury to Richard Baxter, April 2, 1654, *ibid.*, VI, No. 3/5.

[32] George Lawrence, *Peplum Olivarii* . . . (London, 1658), p. 26.

[33] Baxter, *Reliquiae Baxterianae*, Pt. II: p. 197; Powicke, *Richard Baxter*, p. 121; Shaw, *History of the English Church*, 2: p. 86; and [James Hay], *Collonel James Hays Speech to the Parliament upon the Debate concerning Toleration* . . . (n.p., 1655).

[34] Lorenzo Paulucci to Giovanni Sagredo, October 12, 1654, *Calendar of State Papers, Venetian, 1653–1654*, p. 268.

Baxter's sponsor, invited Archbishop Usher to serve, but Usher declined. Broghill then named Baxter. Baxter's colleagues were Stephen Marshall, William Reyner, Francis Cheynell, Thomas Goodwin, John Owen, Philip Nye, Sidrach Simpson, Richard Vines, and Thomas Manton; they were either Independents or Presbyterians.

The conference, which came close to meeting Baxter's ideal, proved a disappointment to Baxter and the Presbyterians. When Baxter arrived in London, he found most of the divines following the leadership of Francis Cheynell and John Owen, two Congregationalists, who had already presented the conference with a draft report. Baxter and Vines opposed the draft report, which was based on the twenty propositions adopted by the Committee for the Propagation of the Gospel in 1652, but their fellow Presbyterians, Marshall, Manton, and Jacomb, showed an inclination to support the Independents. Marshall had shown a surprising degree of latitude as early as 1652.[35] Baxter and Vines apparently tried to incorporate the Anglicans by proposing that the ministers submit the "Creed, the Lord's Prayer and Decalogue as our essentials or Fundamentals, which at least contain all that is necessary to salvation; and hath been by all the ancient Churches taken as the sum of their Religion." The Independents refused to proceed that far along the road to total latitudinarianism. They also rejected the suggestions of Baxter and Vines that ministers and civil magistrates be granted authority to censure and discipline religious offenders. In the end, the ministers submitted twenty proposals which were basically the same as those submitted by the Committee for the Propagation of the Gospel in 1652 and which were adopted by the Congregationalists at their Savoy Conference in 1658.[36] Nothing concrete resulted from the subcommittee's recommendations.

The meeting revealed the disunity among the Presbyterians and the gorge which separated them from the Independents. Some of the Presbyterians were willing to sacrifice much in order to reach an understanding with the Congregational wing of the Independents. The rigid Presbyterians, who were not represented at the conference, would not even consider union if union required desertion of the Solemn League and Covenant. Some of Baxter's supporters suspected a number of his principles.

Although he supported Baxter in 1654 and later, Vines objected to much of Baxter's plans and questioned whether Presbyterians and Independents could ever unite. At some point in 1653 Baxter sent his papers to Vines for his opinion. Vines applauded accommo-

dation as "a great and good work," which he considered likely of success between the Anglicans and the Presbyterians who were not "much distant" in doctrine and worship. The essential differences between Anglicans and Presbyterians, according to Vines, were in matters of government and ordination, and it was very unlikely that the Presbyterians would accept Baxter's plan for modified episcopacy or episcopal superintendency. Vines personally objected to the veto power which Baxter was willing to grant the bishop. He agreed with Baxter that there should not be lay elders, and thereby placed himself in opposition to the Independents, who had both clerical and lay elders. In general, Vines was pessimistic about the prospects for unity.[37] Later developments proved Vines correct on all points. Thomas Gataker wrote Baxter in the same vein as Vines. Burgess, whether Anthony or Cornelius is not clear, suspected Baxter of being an Erastian.[38]

Dissension among the Presbyterians was reflected in the opposition of other Presbyterians to Baxter's activities. William Duncombe wrote from King's College, Cambridge, that Baxter was opposed by the Arminians but that he was most opposed by the strict Calvinists and some learned doctors of the University.[39] The strongest objections to Baxter and his propositions came from the Scottish Presbyterians and their English friends who opposed any retreat from the Solemn League and Covenant and the Presbyterian system established by the Long Parliament. Robert Baillie complained to Simeon Ashe, friend and confidant of the Earl of Manchester, as follows:

I bless God you [in London] have so much as the shew of a Presbyterie and Synod. Why has not all England and Ireland so much? Why want you a General Assemblie? Why have ye no power at all to execute ecclesiastical jurisdiction? not so much as Independents, Anabaptists, or Papists have among their owne. For all of these, as we hear, are tollerate to exercise their discipline among themselves; only you Presbyterians are either restrained or not carefull to use your libertie.

Baillie and the Scottish Presbyterians never really understood the situation in England and were constantly urging the English Presbyterians to attempt politically impossible deeds. Baillie was particularly concerned about Baxter's writings and suggested that Vines and Burgess attempt to convert Baxter from his errors.[40] Ashe's reply indicates that the division between his circle and Baxter's was great, for he told Baillie that Baxter was "doubtless a godly man, though tenacious in his mistakes. Mr. Burgess and Mr. Vines dealt with him to reduce him, but could not convince him

[35] Stephen Marshall, *A Sermon Preached . . . on Easter Monday April 1652 . . .* (London, 1653).

[36] Baxter, *Reliquiae Baxterianae,* Pt. II: pp. 197–205; Baxter MSS, Treatises I, foll. 92–93; and Sir Roger L'Estrange, *L'Estrange His Apology . . .* (London, 1666), p. 124.

[37] Baxter, *Reliquiae Baxterianae,* Pt. II: p. 147.

[38] *Ibid.,* pp. 146–148.

[39] William Duncombe to Richard Baxter, September 12, 1654, Baxter MSS, Letters VI, No. 34.

[40] Robert Baillie to Simeon Ashe, December 31, 1655, *The Letters and Journals of Robert Baillie,* ed. David Laing (3 v., Edinburgh, 1842) 3: pp. 302–306.

to satisfaction." [41]   Two years later Baillie was still complaining that Baxter was harming Presbyterianism more than all the sectaries in England.[42]   It is not surprising, then, that Baxter commented that some of the "ancient Presbyterians" opposed his attempts at comprehension and association.[43]   Time and adversity would reduce the number in opposition to union, but there was still much Presbyterian resistance to compromise in 1660.

Although the proposals for unity through legislation or a clerical assembly failed of favorable reception, Baxter's Worcestershire Association was widely copied. In reality, the association was the application of the larger plan for national union on a local level, but shorn of some of its disciplinary powers.

Who joined the county associations?   To what extent were the associations successful?   The Worcestershire Association of 1653 included fifty-four ministers, several of whom were from neighboring counties.   Since the county had approximately 112 parishes and since fewer than fifty-four of these subscribed, it is apparent that the Worcestershire Association was supported by no more than one-third of the ministers.   Some of the members were not active participants.[44]   Baxter's account of the Worcestershire Association is in general agreement with the foregoing:

though we made our Terms large enough for all, Episcopal, Presbyterians and Independents, there was not one Presbyterian joyned with us that I know of, (for I know but of one in all the County . . .) nor one Independent, (though two or three honest ones said nothing against us) nor one of the New Prelatical way . . . but three or four moderate Conformists that were for the old Episcopacy; and all the rest were meer Catholicks: Men of no Faction, no siding with any Party, but owning that which was good in all, as far as they could discern it; and upon a Concord in so much, laying out themselves for the great ends of their Ministry, the Peoples Edification.[45]

When Baxter's statement and the list of subscribers are checked against the Worcestershire ejectments of 1660 to 1662, Baxter's summary acquires significance and clarity.   Of the fifty-four subscribers to the Worcestershire Association, only twenty-two were ejected after the Restoration.   Eleven of these were licensed as Presbyterians in 1672, and ten others were probably Presbyterians.   The other ejected member was an Anabaptist.   Thirteen of the fifty-four conformed either before August 24, 1662, or afterwards.   It is probable that the remaining eighteen members conformed.   Five of the twenty-two nonconformists

had sons—ten sons in all—who entered the ministry. It is of some significance that eight sons took Anglican orders; one became a Presbyterian, and one a Congregationalist.   The members of the Cambridgeshire Association fall into approximately the same percentages as the members of the Worcestershire Association.   The foregoing analysis of the Worcestershire and Cambridgeshire Associations supports Baxter's statement that the Laudians, the rigid Presbyterians, and the extreme Independents did not participate.   The county associations drew their support from the moderate Presbyterians and the moderate Anglicans, though two Laudians, Thomas Warmestry and Thomas Good, did attend the Worcestershire Association once or twice.[46]

The moderate Presbyterians in Westmorland and Cumberland found that no Independents and few Anglicans would join their association.   A small group, acting independently of Baxter and under the leadership of Richard Gilpin, a Presbyterian, established an association in Cumberland and Westmorland in 1653. This group attempted "some reconciliation at least of different judgments in matters of Church government than formerly," [47] but at its formation the Cumberland and Westmorland Association was predominantly Presbyterian, with the Independents and most of the Anglicans abstaining.[48]

Several things are obvious.   The association movement had slight numerical support, even though it possibly extended to sixteen counties.   There were few permanent defenders of comprehension on such a broad basis.   In some counties the idea was not entertained by either the clergy or the people.[49]   Many who joined the associations were Low Church Anglicans who passed from Laudian rule in 1640 to the restored Anglican government in 1662 without being removed from their churches.   Another large number should be classified as moderate Presbyterian.   Anglican cooperation with moderate Presbyterians in the associations undoubtedly led many of the moderate Presbyterians to assume that they could reach an understanding with the Anglicans.

From 1654 onward some of the Anglicans indicated a willingness to work toward religious unity on less than Laudian terms.   Baxter corresponded indirectly with Archbishop Usher as early as 1652, and in 1654 they agreed that Usher's proposals of 1641 for modified episcopacy would settle the Presbyterian and Anglican

---

[41] Simeon Ashe to Robert Baillie, [January 1656], *ibid.,* pp. 306–307.

[42] Robert Baillie to Simeon Ashe, November 29, 1658, *ibid.,* p. 391.

[43] Baxter, *Reliquiae Baxterianae,* Pt. II: p. 167.

[44] A list of the members of the Worcestershire Association is printed in Powicke, *Richard Baxter,* pp. 173–175.

[45] Baxter, *Reliquiae Baxterianae,* Pt. I: p. 97; Baxter employs Presbyterian here in its strict Scottish sense.

[46] Matthews, *Calamy Revised,* is the source used here.

[47] Cumberland and Westmorland Association, *The Agreement of the Associated Ministers and Churches of the Counties of Cumberland and Westmorland* (London, 1656), p. 27; see also J. Hay Colligan, "The Provincial Meeting of Cumberland and Westmorland," *Congregational Historical Society Transactions,* 4: pp. 159–168.

[48] Baxter, *Reliquiae Baxterianae,* Pt. II: pp. 162–164.

[49] The ministers and people of Herefordshire were for either total episcopacy or nothing approaching episcopacy, Powicke, *Richard Baxter,* p. 145.

disagreements.[50] Baxter then exchanged ideas with Bishop Brownrigge.[51]

In 1656 a small group of moderate Anglicans presented proposals for governmental action. John Gauden, Nicholas Bernard, Archbishop Usher, Secretary of State John Thurloe, perhaps Bishop Brownrigge, and others unidentifiable proposed that the moderate wings of the Anglican, Presbyterian, and Independent parties compromise their differences. The moving force in this Anglican effort was John Gauden, who wrote Nicholas Bernard in 1656:

I find the minds of ministers (however differing in some principles, rather of polity than piety) to be moved toward a fraternall accord as to the maine. . . . Not only Presbyterians and Independents, who seemed more symbolizing, but even episcopall, whose antipathies seemed irreconcible, are upon a very calme temper. . . . I should be glad to see that effected, which then seemed [in 1641] consented to; that the succession of ministeriall order and authority might be preserved most unquestionable by the happy accord of bishops and presbyters; that there might be some presidency and counsell in the government of the church; that sound doctrine, holy lifes, brotherly love, sanctity of dutys, might be restored and preserved to this reformed church, whose decayes and dangers are from that scattered and confused state it hath beene and still is.[52]

The theme throughout Gauden's letter is that Usher's plan for modified episcopacy might prove acceptable to all moderates as the basis for union and compromise.

At some date prior to September, 1656, Gauden went to London, where he obviously conferred with Bernard, Usher, Brownrigge, and perhaps Thurloe. As a result of these conferences, Gauden proposed to bring the Presbyterians and Anglicans together before approaching the Independents. This approach was apparently suggested by what Usher told Gauden of Baxter's visit to London in 1654 when Usher and Baxter agreed in thirty minutes that Usher's proposals of 1641 would settle the Presbyterian and Anglican differences on religious polity,[53] or by the exchange of letters between Baxter and Brownrigge in 1655.[54] In any event, Gauden referred to a Presbyterian minister and a peer, who must be identified as Baxter and Lord Broghill, who had indicated a willingness to accept Usher's plan for reducing episcopacy to synodical government by curtailing the bishop's authority and by increasing the independence of the presbyter.[55]

After a third letter from Gauden on October 10, 1656,[56] Bernard forwarded all Gauden's correspondence to Secretary Thurloe for action,[57] which suggests that Cromwell was at that time considering proposals for government enforcement of unity and discipline. Bernard's action definitely indicates that the government was at least willing to receive proposals for unification of the various groups. The almost immediate publication of Usher's papers indicates that the moderate Anglicans had some reason to hope that the Presbyterians and perhaps others would support an episcopal superintendency. But so far as is known no action was ever taken by the government or the Presbyterians on the proposals of Gauden, Bernard, and Usher.

There is evidence, however, that a number of Presbyterian clergy and laity moved closer to Baxter and the moderate Anglicans in 1656. Early in 1656, John Taylor, a moderate minister, expressed a desire to see a compromise between Presbyterians and Anglicans. He wrote Baxter that

we shall hardly be in any settled condition of combination except some prime presbyter of choise learning, age, experience, prudence & piety . . . may be appointed by lawe, in each fit compass of the land; as suppose, an ordinary county . . . or some less expert, yet sutable to the designe intended. This church officer, if he may not be called a prelate . . . yet he may have a performance in a sort, for the uniting of the church. . . . I shirk not at any lawfull name, so the power be pious & prudentiall. Nor need he lord it over his Brethren authorities. It may suffice him to be a prelate thus far; & in the estimation of his copresbyters, for the eminency of his gifts & graces: which may be such as justly do deserve such a prelacy; & configurally may prove that his judgment & determination will not be hastily opposed, if at all.[58]

This was what Baxter and Usher had agreed on in 1654 and what Vines had predicted would help resolve the Presbyterian and Anglican differences. It was what Gauden, Bernard, Usher, and Brownrigge had proposed to Thurloe.

The most encouraging news came from a Presbyterian politician. Early in September, 1656, Sir Edward Harley, member for Herefordshire in the parliament of 1656, and his friends solicited the aid of Baxter in drawing up bills to "take away the Scandal of Schism" which Harley considered "no les dangerous then the Scandal of the Cros." [59] Harley's request may be directly related to the Anglican proposals already discussed. If so, Harley's letter would strengthen the supposition that Cromwell was considering a more conservative policy in 1656.

[50] Richard Baxter to Sir Edward Harley, September 15, 1656, Baxter MSS, Letters I, No. 34, which has been printed in *Richard Baxter and Puritan Politics*, ed. Richard Schlatter (New Brunswick, N. J., 1957), pp. 46–60; and Baxter, *Reliquiae Baxterianae,* Pt. II: p. 206.

[51] Baxter, *Reliquiae Baxterianae,* Pt. II: pp. 172–178.

[52] John Gauden to Nicholas Bernard, 1656, *A Collection of the State Papers of John Thurloe, Esq.,* ed. Thomas Birch (7 v., London, 1742) 5: p. 598; hereafter cited as *Thurloe State Papers.*

[53] John Gauden to Nicholas Bernard, September, 1656, *ibid.,* pp. 598–599, and Baxter, *Reliquiae Baxterianae,* Pt. II: p. 206.

[54] Baxter, *Reliquiae Baxterianae,* Pt. II: pp. 172–178.

[55] John Gauden to Nicholas Bernard, September, 1656, *Thurloe State Papers* 5: pp. 598–599.

[56] John Gauden to Nicholas Bernard, October 10, 1656, *ibid.,* pp. 600–601.

[57] Nicholas Bernard to John Thurloe, November 17, 1656, *ibid.,* p. 597; and Bernard, *A Letter of Dr. Bernards to a Friend of His at Court* [London, 1660 ?], p. 7.

[58] John Taylor to Richard Baxter, January 5, 1656, Baxter MSS, Letters VI, No. 48.

[59] Sir Edward Harley to Richard Baxter, September 2, 1656, *ibid.,* II, No. 123.

Baxter replied to Harley in a long and interesting letter. By implication Baxter advised Harley to accept the Cromwellian government but to work for its improvement. The forthcoming parliament should pass an act "for securinge Religion in the maine." Parliament should neither permit universal toleration nor be "too forward in imposinge on others." After adopting a broad doctrine, parliament should punish non-conformists by denying them maintenance and public encouragement. Both ministers and laity should be subjected to sterner tests for morality and religious beliefs. Of far more significance, however, was Baxter's suggestion that parliament encourage and promote unification. A committee of parliament should solicit papers from "one or two of the most moderate Byshops, . . . one or two of the most moderate & best esteemed Presbyterians, & as many of the Congregationall way." From these papers could be drawn a plan for prosecution by the parliament. Baxter cited the agreements of the Westmorland and Cumberland ministers and of his own Worcestershire group as proof that peace and unity could be had, and he urged the government to give its assistance to such local efforts. While the consultations were in progress, the parliament should proceed to "settle" the Committee for Approbation of Ministers, which should be enlarged and duplicated in subordinate parts of the country. The Committee for Ejecting Scandalous Ministers should be enlarged, and county committees of the same type should be established. Other disciplinary bodies should be created, and changes should be made in the administration and finance of the parishes.[60] Baxter's long letter and the Anglican papers undoubtedly served as the basis for the unsuccessful attempt by the moderates in the parliament of 1656 to make drastic revisions in the existing religious laws.[61]

The basic features of Baxter's recommendations to Harley and the parliament met with the approval of Edward Reynolds, who finally returned to the Anglican fold, but met with only lukewarm support from John Owen, spokesman for the Congregationalists. In a sermon to the parliament of 1656 Reynolds lamented the state of religion and attacked those who "Cry up a boundless and universal liberty," "Cry down the coercive power of the Magistrate," "Bring into contempt the faithful and able Ministers of the Gospel," "Decry Learning and the Schools of the Prophets," "Cry down the maintenance of the Ministry," and "Put Doctrines, which in their own proper Colours would not be swallowed, into a disguise." Reynolds urged all men who "agree in the main fundamental Doctrines

of truth and godliness, in the substantials of Faith, Worship and Obedience" to live in "mutual love, toleration and forbearance of one another in differences which are not subversive unto faith and godliness" and requested parliament to take action to protect England and its people from the dangers to religion.[62] Owen, on the other hand, contended that God had broken the imposing people and requested parliament not to return to an imposed government, discipline, and worship.[63] Reynolds and Owen had stated the essential differences between the Presbyterians and the Independents. These differences continued to exist to and beyond the Restoration and made the Anglican task easier after 1660. As already indicated, these differences drove the moderate Presbyterians, such as Reynolds, Baxter, and Vines, away from the Independents and toward the moderate Anglicans, such as Gauden, Bernard, and Usher.

Despite the failure of all plans for national union and only limited union at the local level prior to the death of Oliver Cromwell in September, 1658, the Presbyterian reconcilers displayed signs of affection to Richard Cromwell and hopes for the ultimate success of their efforts. Bishop Burnet observed that "both the royalists and the presbyterians fancied [Richard] favoured them, though he pretended to be an independent."[64] On October 11 Edward Reynolds in behalf of Simeon Ashe, Edmund Calamy, Thomas Manton, William Bates, Matthew Poole, William Spurstowe, Lazarus Seaman, William Jenkyn, and other London Presbyterian ministers made an oral address to the new protector.[65] Edward Bowles, Presbyterian chaplain to Lord Fairfax, presented an address from his Yorkshire brethren on November 22.[66] The Presbyterian clergy had never given such approbation to Oliver Cromwell.

The most striking change occurred in Baxter's attitude toward the government. Baxter conferred with Oliver Cromwell in 1654 and gave him frequent advice through Dury, but Baxter consistently refrained from voicing public approval of the senior Cromwell. To Richard Cromwell, Baxter early adopted an attitude of open acceptance. He dedicated no less than three books to the new protector. Each of these was an attempt to persuade Richard to assist in restoring order and unity among the religious parties.

In *A Key for Catholicks* Baxter urged the protector not to tolerate Roman Catholics. The government's

---

[60] Richard Baxter to Sir Edward Harley, September 15, 1656, *ibid.*, I, No. 34.

[61] *Commons Journals* 7: p. 506; Charles Harding Firth, *The Last Years of the Protectorate, 1656–1658* (2 v., London, 1909) 1: pp. 145–147; Shaw, *History of the English Church* 2: pp. 92–97; and William Prynne, *A True and Perfect Narrative* . . . (London, 1659), pp. 57–58.

[62] Edward Reynolds, *The Peace of Jerusalem; a Sermon preached in the Parliament-House* . . . (London, 1657).

[63] John Owen, *God's Work in Founding Zion . . . . A Sermon preached* . . . (Oxford, 1656).

[64] Gilbert Burnet, *Bishop Burnet's History of His Own Times: With Notes by the Earls of Dartmouth and Hardwicke,* ed. M. J. Routh (6 v., 2nd ed., Oxford, 1833) 1: p. 150; hereafter cited as *History of His Own Times.*

[65] *The Publick Intelligencer,* No. 147, p. 912.

[66] *Mercurius Politicus,* No. 443, p. 32.

foreign policy should be one of alliance with Protestant nations and of opposition to Catholic states. At home the government should "compassionate the weak and curable, Punish the uncurable; restrain the forward, but Love and cherish the servants of the Lord." "Godly, Faithfull Magistrates" should be empowered to punish the religious radicals of unorthodox theology and practice. Above all else, the protector should encourage the approved, orthodox ministers and should aid in "the procuring and maintaining an Union and Concord among all the Pastors and Churches in your Dominion." [67]

One month later Baxter outlined his plan for religious polity to the protector. The general exhortation to Richard Cromwell was to avoid all extremes in religion and to work toward the elimination of division so that "there might be no such things as Parties or Separations . . . (though diversity of opinions there will be)." In other words, the Cromwellian church should be as broad as possible without passing from the orthodox to the heterodox. He also assured the younger Cromwell that the several orthodox groups were ready for union and recommended that he consult Baxter's *Confirmation and Restauration* for the "Reforming, Reconciling Truth which must heal us if ever we be healed." Baxter also appealed to the moderates among the Anglican laymen and clergy for their support.[68] In his *Holy Commonwealth*, which went to the press with a dedication to Richard Cromwell after his abdication, Baxter gave overt recognition to the Cromwellian government and urged the creation of a moderate theocracy.[69]

Richard Cromwell's seeming conservativism and the election of numerous Presbyterians to the parliament of 1659 convinced the London Presbyterians that the government might be persuaded to support their movement for a drastic revision of the statutes on religion in the direction of a national establishment. The clergy and their friends in parliament named Thomas Manton to solicit the advice and support of Richard Baxter.[70] Baxter's reply contained much of what he had written Harley in 1656. He presented both negative and affirmative arguments to Manton's propositions. Baxter's reply also indicated a continued feeling that parliament should pass religious legislation only after consulting with representatives of all parties and that parliamentary action should be along latitudinarian lines.[71] Parliament never took up religious matters before Richard, under army pressure, dissolved it on April 22, 1659.

The sincerity of purpose and the hopes of the Presbyterians were well revealed by the multitude of tracts which they published throughout the Cromwellian period, but especially in 1658 and 1659, in favor of union. Thomas Case urged the people of Chatham to "forget all your own private opinions and differences; Divisions have been the sad obstructions of Englands Reformation and Settlement." [72] Daniel Cawdry vied with the Laudian Dr. Henry Hammond for the support of the moderate Anglicans.[73] Edmund Calamy attempted to convert the Congregationalists from total separation. Extreme decentralization, he said, "would quickly bring destruction upon the whole." [74] These examples of Presbyterian propaganda in behalf of union could be multiplied at length.

The Presbyterian efforts for unity brought some concrete progress in 1658 and 1659. The Presbyterian and Independent ministers of Cheshire and Lancashire approached agreement in 1659.[75] The Manchester Classis carried on lengthy discussions with the Anglicans of the area.[76] Some Independents requested Richard Cromwell to effect a settlement of their differences with the Presbyterians.[77] John Dury and the Worcestershire Association renewed their exchange of ideas and proposals on union through both national and local efforts,[78] and Lewis du Moulin, professor of history at Oxford, published a work in which he suggested something similar to Baxter's association plan.[79] Baxter

---

[67] Richard Baxter, Epistle Dedicatory, *A Key for Catholicks* . . . (London, 1659), sigs. a3ᵛ, b1ᵛ.

[68] Richard Baxter, Epistle Dedicatory and Preface, *Five Disputations of Church-Government, and Worship* (London, 1659), sigs. A3ʳ, ᵛ; and *Confirmation and Restauration* . . . (London, 1658). See Baxter, *Reliquiae Baxterianae*, Pt. I: p. 117, for the impact of this on the people.

[69] Richard Baxter, *A Holy Commonwealth* . . . (London, 1659).

[70] Thomas Manton to Richard Baxter, January 27, 1659, Baxter MSS, Letters II, No. 124.

[71] Richard Baxter to Thomas Manton, February 1, 1659, *ibid.*, V, No. 283.

[72] Thomas Case, *Eliah's Abatement: Or, Corruptions in the Saints* . . . (London, 1658), [p. 15].

[73] Daniel Cawdry, *The Account Audited and Discounted* . . . (London, 1658), p. 143.

[74] Edmund Calamy, Preface to Samuel Hudson, *A Vindication of the Essence and Unity of the Church Catholick Visible* . . . (London, 1658).

[75] Adam Martindale, *The Life of Adam Martindale, Written by Himself*, ed. Richard Parkinson, (Manchester, 1845), 4: pp. 112, 117–118, and 122; Henry Newcome, *The Autobiography of Henry Newcome*, ed. Richard Parkinson (2 v., Manchester, 1852) 1: pp. 45, 47, 57, 62–63, 67–68, and 297; and D. T., *Irenicum; or an Essay towards a Brotherly Peace and Union, between Those of the Congregational and Presbyterian Way* . . . ., by Discipulus de Tempore, Junior [pseud.] (London, 1659).

[76] *Minutes of the Manchester Presbyterian Classis, 1646–1660*, ed. William A. Shaw (3 v., Manchester, 1891) 3: pp. 376–399; and anonymous, *The Censures of the Church Revived* . . . (London, 1659).

[77] G[eorge] D[avenport] to William Sancroft, October 15, 1658, British Museum, Harleian MSS 3783, fol. 222; and Shaw, *History of the English Church* 2: pp. 166–178. Hereafter British Museum and Harleian are shortened to B.M. and Harl. respectively.

[78] Richard Baxter, *The Judgement and Advice of the Assembly of the Associated Ministers of Worcester-Shire* . . . (London, 1658).

[79] Lewis du Moulin, *Proposals and Reasons* . . . (London, 1659).

prevailed on John Eliot, the New England Congregationalist, to write his friends in England in behalf of union,[80] and Baxter personally reached a tentative agreement with Philip Ney, a Congregationalist, and Thomas Lambe and William Allen, two Anabaptists.[81] In all probability correspondence now missing or hopelessly scattered would reveal a much broader movement toward union and reconstitution of the Cromwellian church.

The discussions of religious unity were suddenly terminated in 1659. The Savoy Conference of Congregationalists in 1658 widened, rather than lessened, the gap between the Congregationalists and the Presbyterians.[82] By March 15, 1659, John Owen and other Independents had joined the army council in opposing Richard Cromwell.[83] This combination forced Richard to dissolve the parliament of 1659 and then to abdicate. Richard Baxter, Henry Newcomen, and Oliver Heywood thought they were nearing success in their discussions with the Independents and with some Anglicans when the political and religious upheavals of 1659 put an end to all their earlier efforts.[84] In any event, the moderate Presbyterians long held the religious Independents and the political radicals responsible for the political and religious disruptions of 1659, and for the next several years they excluded the various Independent groups from their plans for a broad or comprehensive church. Several years of persecution were required before the Presbyterians and the Congregationalists could meet on friendly terms.

II. PRESBYTERIAN POLITICIANS, 1649–1659

The Royalists counted heavily on Presbyterian help against the Cromwellian government, but such assistance was not forthcoming in effective quantity or quality. Few of the Presbyterians actively supported Charles II between 1649 and 1659; nor did they give more than limited support to Oliver Cromwell, though there was a noticeable improvement in the Presbyterians'

relations with Oliver after 1654. Realizing that the religious and political radicals constituted a threat to peace and security and hoping that Richard would prove more favorable to the Presbyterian cause, both political and religious, many Presbyterians showed an inclination to aid Richard Cromwell during his brief rule. It was Independency and Republicanism, especially in the army, rather than Presbyterianism or Royalism which overthrew the Cromwellian system in 1659 and restored the "Good Old Cause," and it was Presbyterian and moderate opposition to the "Good Old Cause" which brought Charles II back to England in 1660.

The initial reaction of the Presbyterians, both lay and clerical, to Cromwell's *coup d'etat* of December, 1648, was mild in view of their strength and their repeated avowals of allegiance to monarchy and Presbyterianism. Many Presbyterians in the Long Parliament retired after only vocal protest, although some, like William Prynne, published strong attacks on the new government. The clergy printed protests against the execution of Charles I, Pride's Purge, and the Engagement, or in behalf of the Solemn League and Covenant and monarchy.[1] However, a group of London Presbyterian ministers declared a willingness "to live quietly and peaceably in our places, and callings, and to submit to such things as are imposed upon, or required of us, by the powers which are in actual possession . . . ."[2] Some few of the laity became confirmed Royalists.[3] Still others fled abroad. There was no sign, however, of significant and organized resistance by the Presbyterians to the new regime.

Happily for the exiled Stuart, enough Presbyterian Royalists accompanied him into exile to serve as contacts between the king and the Presbyterians in England. All were laymen; not a single Presbyterian minister is known to have fled abroad to join Charles II. As early as October, 1649, Lord Willoughby of Parham, Edward Massey, Richard Graves, Alderman James Bunce of London, and Silas Titus were working actively from abroad for Presbyterian support for the proposed landing of Charles II in Scotland. Titus allegedly had a list of eighty London citizens who promised both money and men if Charles would agree with the Scots.[4]

[80] F. J. Powicke, "Some Unpublished Correspondence of the Rev. Richard Baxter and the Rev. John Eliot, 'The Apostle to the American Indians,' 1656–1682," *Bulletin of the John Rylands Library*, 15 (1931): pp. 138–176, 442–466.

[81] Baxter, *Reliquiae Baxterianae*, Pt. II: pp. 181–193, and Appendix, pp. 51–95.

[82] Matthew Poole to Richard Baxter, August 14, 1658, Baxter MSS, Letters V, No. 218; and Baxter, *Reliquiae Baxterianae*, Pt. I: p. 104.

[83] Arthur Annesley to Henry Cromwell, March 15, 1659, B.M., Lansdowne MSS 823, fol. 251; Lansdowne hereafter shortened to Lans.

[84] Richard Baxter to William Newe, August 6, 1659, Baxter MSS, Letters IV, No. 177; Newcome, *Autobiography* 1: p. 108; and Oliver Heywood, *The Rev. Oliver Heywood, B. A., 1630–1702; His Autobiography, Diaries, Anecdote and Event Books*, ed. J. Horsfall Turner (4 v., Brighouse, Eng., 1882) 1: p. 174.

[1] For examples see Cornelius Burgess, *A Vindication of the Ministers of the Gospel, in and about London* . . . (London, 1649); [London Provincial Assembly], *A Testimony to the Truth of Jesus Christ, and to Our Solemn League and Covenant* . . . (London, 1648); and [Edward Gee], *A Plea for Non-Scribers* . . . (n.p., 1650).

[2] [Edward Reynolds], *The Humble Proposals of Sundry Learned and Pious Divines within this Kingdome* . . . (London, 1650), p. 2.

[3] Godfrey Davies insisted that many Presbyterians turned Royalist as a result of the second Civil War; see his *The Early Stuarts, 1603–1660* (Oxford, 1949), p. 196.

[4] Samuel Rawson Gardiner, *History of the Commonwealth and Protectorate* (4 v., London, 1905) 1: p. 184; hereafter cited as *Commonwealth and Protectorate*.

To the London group must be added the former parliamentary leader of the party, Denzil Holles.[5]

Although the Presbyterian Royalists in exile pressed vigorously for an invasion of Scotland and an agreement with the Scottish Presbyterians, reports from England encouraged the Stuart king to hope for major assistance from the English Presbyterians. One correspondent reported that

the Independents are possessed of all the forts and towns, the navy and treasures. The Presbyterians yet holdeth a silent power by means of the Divines, and the interest of some gentry and nobility, and especially in London and the great towns. . . . Some are rigid for the *jus Divinum* of Presbytery, but the greatest part, weary of trouble and the rod that now hangeth over them, would repent and serve his Majesty; some purely without fraud, others being assured to be freed from their past acts, their livings and offices preserved to them, their moneys laid out in church lands repaid.

The writer went on to assert that an understanding between Royalists and Presbyterians was essential to the success of any rising, for without the latter a foreign army would be required.[6] The same report, in less detail, was sent to Sir Henry Bennet by Abraham Cowley.[7]

The English Presbyterians are said to have figured prominently in the Royalist plans of 1650 for an English insurrection in support of Charles and his Scottish arms. An early biographer, probably a moderate Royalist, of Charles II admitted in 1660 that the plan of 1650 was

chiefly laid by those Presbyterians who had been such dire Opponents of his Majesty's blessed father . . . , viz, the greatest part Presbyterian Ministers, who had most of them formerly belcht out such firebrands from their Pulpits as had set both Church and State in a combustion; but now whether out of a reall sence of their Errour (which I have the charity to believe it was) they had a desire to return to their Allegiance to his Son their lawfull and native Sovereign; or out of an ambition, by joining with their Scottish Brethren (which I am loath to judge) to get the Power again into their hands. . . .[8]

Thomas Coke, who was apprehended by the government in 1650 as a conspirator, made sworn statements, which are not too trustworthy, that Presbyterians were involved in the Royalist conspiracy. Coke insisted that the plan was carried on in London by "some of the nobility and principally by the ministers." The London

ministers named by Coke were Edmund Calamy, Richard Vines, William Jenkyn, Christopher Love, Thomas Cawton, Thomas Gouge, Thomas Case, John Fuller, and one Crawford. These Presbyterians were said to be in correspondence with other clergymen throughout the country, but this correspondence, if it ever existed, cannot now be found.[9]

Although some English Presbyterians joined in the Royalist plans, it is abundantly clear that the mass of them did little to aid Charles II in 1650. Richard Baxter later attributed this to three factors: Cromwell's victory at Dunbar, the fact that the "implacable Cavaliers had made no preparation of the Peoples Mind, by any Significations of Reconciliation, or of probable future Peace," and the coolness of the Laudian divines toward a compromise on religion.[10] In Lancashire and Derbyshire the king's agents were met by Presbyterians who demanded that all papists and prelates be dismissed and that all others be required to swear the Covenant oath.[11] The seriousness of the Presbyterian threat to Cromwell is well reflected by the execution of only one, Christopher Love.[12]

Proof that the English Presbyterians were generally apathetic to the cause of Charles II in Oliver Cromwell's time is found in the draft of a letter of 1655 or 1656 by Silas Titus, Presbyterian agent with Charles II, to his friends in England. The document's preamble reflects the writer's disappointment with his Presbyterian brethren at home:

If we could as easily excuse it to our selves, as we can to all the world besides; we could be silent, as our freindes can desire us, and be as little concern'd for theire interest or safety, as they have pleas'd to be for our Bannishment & sufferings. And if indeed we were soe, whatsoever other fault were in it, we thinke ingratitude could be more of our accusations for we too well know that we are the only persons who suffer for the prosecution of theire principles, that have no support or Countenance from those that make the same professions and have the same Comon Engagements with them. Besides we can not but imagine, but the same prudence and caution which our freindes have hitherto practis'd in abstaining from all manner of Commerce & Correspondency with us will still prevaile with them to persist in this course of indifference towards us; and easily perswade them to allow us still the Honour of suffering, and the Liberty of Complaining, without being themselves concern'd in either.

Even worse, so far as Titus was concerned, some Presbyterians had made "particular under-hand appli-

[5] Sir Edward Nicholas to Earl of Norwich, March 11/21, 1651, *The Nicholas Papers: Correspondence of Sir Edward Nicholas, Secretary of State*, ed. Sir George F. Warner (4 v., London, 1920) 1: p. 227; hereafter cited as *Nicholas Papers*.

[6] Quoted by John Stoughton, *History of Religion in England from the Opening of the Long Parliament to 1850* (8 v., London, 1881) 2: pp. 30–31, who failed to identify the writer but did date the letter as March, 1650; hereafter cited as *History of Religion*.

[7] Abraham Cowley to Henry Bennet, July 13/23 and July 27/August 6, 1650, in T. Brown, *Miscellanea Aulica: Or, a Collection of State-Treatises, never before publish'd* (London, 1702), pp. 144–147.

[8] I. D., *The History of His Sacred Majesty Charles the II . . .* (London, 1660), pp. 93–94.

[9] Historical Manuscripts Commission, *Fourteenth Report, Appendix, Part II, The Manuscripts of His Grace the Duke of Portland* (4 v., London, 1894) 1: pp. 584–585; hereafter cited as H.M.C. and *Portland MSS.*

[10] Baxter, *Reliquiae Baxterianae*, Pt. I: p. 68.

[11] Laurence Echard, *The History of England* (3 v., London, 1707–1718) 2: pp. 704–705; Gardiner, *Commonwealth and Protectorate*, 2: pp. 38–39.

[12] See Christopher Love, *A Cleare and Necessary Vindication of . . . Christopher Love . . .* (London, 1651); and anonymous, *Mr. Love's Case* (London, 1651).

cations for themselves; imagining to save theire owne Cabines though the shippe of their party sinke."

Titus went on to shame his correspondents with the attitudes of the Royalists and Levellers toward the Presbyterians:

The greatest part of the King's partie, & it may be those that will beare downe the Rest, doe not seeme to have abated any thing of theire old Rancour. They style the presbiterians the authors & beginners of all these troubles; a people only Active, Fortunable, Liberal, and Faithfull to theire Engagements, in pulling downe the King & destroying a Lawfull government. . . .

The Republicall partie everie where represent the presbiterians as a Covetous, Lazie, & Cowardly people, unfaithfull to one another, and unusefull to any else. They say that of all parties they are the proudest & think themselves fittest to governe; but of all parties they say they are the unworthiest and meanest, and that dare hazard least either to justifie theire engagements, or obtaine theire ambitions. And besides they spreade it everie where that the great complyers with Cromwell are of that partie, and that he allowes theire ministers tythes to be his oratours; and to set him up King in theire pulpits, where they pull'd downe the Last.

To prevent credence being given to these charges and to prepare for any eventuality, Titus implored the Presbyterians to discard every thought and action which might be contradictory to their oaths to preserve king and parliament.[13]

Some explanation for the passivity which Titus deplored in his Presbyterian correspondents can be found in the inadequate nature of the royal promises to the English Presbyterians. How vague and general these were is illustrated by a letter from Charles II to Titus on September 10, 1656, in which the king stated

I know not how to make any offers to them, till you advise me upon conference with them, or upon your owne observation, how and in what manner I may oblige them, and then they shall finde that I am there frinde. Assure your frindes of the Clargy, whome you finde to be in truth cordiall to me, that they shall finde there owne accounte in serving me, and what preferments you shall promis to them in my name, they may depende upon, and I will make good to them, nor shall any person contribute effectually to my service, whome I will not requite to the full. . . .[14]

Such uncertain rewards were not likely to entice the laity to embark upon an improbable and perilous design, the failure of which would most certainly result in loss of estate and possibly life itself. Nor would a promise of patronage satisfy a clergyman dedicated to a program of ecclesiastical reform.

Certain events in 1657 apparently gave the Royalists new hope for an effective compromise with the Presby-

terians and others. Not the least of these promising incidents was the marriage of the Duke of Buckingham, recently returned to England from abroad, and Mary Fairfax, daughter of the Lord General Fairfax. Lord Fairfax, now cold toward Cromwell, was not a sincere Presbyterian, but his wife and his chaplain, Edward Bowles, were. In view of Buckingham's new and powerful alliance, his Royalist colleagues felt that he could organize the northern Presbyterians for an uprising. The old agency of the exiles—the Sealed Knot, consisting of both Royalists and Presbyterians—was no longer in complete trust, so one closer to the king was sent to appraise the situation. This agent was James Butler, then Marquis of Ormonde, whose mission did not have the full support of the Royalists. Sir Edward Hyde, the closest confidant of Charles II, was

absolutely against the journey, as an unreasonable adventure upon an improbable design, seeing there was no just ground to imagine, that those who had confidently undertaken the greatest matters, were able to perform any thing.[15]

The results of Ormonde's expedition fully justified Hyde's pessimism. No organized Presbyterian party existed. Ormonde found Presbyterians who were opposed to Cromwell, but the malcontents were jealous of each other. His most important discovery was the lack of communication between men of similar views toward the existing government. The Presbyterians were not in agreement as to what demands to place before Charles II. The Earl of Manchester, Lord Denbigh, Sir William Waller, Edward Rossiter, and similar moderates seemed to be content with a royal promise of security for their lives and estates; Lord Saye and Sele, Lord Robartes, and the more rigid Presbyterians wanted confirmation of the Newport terms of 1648.[15a] Alexander Popham was afraid of

---

[13] Draft paper by Silas Titus, B.M., Egerton MSS 1533, foll. 55–56. This document may be roughly dated by the reference made to a recent visit by the republican leaders to Charles II and Spain. Edward Sexby visited both Charles II and Spain in 1655 and again in 1656, so Titus' address to the Presbyterians was written late in 1655 or in 1656.

[14] Charles II to Silas Titus, September 10/20, 1656, B.M., Egerton MSS 1533, fol. 34. Completely in the hand of the king.

[15] Thomas Carte, *An History of the Life of James Duke of Ormonde, from his Birth in 1610, to his Death in 1688* (3 v., London, 1735–1736), 2: p. 170; hereafter cited as *Ormonde.*

[15a] The Treaty of Newport, which deserves study, was the last set of negotiations between the Long Parliament and Charles I. The Long Parliament presented the king with demands that can be traced back to the Nineteen Propositions of 1642, but more particularly to the Hampton Court Propositions of 1647, which were almost identical to those presented at Newcastle in 1646. The king was to cancel certain acts against the Long Parliament and various appointments, grants, and creations. He was to take the Solemn League and Covenant, to agree to the abolition of episcopacy and various features of the Church of England, to accept bills designed to cleanse the king and kingdom of Roman Catholicism and to promote puritanism, to agree to surrender control of the military and naval forces for twenty years, to accept measures agreed on by England and Scotland, to surrender Irish policy to parliament, to surrender Scottish policy to the Scottish Estates, to surrender control of the City of London and the Tower of London, and to accept acts and actions of the Long Parliament since May 22, 1642. A long list of persons was to be imprisoned, fined, or disqualified. In 1647 the Long Parliament added a demand for the sale of church lands, and in 1648 one for the abolition of the Court of Wards and Liveries. After nu-

detection. In brief, Ormonde reported that there was no significant Presbyterian support for an overthrow of Cromwell.[16]

Ormonde's summary of the political situation in England confirms what Titus knew by way of his Presbyterian correspondents. Prior to the death of Oliver Cromwell in September, 1658, there was no Presbyterian party actively working as a body for the restoration of Charles II. Those Presbyterians secretly hoping for change had no common program. Their organization and platform, if any, had been split asunder by the agonizing events of 1643 through 1648. The Presbyterian Royalists were acting as individuals, and they were few in number prior to September, 1658.

One must look elsewhere for most of the Presbyterians. Did they support Cromwell? Did they follow a policy of neutrality and passive obedience? These would appear to be the logical alternatives to active opposition to Oliver Cromwell.

A small group of "Presbyterian" members of the Long Parliament continued to serve in the Rump from 1649 to 1653 and again in 1659. Gardiner noticed that some supporters of a treaty with Charles I in 1648 either remained in the House of Commons or returned after Pride's Purge,[17] and the Venetian minister, Lorenzo Paulucci, commented in 1653 about the "growing power of the Presbyterians in parliament, to the detriment of the more numerous Independents."[18] A modern study of the Rump Parliament, by no means conclusive, was startling in its tentative findings. J. H. Hexter, after a comparison of the eldership lists for the classical organizations and the membership of the Rump, felt that there was sufficient evidence to show that the Presbyterian survivors of Pride's Purge were more numerous than had been thought. He concluded that a "rather high percentage of 'Presbyterians' were Presbyterians; but as we most assuredly should not

expect, an even higher percentage of 'Independents' were Presbyterians."[19]

Hexter's findings suggest why some Presbyterians thus found it possible to submit to or support, even actively, the Cromwellian government. Many of those traditionally called Presbyterians were Erastians in religion. This group included most of the lawyers and some few others who felt that the clergy, whatever their doctrinal position, should exercise less control over the church and none over the state. The so-called Presbyterian party also contained some who were largely indifferent to religious affairs but vigorous in opposing Charles I on civil policy. Lawyers like John Glynn and John Maynard, stalwarts of parliamentary Presbyterianism before 1649, felt no guilt from serving the Protectorate. Sir Thomas Widdrington, an obvious favorite of Oliver Cromwell, could suggest putting the Duke of Gloucester on the throne, and then continue in office after the rejection of his "Presbyterian" plan.[20]

There is evidence that Cromwell approached certain of the Presbyterians, both lay and clerical, early in 1649 with overtures of compromise or peaceful coexistence. According to Edmund Ludlow, Cromwell held a meeting of Presbyterians and Independents, possibly on February 4, 1649, for the purpose of effecting a "reconciliation between the two parties," but failed to accomplish his purpose. Ludlow mentioned a second meeting at a later date at which Cromwell suggested the possibility of seating one of the younger Stuarts on the throne.[21] Clement Walker, Presbyterian historian of Independency, also insisted that there were discussions between Cromwell and the Presbyterians, and added that Cromwell even offered to establish some degree of Presbyterian rule over the church and to readmit the secluded members of the Long Parliament.[22] Although these early efforts failed, Cromwell, according to Ludlow, later "gratified such of the Presbyterian party as were the most complying."[23]

Ludlow's statement is substantiated by the known activities of some Presbyterians. As Cromwell's position became more secure and as he gave evidence of his conservatism by his efforts to loosen the hold of the army, Presbyterian support for his government began to appear. The Nominated or Barebones Parliament of 1653 was notorious for its strong Independency, but those of 1654 and 1656, even after purging, showed Presbyterian acceptance of, and even marked Presbyterian support for, the government. This support was

merous and lengthy exchanges, and some concessions on both sides, both houses voted on December 5, 1648, that the royal answers were a sufficient ground for further negotiations in the direction of a formal treaty, but Coronet Joyce's seizure of the king and Colonel Pride's Purge of the Long Parliament ended the Newport, or Isle of Wight, negotiations. *The Constitutional Documents of the Puritan Revolution, 1625–1660*, ed. Samuel Rawson Gardiner (3rd ed., Oxford, 1958), pp. 290–306; and Samuel Rawson Gardiner, *History of the Great Civil War, 1642–1649* (4 v., New York, 1901) 3: p. 127 ff. and 4: p. 214 ff.

[16] Carte, *Ormonde* 2, p. 178; Firth, *Last Years of the Protectorate* 2: pp. 62–63. Most of Ormonde's reports are calendared in *Calendar of the Clarendon State Papers preserved in the Bodleian Library*, ed. F. J. Routledge (4 v., Oxford, 1932), 4: pp. 8–23; hereafter cited as *Calendar of the Clarendon State Papers*. This work is a continuation of the first three volumes edited by O. Ogle, W. H. Bliss, and W. D. Macray. The concluding volume (5) by Routledge has been completed in three manuscript volumes, filed in the Bodleian Library as Clarendon MSS 15*b*, and will be cited as such later.

[17] Gardiner, *Commonwealth and Protectorate*, 2: p. 173.

[18] Lorenzo Paulucci to Giovanni Sagredo, January 14/24, 1653, *Calendar of State Papers, Venetian, 1653–1654*, p. 12.

[19] J. H. Hexter, "The Problem of the Presbyterian Independents," *American Historical Review* 44: p. 37.

[20] Gardiner, *Commonwealth and Protectorate* 2: p. 75.

[21] Edmund Ludlow, *The Memoirs of Edmund Ludlow, Lieutenant-General of the Horse in the Army of the Commonwealth of England, 1625–1672*, ed. C. H. Firth (2 v., London, 1894) 1: pp. 183–185; hereafter cited as *Memoirs*.

[22] Clement Walker, *The Compleat History of Independency* (London, 1661), Pt. II: p. 157.

[23] Ludlow, *Memoirs* 2: pp. 37–38.

not given without some misgivings. Henry Bartlett, a minister, wrote Baxter in 1654 that

some secluded Members, that are like to be chosen for the future Parliament, [desire] youre judgement & reasons with it; how they may (in respect of the Covenant they tooke to preserve the privilege of Parliament) sit in the next Parliament: whether they ought to declare against those former breaches, or silently passe them by, & go on as things now stand: whether they may establish by their vote the present form of government, or declare against it, or silently pass it by.[24]

Presbyterians took a marked and successful interest in the elections of 1654. It was reported from Wiltshire that the Presbyterians led by their ministers, Humphrey Chambers, Byfield, Strickland, and others unidentified, had

gathered together a great number of people, & taught them their lessons before hand to cry up only those ten men named in their List, and to brand others, as namely Lieut. Gen. Ludlow, Col. Eyre, etc. (who were nominated by approved faithfull men in the County) with the names of Anabaptists, Levellers, to render them odious to the generality of injudicious people, by these false and malitious imputations.

The writer warned his reader to expect a similar combination of Presbyterian laity and clergy elsewhere.[25] In a short time the Wiltshire ministers published an admission of everything charged against them and of collusion with a London Presbyterian clergyman.[26] It is unlikely that the Wiltshire case was an isolated attempt by the Presbyterians to influence the Cromwellian parliament. Gardiner explained the electoral success of the Presbyterians by assuming that the electoral temper was growing conservative and acquaintance with Presbyterian discipline was becoming more distant.[27]

Cromwell did not take alarm at the activity and success of the Presbyterians in 1654. Edmund Ludlow insisted that "the Cavaliers and the imposing clergy, the lawyers and court interest, all joining against that of the commonwealth," worked together for the election of men favorable to the protectorate as opposed to a commonwealth.[28] It is certainly true that the Presbyterians within the parliament of 1654 were numerous enough, and Cromwell was willing, to attempt the erection of a national church along modified Presbyterian lines and to select the Presbyterian Richard Baxter to preach before the parliament.[29] In other words, a significant number of Presbyterians tended

to support Cromwell in 1654, and they received his blessing.[30]

Most of the Presbyterians elected in 1654, including those excluded from the parliament after the election, were returned in 1656. Major General Kelsey complained to Cromwell that "most of the Cavaliers falling in with the Presbyterians against all those persons that owned your Highness and present Government" by major generals had secured the return of unfavorable candidates.[31] Ludlow commented, however, that "the emissaries of the court caused the elections in most places to be decided in favour of such as pleased them," [32] and the evidence is that the court did favor many of the victorious Presbyterian candidates. Cromwell was again changing courses. The major generals were to be dropped. Kelsey did not understand the motives of the more conservative candidates. For example, Henry Haynes, major general in East Anglia, wrote John Thurloe, government manager of the election, that the "honest men . . . will be compelled to take in with the Presbiterian to keepe out the malignant" in Suffolk.[33]

It is true, however, that the council of state intended to purge the parliament of 100 to 120 and that there was a reported plot on the part of the Royalists, Levellers, and some Presbyterians for an invasion and uprising. Thus the court may have favored the candidacies of some Presbyterians only for reasons of temporary expediency and not in the belief that they would support the protectorate.

Despite the seclusion of some Presbyterians, those who supported Cromwell in the parliament of 1656 were "in general . . . Presbyterians rather than Independents." [34] The more ardent advocates of kingship for Cromwell included Sir Richard Onslow,[35] Lord Broghill, John Glynn, and William Pierrepoint,[36] all of whom were generally considered Presbyterians. Onslow, Glynn, and Pierrepoint had, in fact, been purged in 1648. Cromwell rather obviously attempted to cement this relationship with the Presbyterians by naming Viscount Saye and Sele, the Earl of Manchester,

[24] Henry Bartlett to Richard Baxter, June 3, 1654, Baxter MSS, Letters VI, No. 23.
[25] Anonymous, *The Copy of a Letter sent out of Wiltshire to a Gentleman in London* . . . (London, 1654). This may have been written by Edmund Ludlow.
[26] Humphrey Chambers and others, *An Apology for the Ministers of the County of Wilts* . . . (London, 1654).
[27] Gardiner, *Commonwealth and Protectorate* 3: p. 176.
[28] Ludlow, *Memoirs* 1: pp. 388–389.
[29] See preceding chapter.
[30] Sir Edward Nicholas was completely baffled by this election, being unable to understand why Cromwell permitted the Presbyterians to be returned. The elections caused some of Charles' advisers to urge "extraordinary compliance with the Presbyterian party, because so many of them are chosen to sit in this mock Parliament." Sir Edward Nicholas to Joseph Jane, August 22/September 1, 1654, *Calendar of State Papers, Domestic Series, 1654–1662* (London, 1861–1886) **1654**: pp. 324–325; hereafter cited as *C.S.P. Dom.*
[31] Major General Thomas Kelsey to Oliver Cromwell, August 26, 1656, quoted by Stoughton, *History of Religion* 2: pp. 122–123.
[32] Ludlow, *Memoirs* 2: p. 17.
[33] Major General Henry Haynes to John Thurloe, July 19, 1656, *Thurloe State Papers* 5: p. 230.
[34] Firth, *Last Years of the Protectorate* 1: p. 73.
[35] *Ibid.*, p. 139.
[36] Bulstrode Whitelocke, *Memorials of English Affairs* (4 v., Oxford, 1853) 4: p. 289; *Thurloe State Papers* 6: pp. 37–38.

Lord Wharton, Lord Broghill, John Glynn, Sir Richard Onslow, Sir Gilbert Gerard, William Pierrepoint, and Alexander Popham to his House of Lords in December, 1657.[37]

Not all Presbyterians were reconcilable. William Prynne indicated his opposition to the plan to make Cromwell king by publishing his *King Richard the Third Revived* in 1657.[38] Wharton, more an Independent than a Presbyterian in religion, inquired of Saye and Sele whether they, as ancient lords, should accept seats in the new house. Saye and Sele had no doubts whatsoever; he flatly refused to imply sanction to any upstart's lords by joining with them.[39]

This survey of Presbyterian lay activity during the rule of Oliver Cromwell offers one major conclusion. Instead of one party, there were many Presbyterian groups or factions. Some few actively supported the royal cause. Others, after a brief period of uncertainty, cooperated with the more conservative Independents and liberal Royalists to make the best of the existing government. Another group, perhaps the largest, remained passively obedient whenever possible. The important thing, however, is that the Presbyterians, as a political unit, entered the crucial pre-Restoration period totally demoralized and shattered.

The political radicalism of the English army, the ambitions of the officers, and the religious Independency of both officers and men caused the Presbyterians to give Richard Cromwell, who was considered preferable to anyone then available, more support than they had given his father. The political feeling of the army is well reflected in General Charles Fleetwood's statement that the "army have a great desire that the good old spirit may still be kept alive to carry on their work," [40] and in the Venetian minister's report that the army was discontented as early as October 15, 1658.[41] The radical and ambitious officers were responsible for keeping Henry Cromwell in Ireland against his wishes and those of the conservative elements in the government.[42] In religion the army was allied with the Independents. John Owen, a leading Congregational minister, formed a separate church for the army

officers at Wallingford House.[43] The army's religious policy is contained in Fleetwood's statement that "it is farre from us to incourg an imposing spirit in any; it is both against principles & practise of us." [44] Thurloe and other conservative advisers of Richard Cromwell were alarmed by the army's religious and political radicalism.[45]

George Monck, commander of the Scottish Army, was so fearful of what the English army might do that he urged Richard to counterbalance the radicals by forming new alliances with the Presbyterians. He advised the protector to call an assembly of divines, when he summoned a parliament, "to agree upon some way of union and accommodation, that we may have unity in things necessary, liberty in things unnecessary, and charity in all; which will put a stop to that progresse of blasphemy and profanes, that I feare is too frequent in many places by the great extent of toleration . . . ." At the same time the government should "countenance and favour some of the gravest sort of moderate Presbyterian divines" such as Reynolds, Calamy, Cooper, and Manton. The new peers should be balanced by the addition of "the most prudent of the old lords" and others, including Pierrepoint, Sir George Booth, Sir John Hobart, Richard Hampden, Edward Baynton, Popham, and Robert Rolle, each of whom was a Presbyterian of sorts. The council of state should be altered by the inclusion of a few Presbyterians. Monck also recommended a reduction in the military forces.[46]

Despite the government's failure to adopt Monck's recommendations, many Presbyterians grew more favorable to Richard Cromwell as time passed. According to Richard Baxter, everyone

wondred to see all so quiet, in so dangerous a Time. Many sober Men that called his Father no better than a Trayterous Hypocrite, did begin to think that they owed him Subjection. They knew that the King was by Birth their Rightful Sovereign; and resolved to do their best while there was hopes to introduce him, and defend him. . . . [But they marvelled at providence and] thought that it is not left to our liberty, whether we will have a Government, or not; but that Government is of Divine Appointment; and the Family, Person or Species is but of a subservient, less necessary determination: And that if we cannot have him that we would have, it followeth not that we may be without . . . .[47]

Baxter was justifying, as best he could, his own acknowledgment of Richard's *de facto* position, but his statement unquestionably applied to many men already beginning to forget Charles Stuart. As early as Novem-

[37] Whitelocke, *Memorials of English Affairs* 4: pp. 313–314, where a list of Cromwell's appointees is printed.

[38] [William Prynne], *King Richard the Third Revived* . . . (London, 1657).

[39] Lord Saye and Sele to Lord Wharton, December 29, 1657, printed by C. H. Firth in the *English Historical Review* 10: pp. 106–107.

[40] Charles Fleetwood to Henry Cromwell, October 12, 1658, B.M., Additional MSS 43,724, fol. 57; Additional is hereafter shortened to Add.

[41] Francesco Giavarina to Doge and Senate, October 15/25, 1658, *Calendar of State Papers, Venetian* 31: pp. 254–256.

[42] Sir Francis Russell to Henry Cromwell, October 5, 1658, B.M., Lans. MSS 823, fol. 122; Sir Henry Russell to Henry Cromwell, November 1, 1658, *ibid.*, fol. 138; Charles Fleetwood to Henry Cromwell, October 10, 1658, B. M., Add. MSS 43,724, fol. 59; and Charles Fleetwood to Henry Cromwell, October 26, 1658, *ibid.*, fol. 61.

[43] Arthur Annesley to Henry Cromwell, March 15, 1659, B.M., Lans. MSS 823, fol. 251.

[44] Charles Fleetwood to Henry Cromwell, [October, 1658], B.M., Add. MSS 43,724, fol. 63.

[45] Arthur Annesley to Henry Cromwell, March 15, 1659, B.M., Lans. MSS 823, fol. 251.

[46] *Thurloe State Papers* 7: p. 388; according to the editor, Birch, the paper was in the hand of Dr. Thomas Clarges, Monck's brother-in-law, and was delivered to Thurloe.

[47] Baxter, *Reliquiae Baxterianae*, Pt. I: p. 100.

ber 9, Thomas Gorges, a fairly conservative politician, remarked that the protector was gaining with the sober party, and was thereby checking "specious pretences or designs of some persons who as yet have noe apparent footing." [48]

Richard's early successes made the Royalists despondent. Hyde wrote,

We have not yet found that advantage by Cromwell's death as we reasonably hoped, nay rather, we are the worse for it, and the less esteemed, people imagining by the great calm that hath followed, that the nation is united, and that in truth the King hath very few friends. [49]

A major cause for the Royalist despair was the adherence of many Presbyterians to the banner of Richard Cromwell and the indifference of others to the king across the waters. The Presbyterian ministers lost no time in paying vocal tribute to the new ruler. To the Royalist Lord Insequin in Paris it appeared that "divers of the Presbyterians are not so well inclined as last year, though still violent against Cromwell and the Army." [50]

For clear evidence of Presbyterian support for Richard, however, it will be necessary to turn to the elections and parliament of 1659. The calling of this parliament was to have fatal consequences. It was summoned only after due consideration of other possible solutions to the government's problems. Wars, at home and abroad, added the burden of costly troops and ships to the customary expenses of government. Fleetwood wrote Henry Cromwell that "the necessity of our affayres leads us to this choyce" and that no money could be sent to Ireland until new revenue was raised. [51]

Fortunately, there are several surviving estimates of party divisions within the commons of 1659. A disinterested observer, Francesco Giavarina, asserted that "several have been chosen who have always shown a greater leaning for the royal party than for the present," [52] and two weeks later remarked that the parliament "is composed of members all differing in their beliefs and religion." [53] The strongest single element was the legal party of 150 lawyers, "more

than ever before," [54] and one Royalist agent said all of the lawyer members were of the court party. [55] This would place the Presbyterian lawyers in accord with the protector. The Royalists were estimated at more than forty by William Rumbold, [56] but this statement should be compared with the report that the "strongest party in the Parliament is that of moderate men, who would call in the King if they durst, but will consent to Cromwell's being Protector for the sake of peace." Moderate in this case would include the Presbyterians, and it is significant that Henry Slingsby, a Royalist agent, recognized that the Presbyterians intended to support the existing government rather than risk upheaval. [57]

The most complete breakdown of the parliament comes from the pen of Alan Broderick, who informed Hyde that there were

47 true patriots of liberty, 23 of them highly exasperated at the present government, 24 of meeker spirits. Counterfeit Commonwealth-men and such neuters as usually occur from 100 to 140 (as the House fills), Court lawyers 72 certain, with many contingent officers of State and Army 100 and odd. Many double elections not supplied, many absent by design, many on their necessary occasions. [58]

In other words, the parliament included 47 Royalists, 172 court politicians or other adherents of the court, and approximately 100 to 140 radical opponents of the court. These estimates correspond roughly to the division votes on all major bills.

The general strength of the Presbyterians in this parliament is suggested by the selection of three Presbyterians, Reynolds, Manton, and Calamy, to only one Independent, Owen, to preach at the opening session and of Cooper, a Presbyterian, to pray every day. [59] This picture is borne out by the membership of the committee appointed to draft a declaration for a fast. The Presbyterians dominated the committee, and its report, adopted by the Commons with only slight change, carried mild Presbyterian overtones. [60] Moreover, the Commons ordered the City of London to restore Major General Richard Brown, an avowed Presbyterian, to the offices which had been denied him for several years. [61]

With few exceptions, individuals cannot be assigned

[48] Thomas Gorges to Henry Cromwell, November 9, 1658, B.M., Lans. MSS 823, fol. 145.

[49] Sir Edward Hyde to [William Howard], January 11/21, 1659, *State Papers Collected by Edward, Earl of Clarendon*, ed. R. Scrope and T. Monkhouse (3 v., Oxford, 1767–1786) 3: p. 407; hereafter cited as *Clarendon State Papers*. Letters printed in this work have been checked against the *Calendar of the Clarendon State Papers*, and in most cases against the originals in the Bodleian Library, and references to one may incorporate information from all three sources.

[50] Lord Insequin to Sir Edward Hyde, December 31/January 10, 1658/1659, *Calendar of the Clarendon State Papers* 4: p. 126.

[51] Charles Fleetwood to Henry Cromwell, [1658], B.M., Add. MSS 43,724, fol. 71.

[52] Francesco Giavarina to Doge and Senate, January 14/24, 1659, *Calendar of State Papers, Venetian* 31: pp. 284–285.

[53] Francesco Giavarina to Doge and Senate, January 27/February 7, 1659, *ibid.*, pp. 287–289.

[54] [Dr. Moore to Sir Edward Hyde], January 28, 1659, *Calendar of Clarendon State Papers* 4: p. 140.

[55] [Henry Slingsby to Sir Edward Hyde], February 18, 1659, *Clarendon State Papers* 3: p. 425.

[56] [William Rumbold to Marquis of Ormonde], February 18, 1659, *Calendar of the Clarendon State Papers* 4: p. 151.

[57] [Henry Slingsby to Sir Edward Hyde], February 10, 1659, *ibid.*, p. 146.

[58] [Alan Broderick to Sir Edward Hyde], March 18, 1659, *Clarendon State Papers* 3: p. 440. In a letter of March 25 Broderick told Hyde that only five knights of the shire supported the government, *Calendar of the Clarendon State Papers* 4: pp. 166–167.

[59] *Commons Journals* 7: pp. 594–595.

[60] *Ibid.*, pp. 622–625.

[61] Whitelocke, *Memorials of English Affairs* 4: p. 341.

to any party in this parliament, because of much cross-voting.[62] Some members, however, rather consistently supported or opposed the court. John Maynard, lawyer and Presbyterian, was the protector's spokesman and leader in the commons.[63] Lord Aungier, Richard Norton, and Arthur Annesley, all Presbyterians, apparently supported the desires of Henry Cromwell, and probably those of the lord protector.[64] Thomas Grove, Baxter's friend, was sufficiently in favor to ask the lord lieutenant of Ireland to advance his brother's interest in Ireland.[65] Another Presbyterian, Andrew Marvell, was an officeholder, and could be relied on by the court.

Some Presbyterians were active debaters in behalf of the government. On February 7, when Sir Arthur Haselrigge, Thomas Scot, and Colonel White spoke for four hours against the bill to recognize Richard Cromwell as lord protector, they were "briefly & fully" answered by the Presbyterians John Bulkeley, Robert Beake, a friend of Richard Baxter, and Serjeant John Maynard.[66] This one example could be multiplied, but the list of tellers should suffice. Tellers for the government on important measures included Arthur Annesley, John Bulkeley, John Maynard, Thomas Grove, John Trevor, Edward Rossiter, Richard Hampden, Sir Richard Temple, Francis Gerard, and Hugh Boscawen, all of whom were men usually viewed as Presbyterians. It should be added, however, that Annesley, Sir George Booth, and Lord Fairfax served as tellers in opposition to the government on some measures.[67]

The disunity among the Presbyterians in 1659 is best revealed by their division on the question of the "Other House," as the peers were called. It was reported to Henry Cromwell that "many of the country gentlemen" were very active in asserting the rights of the ancient, hereditary lords to sit in the "Other House." The leading advocates were Booth, Hungerford, Knightley, Tirrell, William Morice, Annesley, and Edward Turner, a secret Royalist. These men and their followers joined with the Commonwealth party, who had been against the *Petition and Advice,* in opposition to the bill to recognize the nominated lords. Another group of Presbyterians, Bulkeley, Grove, John

Swinfen, Thomas Bampfield, Samuel Godfrey, and "several others," joined the court officers.[68]

The reason for the battle about the composition of the "Other House" was the high number of army officers summoned to it by Richard Cromwell. The readmission of the old peers would have provided a counterbalance to the power of the army, as Monck had recommended to the protector. An examination of the debates reveals strong Presbyterian sentiment for recognition of the protectorate, and an equally strong desire to curb the military by placing it under civil authority. James Stephens, Annesley, Sir John Northcote, Samuel Gott, and Henry Hungerford addressed the commons in such terms.[69]

Terrified by the support given the protector by the conservatives, opposed to a protectorate, and ambitious for power, the army and its following forced Richard to dissolve his parliament and then to abdicate. The left-wing elements, Independents, Republicans, and Fifth Monarchists, repeatedly broadcast the accusation that the Presbyterians, Cavaliers, and the court party were attempting to restore monarchy by using either Richard Cromwell or Charles II and by reinstating the old peers.[70] This charge served well as a cover for the army's general dissatisfaction with both parliament and protector and its ambition for power. Acute observers had predicted, almost from the first day of the parliamentary session, that the army would use force against the parliament, and perhaps the protector.[71] Richard at first seemed determined to combine with the parliament in opposing the army council, which he once ordered dissolved. This action was reported as "very satisfactory to the house and well pleasing" to the predominantly Presbyterian City of London which was "firmly united to his Highnesse and to the parliament."[72] The commons, with the Presbyterians Boscawen and Rossiter acting as tellers for the majority, actually approved the protector's decree to the army

[62] See Thomas Burton, *Diary of Thomas Burton, Esq., Member in the Parliaments of Oliver and Richard Cromwell, from 1656 to 1659,* ed. John Towill Rutt (4 v., London, 1828) 3 and 4; hereafter cited as *Diary of Thomas Burton.*

[63] [Alan Broderick to Sir Edward Hyde], March 18, 1659, *Clarendon State Papers* 3: p. 440.

[64] Francis Lord Aungier to Henry Cromwell, February 15, 1659, B.M., Lans. MSS 823, fol. 218; Richard Norton to Henry Cromwell, February 7, 1659, *ibid.,* fol. 208; and Arthur Annesley to Henry Cromwell, February 15, 1659, *ibid.,* fol. 216.

[65] Thomas Grove to Henry Cromwell, March 1, 1659, *ibid.,* fol. 237.

[66] Gilbert Mabbott to Henry Cromwell, February 8, 1659, *ibid.,* fol. 212.

[67] *Commons Journals* 7: pp. 603–641.

[68] Sir Hierome Sankey to Henry Cromwell, March 8, 1659, B.M., Lans. MSS 823, fol. 247. See also Richard Norton to Henry Cromwell, February 7, 1659, *ibid.,* fol. 208; Arthur Annesley to Henry Cromwell, February 15, 1659, *ibid.,* fol. 216; and John Thurloe to George Downing, March 4, 1659, B. M., Add. MSS 22,919, fol. 86.

[69] *Diary of Thomas Burton* 4: pp. 11, 27, 33–34, 56–57, 63–65.

[70] Anonymous, *An Invocation to the Officers of the Army . . . in a Letter Presented to them on Wednesday 20 April 1659* (London, 1659), pp. 1–2; anonymous, *A Faithful Searching Home Word . . .* (n.p., 1659), p. 22; Henry Gregory, "A briefe Narrative of the Trayalls of King Charls the Second in time of his Banishment, & before his Returne to his Three Kingdomes," B.M., Add. MSS 19,526, fol. 23; and John Thurloe to George Downing, April 29, 1659, *ibid.,* 22,919, fol. 96.

[71] W. Mills to Mrs. Elizabeth Henson, March 11, 1659, *ibid.,* 15,750, foll. 46–47; and Sir Anthony Morgan to Henry Cromwell, March 29, 1659, B.M., Lans. MSS 823, fol. 279.

[72] Dr. Dudley Loftus to Henry Cromwell, April 19, 1659, *ibid.,* fol. 297; see also Sir Anthony Morgan to Henry Cromwell, April 19, 1659, *ibid.,* foll. 301–302.

council by a vote of 163 to 87 on April 18,[73] but time was running out.

Richard lacked the courage to withstand the mounting pressure by the army to dissolve his parliament and to recall the old Rump Parliament which his father had dismissed in 1653.[74] Whitelocke insisted, correctly it seems, that the army's remonstrance of April 6 about pay, enemies of the state, and other grievances was the beginning of Richard's collapse and that it was brought on by his relatives Fleetwood and Desborough.[75] Edward Montagu, later Earl of Sandwich, secretly maintained that Richard could have prevented his personal disaster by proroguing parliament rather than dissolving it.[76]

Both Whitelocke and Montagu's analyses of the situation surely involved the supposition that the Presbyterians would have continued to serve the protectorate, in preference to anything then obtainable. David Masson and Louise Fargo Brown, by implication, arrived at the same conclusion,[77] and the evidence examined here can support no other thesis. The Presbyterian clergy had drawn closer to the protectorate, and even to the Independents, from the time of the dismissal of the Barebones Parliament. The clergy asked only that a broad national church with disciplinary power be created; they felt they had more to gain from a possible settlement with Richard Cromwell in 1659 than from the uncertainties that would follow his removal. A large block of the Presbyterian politicians, including most of their lawyer associates, rallied to the defense of the protectorate by April, 1659. They wanted, most of all, the immediate reduction of the military to its proper subordination to the civil power.[78] In order to accomplish this and other ends, they would have been forced to bestow some monarchical power upon Richard Cromwell. Would they have done so? Some had been urging kingship upon Oliver before his death. Why not, then, upon his son?

All evidence indicates that the connection between Charles II and the English Presbyterians had weakened considerably by 1659. The Royalists had expected great things, but they received nothing immediately,

from the death of Oliver Cromwell. In fact, the Royalists lost ground. Richard Baxter, who expressed Royalist inclinations in 1656, even provided the Presbyterians with a reasoned justification, in his *Holy Commonwealth*, for converting the protectorate into a theocratic monarchy in 1659. Baxter clearly stated his allegiance to the protector, using the argument that a "full and free parliament had recognized the new ruler." [79] A single quotation from the *Holy Commonwealth* is sufficient to indicate Baxter's basic position:

If the whole Family, with whom the People were in Covenant be extirpated, *or become uncapable, the People may new forme the Government as they please,* (so they contradict not the Law of God:) not by Authority, but by Contract with the next chosen Governours; nor as Subjects, but as Free men, the Government being dissolved.[80]

These conditions, he felt, had been fulfilled by the parliament of 1659 in approving the *Humble Petition and Advice,* and, as he told Richard, "the Nation generally rejoyceth in your peaceable entrance upon the Government." [81] A new dynasty, owing much to the Presbyterians, had been created, and Baxter, a man widely respected by the members of Richard's parliament, was busily engaged in justifying its existence when the army council forced the protector to dissolve the parliament on April 22 and finally to abdicate.

The events of April and May, 1659, offered the Presbyterians, whether lay or clerical, little choice. With the army, championed by Republicans and Independents, in power the Presbyterians were once again in total opposition. The clergy's efforts for a broad religious union fell with the protector, and their parliamentary allies fared no better. The "Good Old Cause" of republican rule in both church and state had once more reared its ugly head, and the Presbyterians had already rejected the "Good Old Cause" in 1649.

III. THE GOOD OLD CAUSE

The dissolution of parliament on April 22, 1659, signified the victory of the army, the Independents, and the Republicans over the protectorate. It put an end to the efforts to reconcile the Presbyterians to the new order and to the plans for religious union. It placed the Presbyterians, both lay and clerical, in complete opposition for the first time since 1648. It also forced professional soldiers and civil servants like George Monck, Edward Montagu, Lord Broghill, Lord Falconbridge, Richard Ingoldsby, and William Lockhart, who were moderates, to seek an escape from anarchy, without giving way to an unconditional restoration of monarchy by intolerant Scots and foreign

[73] *Commons Journals* 7 : p. 641.

[74] Richard was characterized by the Venetian minister as "not the man to take such vigorous measures as his father, as he does not entirely share the sentiments of the deceased, nor does he inspire such fear," Francesco Giavarina to Doge and Senate, January 21/31, 1659, *Calendar of State Papers, Venetian* 31 : p. 286.

[75] Whitelocke, *Memorials of English Affairs* 4 : pp. 341–342.

[76] See F. R. Harris, *The Life of Edward Montagu, K. G., First Earl of Sandwich, 1625–1672* (2 v., London, 1912) 1 : pp. 130–131, who quotes from Montagu's manuscript journal.

[77] David Masson, *The Life of John Milton* (7 v., London, 1859–1894) 5 : p. 436; and Louise Fargo Brown, *The First Earl of Shaftesbury* (New York, 1933), p. 76.

[78] Godfrey Davies, "The Election of Richard Cromwell's Parliament, 1658–9," *English Historical Review* 63 : p. 501.

[79] Baxter, *Holy Commonwealth*, p. 484.

[80] *Ibid.*, p. 451 ; italics added.

[81] Baxter, *Five Disputations of Church-Government, and Worship,* [p. 4].

arms.[1] It meant the victory of the Presbyterian monarchists, like William Prynne, over their drifting and
temporizing brethren, and the hostility of the Presbyterian monarchists toward republicanism and of the
Presbyterian clergy toward unregulated Independency
was such that all branches of Presbyterianism ran
headlong into an alliance with Charles II and the
Anglicans. By January, 1660, the Presbyterian-Royalist
alliance, with an assist from Monck, had unseated the
army and the Good Old Cause of republicanism and
Independency.

The Royalist hopes for support from the English
Presbyterians reached their nadir in January, 1659,
when the accord between the Presbyterians and the
protectorate was at its zenith. Almost a year before
Oliver Cromwell's death Sir Edward Nicholas complained that Oliver was "absolutely master of all England and secure against all intestine opposition" and
that Charles II would not be able to enter the kingdom
so long as Oliver lived.[2] The death of Oliver Cromwell
and the accession of Richard Cromwell failed to change
the relations between Presbyterians and Royalists, and
a great distance continued to separate them until the
fears of the Presbyterians were awakened early in
1659.[3]

Even while the conservative and radical forces were
fighting for and against the life of the parliament of
1659 and the protectorate, a new drive for an alliance
between Presbyterians and Royalists was set in motion,
and some favorable news was soon reaching the Royalists in exile. New strength for the royal cause came
in the person of John Mordaunt and those who, like
him, moved toward an understanding between the
Presbyterians and Royalists. Mordaunt was linked by
birth and background to both the parties he sought to
unite. His father, the first Earl of Peterborough, was
a Parliamentarian until his death in 1643. Mordaunt's
brother, the second Earl, was an active Royalist till
1646 and again in 1648. Young Mordaunt joined
the Royalist plot of 1657, despite the opposition of
his Puritan mother, upon whom he was entirely dependent financially. Thenceforward, he became further
implicated in the Royalist intrigues. During the winter
of 1658–1659, Mordaunt worked toward a Presbyterian-
Royalist alliance,[4] and it was his request for "some
wise and powerful person" to lead the movement for
the restoration of Charles II [5] that produced the joint

Presbyterian-Royalist "Plenepotentiary or Great Trust
and Commission" to aid Mordaunt and others in negotiating with the Presbyterians and all who might be
brought to join in a rising against the government.[6]

By late March, 1659, Mordaunt was reporting favorable news from England. Sir William Waller, speaking
in behalf of the Presbyterian monarchists, assured
Mordaunt that "all the restrictions, the fears of the
most guilty of the Presbyterians will at first tye your
Majesty to, will suddenly and visibly be taken off,
. . . and the next free Parliament will restore you
fully to your rights and prerogatives." Most of the
Royalists, according to Mordaunt, were not averse to
any honorable terms the Presbyterians might offer.[7]

Welding a cohesive party from divergent forces
proved very difficult, however. Mordaunt complained
of the lukewarmness of the Royalists who appeared to
scruple at acting with "the Presbyterians, or those
who were so." [8] Edward Massey, a Royalist with a
Presbyterian background, wrote that

the Presbiter party in general are naught and the best of
them do play their game with so much precaution that with
Sir William Waller their expectation to have the worke
play to their hand that I can hope little of good by them,
I meane the great ones, and wish that Major General
Browne prove to answer his Majesty's expectation. For
I am well assured that, if he would do anything, the citty
is apt enough to take fire . . . .[9]

Mordaunt agreed with Massey, but, as he informed
Charles II, the alliance with the Presbyterians "seemed
our best hope, and the belief we have of the integrity
of some of the leading men of them, made us the more
willing to try their power." [10] From this rather in-
auspicious beginning great things were to come, but
not until the army radicals had unseated both parliament and protector.

Various obstacles continued to trouble the pending
alliance through April, 1659. Silas Titus, the Presbyterian agent with the exiled king, was no longer
trusted by the Presbyterians,[11] and the Presbyterian
and Cavalier agents of the king refused to cooperate
with each other.[12] Hyde even feared that the Presby-

---

[1] Godfrey Davies, "The Army and the Downfall of Richard
Cromwell," *Huntington Library Bulletin,* No. 7: pp. 131–167.

[2] Sir Edward Nicholas to Sir Edward Hyde, August 31/Sep-
tember 10, 1657, *Nicholas Papers* 4: p. 13.

[3] Sir Edward Hyde to [William Howard], January 11/21,
1659, *Clarendon State Papers* 3: p. 407; and Lord Insequin to
Sir Edward Hyde, December 31/January 10, 1658/1659, *Calendar of the Clarendon State Papers* 4: p. 126.

[4] *The Letter-Book of John Viscount Mordaunt, 1658–1660,* ed.
Mary Coate (London, 1945), pp. vii–xi; hereafter cited as
Mordaunt Letter-Book.

[5] John Mordaunt to Marquis of Ormonde, February 18, 1659,
Clarendon State Papers 3: p. 426.

[6] The members of this body were Lord Belasye, Colonel John
Russell, Sir William Compton, Sir Richard Willis (all members
of the old Sealed Knot), Lord Loughborough, and Mordaunt.
In June Lord Willoughby of Parham, a Presbyterian, Andrew
Newport, Job Charlton, and William Legge were added, and in
July Sir John Grenville, Sir Thomas Peyton, and William Rum-
bold were added, *Mordaunt Letter-Book,* p. 3.

[7] John Mordaunt to Charles II, March 24, 1659, *Clarendon
State Papers* 3: pp. 443–445.

[8] Viscount Mordaunt to Sir Edward Nicholas, March 30,
1659, *ibid.,* p. 446.

[9] Edward Massey to Sir Edward Nicholas, April 4, 1659,
Nicholas Papers 4: p. 98.

[10] Viscount Mordaunt to Charles II, April 6, 1659, *Clarendon
State Papers* 3: p. 450.

[11] Viscount Mordaunt to Sir Edward Hyde, April 14, 1659,
ibid., p. 453.

[12] T. Ross to Colonel Gervase Holles, April 20/30, 1659,
H.M.C., *Calendar of the Manuscripts of the Marquis of Bath*

terians were seeking an understanding with the Catholics,[13] a frightening possibility that remained in Hyde's mind until long after the Restoration. Thus matters stood when Richard Cromwell dissolved his parliament on April 22, 1659.

Anticipating events in England, Hyde had already provided Mordaunt with instructions. Hyde was pleased that the Presbyterians and Republicans watched each other so warily, and was certain that the wise men of each party would be fearful lest the enemy "gallop so fast towards the King's interest, that they may become less considerable." Future events proved Hyde correct. In the event that the army turned against the protector and his parliament, Mordaunt was to find some of all parties to protest for the privileges of parliament by word and force.[14] The Presbyterians had long defended the privileges and rights of parliament. They needed no prodding from any Royalist to stir them to action against those who meddled with the elected branch of government.

The re-emergence of the Good Old Cause of republicanism made unnecessary Hyde's instructions to Mordaunt. Only eight days after the army council compelled Richard Cromwell to dissolve his parliament, William Prynne, long an antagonist of the Good Old Cause, anonymously published an attack against the army and its activities.[15]

When the army council summoned the Rump Parliament, which had represented the Good Old Cause ten years before, on May 7, 1659, it stirred William Prynne and his fellow Presbyterians to cooperation among themselves, eventually to cooperation with the Royalists, and to action against the Rump Parliament and the army council. Prynne learned of the army's plan to reseat the Rump Parliament only after it had been executed. Approximately thirty of the Presbyterian members secluded from parliament in 1648 met almost immediately and agreed that "about 12 or 14" of them should repair to the commons and inquire "upon what account they did sit there thus sodainly and unexpectedly, without giving any convenient notice or summons to all the rest of the Members to sit with them?" If the Rump's answer was unsatisfactory, the thirty were to meet again and to vote on whether to contact all surviving members of the Long Parliament. The thirty further resolved, once all survivors were present, to debate whether the Long Parliament lost all pretense to legality upon the death of Charles I.

They preferred to consider the Long Parliament legally dissolved by the death of the king, but considered a full Long Parliament better than the Rump.[16]

Under the above instructions, Prynne, Sir George Booth, Arthur Annesley, Sir John Evelyn, Thomas Gewen, Charles Rich, George Montagu, Richard Knightley, Henry Hungerford, and one or two others not named went to the lobby door of the commons on May 7 with the intention of taking the seats from which they had been secluded since 1648. Upon arrival they found the door locked, but, with some resourcefulness, Prynne, Booth, and Annesley succeeded in slipping through when the door was opened to permit the departure of Philip Nye, the Congregational minister. Prynne thereupon unbolted the door to admit the remainder of his followers. Within the lobby they found James and John Herbert, secluded members, who resolved to join the Prynne group. Advancing toward the commons, the secluded members found the entrance blocked by army guards, who at last agreed to submit their names to the speaker. Prynne debated at length with the guards, but to no avail. General Lambert informed Knightley, as the group was leaving, that their entrance into the commons at that time would only lead to disturbance, but implied that the army council would probably remove the guard within a few days.[17]

Thwarted in their original strategy, the secluded members decided to meet at Lincoln's Inn, where Prynne was a bencher, at four that afternoon. Each man had instructions to ascertain how many of the secluded members were in London and the total number of survivors of the Long Parliament. The tabulated results showed eighty members in the City and a total of more than 200 survivors. It was decided that all survivors should be summoned, and a committee of ten was appointed to manage the business. This committee made a separate decision to reappear at the commons on Monday morning, at which time Prynne acted as the delegation's leader. Finding the doors open, Prynne persuaded Annesley and Hungerford to accompany him in a second assault upon the Rump. The other members of the group, less daring than these three, urged sending a letter to the speaker.

Prynne, Hungerford, and Annesley, disdainful of any physical harm that might befall them, advanced boldly onto the floor of the commons. Hungerford and Annesley left shortly, and upon their return found the door barred. Prynne, trapped inside and not wishing to surrender without a fight, instigated a debate on the nature and meaning of the statute by which Charles I had abandoned any right to dissolve the Long Parliament without its permission. The Presbyterian lawyer contended that the Long Parliament

preserved at Longleat, Wiltshire (2 v., London, 1907) 2: p. 131; and Sir Edward Hyde to Viscount Mordaunt, April 23/May 3, 1659, H.M.C., *Tenth Report, Appendix, Part VI* (London, 1887), p. 193; hereafter cited as *Bath MSS* and *Tenth Report* respectively.

[13] Sir Edward Hyde to Viscount Mordaunt, April 29/May 9, 1659, *Clarendon State Papers* 3: p. 464.

[14] Sir Edward Hyde to Viscount Mordaunt, April 23/May 3, 1659, H.M.C., *Tenth Report, Appendix, Part VI*, pp. 195–197.

[15] [William Prynne], *The true Good Old Cause rightly stated, and the False un-cased* (London, 1659).

[16] William Prynne, *A true and perfect Narrative*, pp. 1–4; supplemented by [Arthur Annesley ?], *England's Confusion: Or a True and Impartial Relation of the Traverses of State in England . . .* (London, 1659).

[17] Prynne, *A true and perfect Narrative*, pp. 5–7.

expired with the death of Charles I. Not knowing what to do with the invincible old lawyer, the Rump tried to ignore him, but Prynne's determination to resume his old seat resulted in a postponement of all formal business until after lunch. While Prynne dined, the Rump stole quietly back into the Commons, posting a guard to keep out the intruders.[18]

The secluded members made no further attempt to thrust themselves among the Rump. Unarmed and vastly outnumbered by the army, they preferred the wiser course of verbal attack and denunciation. The forced resignation of Richard Cromwell on May 25 [19] further strengthened the army's grasp on the nation. Richard's fall virtually destroyed any sign of a Protectorate party, and thus helped to clear away some of of the confusion. As between Presbyterian and Independent politician, there was no longer any question of a tacit compromise. Battle had begun; there would be no retreat. Equally significant results of the restoration of the Rump and the fall of the Protectorate were the reunion of the moderate Presbyterians under a single banner, but without responsible leadership, and the reappearance of William Prynne as the recognized propagandist of his party.

Prynne, who had gained his first eminence in 1637 as a Puritan martyr, took full advantage of his renewed seclusion, which he repeatedly cited as evidence that military and republican tyranny was worse than anything ever suffered under monarchy. The original struggle to Prynne had been a defense of the king, kingdom, parliament, and lawful privileges, but, as an army officer confessed to him, the army's cause was entirely different from that which had attracted the Long Parliament in 1642.[20]

As a lawyer by training and an antiquarian by interest, Prynne was somewhat naturally opposed to any radical change in the government. He was terrified by the commonwealth proposals of James Harrington,[21] which he attacked.[22] He had once been able to defend the assumption of vast powers by parliament,[23] but the pendulum of Prynne's thoughts was now swinging in the opposite direction. The Long Parliament, he now insisted, could not survive its creator. Every act since January, 1649, was illegal. These were the fears of a man who longed for the supremacy of law and civil authority over the might of the sword and the disruptive forces of a nonconforming multitude.[24]

In a more positive vein, Prynne demanded that all laws against Roman Catholics be executed. Put no arms in the hands of Anabaptists or Quakers, he urged, "lest London become another Munster, and England another Germanie." The only permanent solution was to restore the "antient, hereditary, just, legal Kingship, King, Governors, Government, with all their necessary invaded Prerogatives, Lands, Revenues, Rights, Jurisdictions" and to preserve them inviolably.[25] Such a government would be a mixture of the three known forms of polity, absolute monarchy, aristocracy, and democracy, with the conveniences of all and the inconveniences of none.[26] Prynne suggested that all men cease paying taxes to the army until it once again subordinated itself to civil power, accurately predicting that this course would produce an impasse in the government and result in its collapse through dissension among the unpaid soldiers.[27]

A somewhat similar attack was made on the army and the Rump by Richard Baxter. His *Holy Commonwealth,* originally intended for the guidance of Richard Cromwell, appeared in July, 1659, with a last minute prefatory attack on the army and Rump for their various activities since 1648.[28]

The Presbyterian war against the second Commonwealth did not go unnoticed. The Presbyterian attacks provoked an editorial reply from *The Faithfull Scout,* an Independent newspaper,[29] and captured the attention of the Venetian minister, who described the Presbyterian activities as follows:

restless and dissatisfied they are making cliques into which they draw many others who are not well affected, and so they cabal and plot further disturbances and issue without the slightest fear, biting broadsides which cannot fail to do considerable damage to the state.[30]

A Royalist wrote very ecstatically to Nicholas that Prynne's "quill doth the best present right to our Egle and, tho his eares are lost, he heares nowe very well and speakes more loyalty to a generall reception then any other." [31] Such plaudits from the Royalist camp,

[18] *Ibid.,* pp. 8–14.

[19] *Commons Journals* 7: p. 664.

[20] Prynne, *A true and perfect Narrative,* p. 17.

[21] [James Harrington], *A Proposition in order to the Proposing of a Commonwealth or Democracie* (n.p., 1659), which appeared about June 14.

[22] [William Prynne], *An Answer to a Proposition in order to the proposing of a Commonwealth or Democracy* (London, 1659), which appeared about June 17.

[23] William Prynne, *The Soveraigne Power of Parliaments and Kingdoms . . .* (London, 1643).

[24] Prynne, *A true and perfect Narrative,* pp. 25–26.

[25] *Ibid.,* pp. 58–59.

[26] *Ibid.,* pp. 85–89.

[27] William Prynne, *The Re-publicans and others spurious Good Old Cause, briefly and truly Anatomized . . .* (London, 1659).

[28] Baxter, Preface to the Army and others, *Holy Commonwealth.*

[29] *The Faithful Scout,* No. 4, p. 26; *The Loyall Scout,* No. 15, p. 109, said: "The Printed Papers of Mr. William Pryn hath taken a great Impression upon the hearts of many, tending much to Insurrections; whereas on the contrary, there ought to be a mutual Union, for the preventing of new Commotions in regard the Enemy is numerous beyond the Seas."

[30] Francesco Giavarina to Doge and Senate, May 20/30, 1659, *Calendar of State Papers, Venetian* 32: p. 24.

[31] W. Miles to Sir Edward Nicholas, June 17, 1659, *Nicholas Papers* 4: p. 157. For additional praise of Prynne's activities see Gregory, "A briefe Narrative of the Tryalls of King Charls the Second," B.M., Add. MSS 19,526, fol. 23; and William Younger, *A Brief View of the late troubles and confusions in England . . .* (London, 1660), p. 99.

and continued and increasing bitterness between Presbyterians and Independents, foredoomed the Presbyterians to an eventual alliance with the old Cavaliers.

The reseating of the Rump Parliament, and the Presbyterian reaction thereto, hastened the discussions between Presbyterians and Royalists and produced a Presbyterian-Royalist plan for a military move against the Commonwealth. New Presbyterian names and proposals appeared in the Royalist correspondence. As early as May 2 Mordaunt was discussing the probable conversion of Robert Harley, who was already planting seeds of disunity among the junior officers of the army, though still insisting on concessions from the absent monarch. Lord Willoughby, Sir William Waller, and Sir George Booth, Presbyterians of differing degrees, were given royal commissions. Colonel Richard Norton was seen in connection with an intended rising.[32]

By June 16, when he submitted a report to Hyde, Mordaunt had almost completed his alliances. Presbyterians holding positions of some importance in the plot included Booth, Willoughby, Manchester, Warwick, Saye and Sele, Robartes, Maynard, Sir John Northcote, the Boscawens, John Rolle, and Edward Rossiter. These Presbyterian leaders requested royal adoption of the terms submitted to Charles I at Newport in 1648, but they accepted the king's commission without receiving any definite concessions from Charles II.[33]

From the various discussions between Presbyterians and Royalists slowly evolved concrete conditions of cooperation. William Rumbold wrote Hyde that a secluded member of the Long Parliament had informed Sir William Compton on June 15 that he and his fellow outcasts planned to oppose the Rump by force within three weeks, or whenever the Royalists could be readied. They intended to issue a manifesto insisting on the Isle of Wight treaty as the basis for readmitting the Stuart line. Secretly, however, their plan was to bring Charles home and then submit the various issues to a freely elected parliament. When the secluded member suggested that a declaration from the king be issued "for the satisfaction of the people," Compton urged the informant to set down the terms desired by his group. These suggestions were transmitted to Rumbold, via Andrew Newport, and edited by Job Charlton, for submission to Hyde and Charles II.[34]

The exiled court had reason to avoid public declarations that might alienate as well as attract support. Seven days prior to Compton's interview with the secluded member, Slingsby had reported to Hyde that some Anabaptists were willing to cooperate with the Royalists if the king would declare in behalf of tender consciences and pardon all but a few royally excepted persons.[35] Hyde's reply was that the

publishing any declaration till the King be in a posture to receive those into his protection who are willing to serve him, is a very difficult point, and may do more harm than good, and that which pleases one may displease two more, therefore all that for the present is to be done is underhand, to satisfy as many particular men as we can that they may satisfy others; and the giving liberty of conscience is as much insinuated to those who are likely to be believed as we can, and you shall do well to assure as many as you can converse with that they may depend upon that indulgence from the King.[36]

Although he definitely committed the king to a policy of indulgence and authorized Slingsby to reassure the Anabaptists of religious toleration, Hyde, as late as June 17, would not agree to a royal declaration. Hyde preferred private to public negotiation.

The Presbyterians were more important to the royal cause than the Anabaptists, and their request for a royal declaration forced Hyde to reverse his stand on a declaration in order to win the Presbyterians over to cooperation with the Royalists. "I like well the discourse that was made to you by the member of the old Parliament," Hyde replied to Rumbold on June 24. Hyde cared not what "specious declaration" was made by the secluded members if they would "really . . . serve the King," and announced his eagerness to receive the proposed heads of a royal declaration.[37]

Importuned for a royal declaration by others as well as the Presbyterians, Hyde dispatched one to Rumbold on July 18. The preamble and the section on religion and liberty of conscience were to be composed by agents in England, who would be better acquainted with the "humours and satisfaction of the persons concerned." The agents were to write the completed proclamation over the king's signature on an otherwise blank sheet of paper and to have the document printed.[38] The declaration probably agreed with a draft dated July 19 among the Clarendon manuscripts. This draft promised that all persons except those attainted as judges of Charles I would be granted a free pardon, that those who performed meritorious service would be rewarded, and that no one

---

[32] Viscount Mordaunt to Sir Edward Hyde, May 2, 1659, *Clarendon State Papers* 3: pp. 459–461; *Mordaunt Letter-Book*, pp. 10–11; *Calendar of the Clarendon State Papers* 4: p. 194; as may be gathered from the multiplicity of references on the Mordaunt letter, their editors have omitted various passages or have failed to collate drafts with the finished document. For Norton see Sir Edward Hyde to Viscount Mordaunt, May 25/June 4, 1659, H.M.C., *Tenth Report, Appendix, Part VI*, p. 203.

[33] Viscount Mordaunt to Sir Edward Hyde, June 16, 1659, *Clarendon State Papers* 3: pp. 489–490.

[34] William Rumbold to Sir Edward Hyde, June 17, 1659, *ibid.*, p. 492.

[35] Henry Slingsby to Sir Edward Hyde, June 10, 1659, *Calendar of the Clarendon State Papers* 4: p. 231.

[36] Sir Edward Hyde to Henry Slingsby, June 17/27, 1659, *Clarendon State Papers* 3: p. 507.

[37] Sir Edward Hyde to William Rumbold, June 24/July 4, 1659, *ibid.*, pp. 513–514.

[38] Sir Edward Hyde to William Rumbold, July 18/28, 1659, *ibid.*, pp. 535–536.

who did not disturb the public peace would be punished for differences of religious opinion.[39] A declaration similar to the aforementioned documents circulated in England in July or August, 1659, and was unofficially published in October of the same year.[40]

Less openly, and on an individual basis, the king and his agents made, or were prepared to offer, additional promises in an attempt to mollify the apprehensions of various Englishmen, including the Presbyterians. Those who engaged in restoring Charles would be recompensed for whatever they might forfeit by any restoration of crown and church lands.[41] On the eve of his planned invasion of England, Charles commanded his brother, the Duke of York, to offer pardons and rewards liberally and to permit unpardonable persons who performed outstanding service to dispose of their property in England before going into exile.[42] Agents, like William Howard, assured people that the king intended to provide "civil and Christian liberty" in matters of religion.[43] There was nothing ambiguous about these statements.

General appeals through declarations might succeed with the multitude, but direct and specific promises were necessary for the conversion of leading men. Many leading figures arranged private agreements with the exiled Stuart.[44] Persistent efforts were made by the king and his agents to win key Presbyterians over to the royal cause by offers of great honor and office.[45] In many cases the king was successful. Most men who responded to the king's overtures brought others with them, especially since the Presbyterians were "quite out of favour" with the government.[46]

Although many of the Presbyterian laymen allied themselves with the Royalists throughout the winter and spring of 1659, the Presbyterian clergy followed a silent course until June. No overtures were made to them by the king, and they initiated none. Then suddenly the Presbyterian pulpits began to resound with bitter denunciations against the Rump government. The ostensible cause was a threatened attack upon the tithe system, but underneath there must have been some connection with the Presbyterian-Royalist rising planned for August, as well as a general irritation with the Independents for upsetting the plans for religious union. Independents, Quakers, and Fifth Monarchists petitioned the Rump to abolish tithes.[47] The republican followers of Henry Nevill reportedly considered the diversion of tithes into the exchequer so as to pay the soldiers. "This," wrote a Royalist, "exasperates the Presbyterians, who are now more unanimous than ever against the present government."[48] From York came a report that the Presbyterian clergy were holding "many and great meetings, are very high. Preach division and distraction."[49] On June 15 a terrified Chesterfield man reported that the clerical movement against the government had spread to his region. Twenty-three ministers under the leadership of Edward Bowles, chaplain to Lord Fairfax, met at Bradford, reportedly for the purpose of forming a petition in defense of religious maintenance. Laymen feared that the abolition of tithes might lead to the loss of their leased glebe and tithe lands.[50]

The threatened destruction of the tithe system, as earlier in the 1650's, awakened the Presbyterians and widened the gap between them and the Independents. William Prynne pictured the petitioners for tithe abolition as "poor mecanical persons" in no way responsible for the payment of church maintenance, more opposed to ministry than tithes, sectaries rather than true Protestants. He reasoned that the tithes would only be transferred from their legitimate and divinely ordained purpose to a sacrilegious use, and Prynne was not alone in this position.[51] The Presbyterian Samuel Clarke was afraid that the abolition of tithes would be only the forerunner for further religious fragmentation and asserted that "a Kingdom divided against itself cannot stand." Fear of sectaries, separatism, and papists drove Clarke and many of his fellow Presbyterians to cry out for uniformity and strengthened magisterial power over the religious activities of the people.[52] It was this same fear of fanaticism, according

[39] Draft of a Proclamation, July 19/29, 1659, *Calendar of the Clarendon State Papers* 4: p. 288.

[40] S. L., *A Letter to the Right Honorable the Lord Lambert* . . . (n.p., 1659). The letter, dated October 14, states that the enclosed declaration by the king has been in the writer's town for three months.

[41] Charles II to Viscount Mordaunt, July, 1659, *Clarendon State Papers* 3: pp. 512–513.

[42] Charles II to Duke of York, July 9/19, 1659, *ibid.*, p. 529.

[43] William Howard to Sir Edward Hyde, July 1, 1659, *Calendar of the Clarendon State Papers* 4: p. 258.

[44] Sir Edward Hyde to Viscount Mordaunt, May 13/23, 1659, *Clarendon State Papers* 3: pp. 475–476.

[45] Charles II to Edward Montagu, June 24/July 4, 1659, *Calendar of the Clarendon State Papers* 4: p. 246; Sir Edward Hyde to Edward Villiers, June 10/20, 1659, *ibid.*, pp. 228–229; and Sir Edward Hyde to Viscount Mordaunt, April 29/May 9, 1659, *Clarendon State Papers* 3: p. 464.

[46] Sir Edward Hyde to M. de Marces, July 2/12, 1659, *C.S.P.Dom, 1659–1660*, p. 5.

[47] Typical of these was Peter Cornelius, *The Way to the Peace and Settlement of these Nations* . . . (London, 1659), which urged that all persons be permitted to purchase their estates free from tithes. As late as October 7 some Warwick Independents petitioned for the abolition of the tithe system, *The Publick Intelligencer*, No. 23, p. 182.

[48] Alan Broderick to Sir Edward Hyde, June 24, 1659, *Clarendon State Papers* 3: p. 505.

[49] Joseph Pease to Adam Baynes, June 13, 1659, B.M., Add. MSS 21,425, fol. 72.

[50] Ant. Devenere (?) to Adam Baynes, June 15, 1659, *ibid.*, fol. 73.

[51] William Prynne, *Ten Considerable Quaeries concerning Tithes*, . . . (London, 1659). Similar views are found in the anonymous *Twelve Seasonable Quaeries Proposed to all True Zealous Protestants and English Free-men* . . . (n.p., 1659); and Giles Firmin, *Tythes vindicated from Anti-Christianisme and Oppression* . . . (London, 1659).

[52] Samuel Clarke, *Golden Apples* . . . (London, 1659), [pp. 4–5].

to Richard Baxter,[53] that made possible the Presbyterian alliance with the Royalists in the summer of 1659.

The awakening of the Presbyterian pamphleteers and clergy gave impetus to the Presbyterian-Royalist alliance for an uprising timed for August 1. At the final meeting of the Trust on July 24, Sir Richard Willis objected to the plan because of the nearness of the harvest season and because it was "totally Presbyterian." His group, consisting of several important men, withdrew; Mordaunt submitted, however, to the insistence of Major General Brown and Lord Willoughby, who headed the most considerable element, the Presbyterians, and who felt that Willis would betray, if he had not already done so, the entire campaign in order to prevent the Presbyterians from making any favorable impression on Charles II.[54]

The Presbyterian-Royalist rising of August 1 failed to progress as its leaders had planned. The government learned of the plot not later than July 9, when the council of state sent a warning to the militia of at least twenty-nine counties.[55] The capitulation of Henry Cromwell permitted the council to strengthen its English defenses by withdrawing men from Ireland and Dunkirk.[56] Thus prepared, the government was able to frustrate the insurrection before it could gain any momentum. News of a rendezvous in the Forest of Dean sent Colonel Okey thence with fifteen troops of horse. Arrests were made at Tunbridge and London on July 27 and 30.[57] The news journals carried stories of Massey and his forces in Gloucester and Bristol as early as July 28.[58] The Surrey contingent received a severe shock on the opening day of the campaign when several groups were surprised at their first muster.[59] So alert and successful was the government that no force of size survived south of the Thames. Massey's escape in the west failed to revive a cause already lost there.[60]

Only in the heart of Presbyterianism, Cheshire and Lancashire, did the rising gain any headway. There the movement was headed by Sir George Booth of Chester and Sir Thomas Middleton of Chirk Castle, Wales. Booth justified his participation as an attempt to obtain what was rightfully his: admission to the parliament, exemption of his property from illegal taxation, and freedom from the rule of the "meanest and most fanatick Spirits of the Nation." Booth insisted that the salvation of England rested upon the admission of the secluded members of parliament or the election of a new parliament.[61] In all this, Booth represented the spirit that was to produce the Stuart Restoration. His forces issued a declaration protesting against all coercive power in matters of religion and declaring in favor of numerous legal, economic, and political reforms. Booth's followers went so far as to hope that "all Parties, Sects, and Sorts" might be united in the "common Brotherhood of English Freedom and Right."[62] These statements by the troops were designed, of course, to lessen the opposition of the people in Lancashire and Cheshire to the Presbyterians and Royalists.

The "great Incendiaries" of the Lancashire-Cheshire area were the Presbyterian clergy. "This is not *Bellum Episcopale*, but *Bellum Presbiteriale*," was the report from Manchester.[63] In Lancashire the clergy revived the Civil War theme of "curse ye Meros" against the Independents.[64] Prominent among the ministers were Harrison, Herrick, and Newcomen, all of whom were leading Presbyterians of the region.[65] Zachary Crofton, a London Presbyterian, mysteriously appeared in Chester at this time and preached, so it was charged, to Booth's men.[66] The actions of the Presbyterian clergy further widened the breach between them and the Independents in that area and "rendered all former endeavours fruitless and an engagement almost hopeless."[67] By acting against the Independents and the Republicans the Presbyterians, both lay and clerical, moved well within the reach of the Royalists and Anglicans. This elementary fact was either ignored or unrecognized by some Presbyterians in 1659.

The Lancashire-Cheshire phase of the insurrection was more successful than all the other efforts combined. Much of this success must be attributed to the willing cooperation of the clergy and laity. While his counterparts in other sections numbered their adherents in hundreds or less, Booth raised a force of between 4,000 and 5,000. This following enabled Booth to remain in the field until overcome by Lambert's superior force at Winnington Bridge, Nantwich, on August 19.[68] Middleton, at Chirk Castle with a smaller contingent, held out until August 24.[69] The rising thus came to

[53] Baxter, *Reliquiae Baxterianae*, Pt. II: p. 207.

[54] Viscount Mordaunt to Hartgill Baron, July 26, 1659, *Mordaunt Letter-Book*, p. 31.

[55] *C.S.P.Dom., 1659–1660*, pp. 5–6.

[56] President Whitelock to Lieutenant General Ludlow, August 4, 1659, *ibid.*, p. 73; and President Whitelock to Sir Brice Cockraine, August 4, 1659, *ibid.*, p. 74.

[57] *The Weekly Post*, No. 13: pp. 105–111.

[58] *The Loyall Scout*, No. 13: p. 112; and *The Weekly Intelligencer*, No. 13: p. 101.

[59] *The Loyall Scout*, No. 14: p. 116.

[60] *The Clarke Papers*, ed. C. H. Firth (4 v., London, 1891–1894) 4: p. 36.

[61] Sir George Booth, *A Letter from Sir George Booth to a friend of his, . . .* (n.p., 1659).

[62] Anonymous, *An Express from the Knights and Gentlemen now engaged with Sir George Booth; . . .* (n.p., 1659).

[63] *The Publick Intelligencer*, No. 188: p. 640.

[64] *The Weekly Post*, No. 14: p. 116.

[65] *Ibid.*, No. 16: p. 130.

[66] Crofton denied the charge in his *Faelix scelus, Querela piorum, et Auscultatio Divina . . .* (London, 1660), [p. 26], but he was probably guilty.

[67] Heywood, *Autobiography* 1: p. 174; see also Martindale, *Life of Adam Martindale*, pp. 131–133.

[68] George Thompson to William Lockhart, August 22, 1659, *C.S.P.Dom., 1659–1660*, p. 136.

[69] *The Loyall Scout*, No. 16: p. 146.

an early failure, leaving the Rump still in power and hundreds of Presbyterians and Royalists under arrest.

Failure stemmed from numerous causes. The withdrawal of Willis and Compton left Booth's flank open to attack from the Midlands. The early seizure of Massey and How prevented the allies from opening a western port for the landing of troops from abroad, and a similar failure in the south prevented a landing south of the Thames. The London Presbyterians were unable, or afraid, to move, and Alderman Bunce's appeal to the London ministers arrived after the fall of Booth and Middleton.[70] Colonel Gervase Holles, intended as the Royalist leader in Lincolnshire, did not receive his instructions from Hyde until August 18.[71] The king's indecisiveness, displayed by his delay at Calais until assured of victory, cost the rising countless men. In the absence of a prominent and capable leader the insurrection wasted its strength through uncoordinated and unsustained efforts by men who suspected each other. Even the elements proved contrary. York and Ormonde were prevented from crossing the Channel with French and exiled Royalist troops, whose arrival and use at the right moment could have provided the momentum necessary for the unseating of the Rump and army.

Upon hearing that the rising had failed, the Royalists began preparing for a new attempt. Charles II turned southward from Calais to seek aid from the French and Spanish, who were then engaged in peace negotiations at Fuentarabia.[72] The royal agents in England endeavored to recover something from the languishing hopes of their fellow Royalists and the Presbyterians. Slingsby referred to the Presbyterians as a "dejected people," but still hoped to squeeze money from the more wealthy ones. "The best instruments," he wrote, "are some zealous Presbyterian ministers."[73]

The Royalist appeals to the Presbyterian clergy met with mixed results because of some lukewarm negotiations between the Presbyterians and the Independents. When the Presbyterian and Independent discussions failed to produce any agreement, the Presbyterians were compelled to turn to the Royalists and the Anglicans.

Richard Baxter, in danger of arrest in July,[74] held lingering hopes of converting the Anabaptists, and complained of being "left all most alone to contend" with Thomas Pierce, Henry Stubbs, the papists, and the sectaries. "Deare Brother," he wrote William Newe," pray hard, if you would not have popery set up in England,"[75] a statement which indicates Baxter's concern about Laudianism, Catholicism, and Independency. In the summer of 1659 Baxter tried to effect a compromise with Dr. Henry Hammond and the Laudians, through Sir Ralph Clare of Kidderminster. Hammond flatly rejected Baxter's overtures. Sir Ralph assured Baxter that a restored episcopacy would never possess prelatical excesses, but the Presbyterian from Kidderminster was not to be convinced by vague statements.[76] Baxter's activities indicate that he had grasped some of the hard facts of the political trend but that he had not accurately calculated the speed with which England was drifting back to monarchy and episcopacy. Further, Baxter was not an eager drifter.

A number of the London Presbyterian ministers held meetings with Independent clergy. Sir Archibald Johnston, then a member of the council of state for all three kingdoms, learned on September 6 that some London Presbyterians, Independents, and Anabaptists, whom he later identified as Seaman, Reynolds, Calamy, Jenkyn, Jacomb, Owen, Caryl, Griffith, Dean, Jessey, and Griffin, had already held a meeting for reconciling their differences and for cooperating against the Quakers.[77] William Allen, an Anabaptist, wrote Baxter on September 7 about the negotiations. Baxter, it seems, had written Allen on August 14 concerning further efforts at union. Allen begged Baxter to journey to London "to help on the work of accommocion which drives so heavily." Lazarus Seaman, the Presbyterian most favorable to Allen's efforts, was "under some discouragement from the indifferencie of his brethren," and was insisting that the project needed the assistance and support of leading men in the army and the Rump to replace Whalley and Goffe, two falling figures, who had been "several times at the meeting." The participation of Whalley and Goffe and the backwardness of the Presbyterians suggest that the whole affair was one of Independent desperation, a suspicion partly substantiated by Allen's statement that the enemy planned to destroy the publicly supported ministry.[78] There is also some reason to suspect that Seaman and the rigid Presbyterians, who later opposed the plan for modifying episcopacy, were attempting to ward off a restoration of monarchy and episcopacy by uniting

[70] Alderman James Bunce to Edmund Calamy, James Nalton, Simeon Ashe, William Taylor, Thomas Watson, William Jenkyn, Matthew Newcomen, Matthew Haviland, and others, August 26/September 5, 1659, *Calendar of the Clarendon State Papers* 4: p. 340.

[71] Sir Edward Hyde to Colonel Gervase Holles, August 18/28, 1659, H.M.C., *Bath MSS* 2: pp. 137–138.

[72] See F. J. Routledge, *England and the Treaty of the Pyrenees* (Liverpool, 1953), for the latest material on this subject.

[73] Henry Slingsby to Sir Edward Hyde, August 26, 1659, *Clarendon State Papers* 3: p. 546.

[74] William Newe to Richard Baxter, July 5, 1659, Baxter MSS, Letters IV, No. 176.

[75] Richard Baxter to William Newe, August 6, 1659, *ibid.*, No. 177.

[76] Baxter, *Reliquiae Baxterianae*, Pt. II: pp. 208–214.

[77] Sir Archibald Johnston, *Diary of Sir Archibald Johnston of Wariston, 1655–1660*, ed. James D. Ogilvie (Edinburgh, 1940), pp. 134–135. Johnston was then a member of the council of state for all three kingdoms.

[78] W[illiam] A[llen] to Richard Baxter, September 7, 1659, Baxter MSS, Letters III, No. 47/24.

at least part of the Presbyterians with the moderate Independents. In any event, the discussions failed to progress beyond preliminaries.

In the realm of secular politics the tide was running ever faster in the direction of a restoration of monarchy. Mordaunt was essentially correct when he informed Charles II that "the less violent party of the very Schismaticks, all the Presbyterians, and most of the House will join with you." [79] One reason for the swing toward royalism was the struggle among the army officers and the radical politicians for power.[80] As Mordaunt predicted,[81] it was only a question of time before the quarreling factions resorted to force against each other. Lambert's ejection of the Rump on October 13 was the fulfillment of Mordaunt's prediction.

Lambert's action of October 13 was the signal for renewed effort by both the Presbyterians and the king's agents. Mordaunt received news of Lambert's expulsion of the Rump on October 18 in Calais, and returned to London by October 22 for the purpose of organizing a new Presbyterian-Royalist alliance.[82] He immediately summoned Silas Titus and Edward Massey, Presbyterians in exile, to return to England to work with the Presbyterians.[83] Everywhere the Presbyterians, or those so-called, were making personal treaties with the king. Sir Henry Yelverton and the Earl of Manchester made tentative alliances with Charles.[84] Sir Thomas Middleton, a Parliamentary general in the Civil War, went abroad to consult Charles II, and convinced the exiled court that he was trustworthy.[85] Captain Arnold Breames, who served both the Long Parliament and Cromwell against Charles I and II, so persuaded Charles II of his new loyalty that he became an intermediary between the king and Admiral Lawson.[86] Such cases are so numerous that it is safe to assume that by November, 1659, most Presbyterian laymen had some connection, either direct or indirect, with the Royalist camp.

Realizing that the army could not be removed from power without military assistance, both the Presbyterians and the Royalists looked to George Monck and his forces for aid. In September, 1658, Lord Culpepper recommended to Hyde that Monck be attached to Charles II by rewards. The king, he said, should not scruple at any method employed by Monck for a restoration of Charles, for "when he is engaged past retreat, he will want you, as much as you will want him, & you may mold him into what form you please." [87] It was not until about June, 1659, however, that the Royalists decided to approach Monck.[88] After Nicholas Monck, the General's brother who held a religious living through Sir John Grenville, had agreed to act as agent between the king and General Monck, a commission was given to Lord Falconbridge, Sir John Grenville, and Lord Bellasis, Falconbridge's uncle, to open negotiations with Monck. They were authorized to offer Monck land and a title.[89] Falconbridge, who was Richard Cromwell's brother-in-law, was particularly important to the king's purpose because of his friendship with Monck and with Fairfax and the Yorkshire Presbyterians. Falconbridge's participation must mean that Fairfax and the Yorkshire Presbyterians, who had correspondence of their own with Monck, knew at least the general nature of the plan, if they were not privy to all of it.

Nicholas Monck departed for Scotland about August 5 and returned to England prior to October 13.[90] According to the reports sent Hyde by his agents, the General made no commitment whatsoever to his brother.[91] The Royalists did succeed, however, in influencing Monck's actions by winning over some of his officers.[92]

Although he apparently made no formal commit-

[79] Viscount Mordaunt to Charles II, October 1/11, 1659, *A Collection of Original Letters and Papers, Concerning the Affairs of England from the year 1641 to 1660. Found among the Duke of Ormonde's Papers,* ed. Thomas Carte (2 v., London, 1739) 2 : p. 226; hereafter cited as *Ormonde Papers.*

[80] Viscount Mordaunt to Duke of York, October 3, 1659, *Mordaunt Letter-Book,* pp. 48–49; although written from Calais, the letter is dated according to the Old Style.

[81] Viscount Mordaunt to Charles II, October 9/19, 1659, *ibid.,* pp. 64–67.

[82] Viscount Mordaunt to Sir Edward Hyde, October 26, 1659, *ibid.,* pp. 75–76.

[83] Viscount Mordaunt to Silas Titus, October 24, 1659, *ibid.,* pp. 71–72; and Viscount Mordaunt to Edward Massey, October 25, 1659, *ibid.,* p. 73.

[84] Dr. John Barwick to Charles II, October 25, 1659, *ibid.;* T. Ross to Colonel Gervase Holles, August 14/24, 1659, H.M.C., *Bath MSS* 2 : p. 136.

[85] Viscount Mordaunt to Charles II, October 27, 1659, *Mordaunt Letter-Book,* p. 78; Sir Edward Hyde to Dr. John Barwick, November 11/21, 1659, Peter Barwick, *The Life of the Reverend Dr. John Barwick . . .* (London, 1724), pp. 453–461.

[86] Charles II to Sir Arnold Breames, October 23/November 3, 1659, *Mordaunt Letter-Book,* p. 89–90.

[87] Lord Culpepper to Sir Edward Hyde, September 10/20, 1658, B.M., Stowe MSS 185, fol. 134.

[88] Thomas Skinner, *Life of General Monck, late Duke of Albemarle,* ed. W. Webster (London and Dublin, 1723), pp. 90–92.

[89] Captain John Skelton to Sir Edward Hyde, October 18/28, 1658, *Clarendon State Papers* 3 : pp. 420–421; Sir John Grenville to Sir Edward Hyde, December 10, 1658, *Calendar of the Clarendon State Papers* 4 : p. 119; Sir John Grenville to Sir Edward Hyde, July 8, 1659, *ibid.,* p. 263; Sir Edward Hyde to Lord Bellasis, July 11/21, 1659, *ibid.,* p. 268; Charles II to Lord Falconbridge, Lord Bellasis, and Sir John Grenville, [*ca.* July 11/21, 1659], *Clarendon State Papers* 3 : pp. 417–418.

[90] Sir John Grenville to Sir Edward Hyde, August 19, 1659, *Clarendon State Papers* 3 : pp. 543–544; Dr. John Barwick to Charles II, October 13, 1659, *Mordaunt Letter-Book,* p. 59.

[91] William Rumbold to Charles II, September 5, 1659, *Calendar of the Clarendon State Papers* 4 : p. 359; Dr. John Barwick to Charles II, October 13, 1659, *Mordaunt Letter-Book,* p. 59.

[92] Dr. John Barwick to Charles II, June 20, 1659, *Calendar of the Clarendon State Papers* 4 : p. 242; Dr. John Barwick to Sir Edward Hyde, October 14, 1659, *ibid.,* p. 410.

ment to anyone, Monck by his display of loyalty to the Rump Parliament and of opposition to General Lambert played into the hands of the Presbyterian-Royalist alliance. The Commonwealth party feared that Monck intended something more than a restoration of the Rump.[93] The Royalists were doubtful of Monck's secret intentions, but they applauded his resistance to Lambert and the English army.[94] The Presbyterians interpreted Monck's actions as favorable to themselves. In an effort to neutralize Monck, the Independents sent two ministers, Joseph Caryl and Matthew Barker, and two preaching officers, Whalley and Goffe, to negotiate with Monck and his forces.[95] Mordaunt, commenting on these developments on October 31, warned Hyde that a Presbyterian cabal was attempting to secure Monck's support for a conditional restoration of Charles II.

While they were trying to win Monck to their side of the Presbyterian-Royalist alliance, the Presbyterians were once again negotiating with the king and his agents for royal acceptance of the Newport terms of 1648 as the basis for the restoration of monarchy. Involved in these negotiations were William Pierrepoint, the Earls of Northumberland, Bedford, Clare, Manchester, and other persons not mentioned by name.[96] Feeling that the Presbyterians would be content with far less, Hyde replied that the king would not accept the Newport terms as the conditions for his restoration.[97] At some date prior to November 25 the principal Presbyterians discussed "some way of accommodation which [would] be advantageous to the king," [98] but Broderick made it clear on December 16 that the Presbyterians had failed to arrive at any generally acceptable proposals to submit to the king. "They promise nothing but generals, never descending to particulars . . .; beside, they demand nothing," was Broderick's report on the Presbyterian position. "Religion," he continued, "though the sacred pretext to the earlier part of the War, they lay aside (at least in great

measure) treating of single interests." [99] Rebuffed on the Newport terms by the king, the Presbyterian laymen found it difficult to assume anything more than a negative attitude toward the existing situation and the Royalist pretensions. The clergy and their claims were not being given serious consideration by the Presbyterian laymen, who were bartering for individual rewards or pardons for past actions. Except for scattered groups, the Presbyterians had no common organization or program. These facts permitted and encouraged Hyde and Charles II to play a waiting game.

As the Presbyterians stood undecided and divided, public opinion and events moved rapidly toward parliamentary government as opposed to military rule. The threat of war between Monck and Lambert proved false as Lambert's army disintegrated and Monck's popularity grew. In London bitterness between the apprentices and the army, stirred up by the Presbyterians and Royalists,[100] produced riots and disorder.[101] Through a combination of events, declarations from Portsmouth and elsewhere,[102] the deployment of Admiral Lawson's fleet in the Thames, and assistance from some military units,[103] the twice unseated Rump Parliament was suddenly restored on December 26.[104] The old secluded members remained outside. The Presbyterian struggle, in conjunction with the Royalists, against the Good Old Cause of republicanism and Independency had succeeded in so far as the army council was concerned. Only a few troops remained loyal to the Rump, and without military support the Rump could not survive. The army and the Good Old Cause had been vanquished. England's future rested with the Presbyterian monarchists, the Royalists, and General George Monck and his army, but no one was in a position in January, 1660, to predict where the political and religious balance might lie at the moment or in the future.

IV. A FREE PARLIAMENT

Throughout the months of the second Commonwealth the Presbyterians, as adherents to the concept of the sovereignty of law, had clamored for a free, or at least a full, parliament, with knowledge that a free and full parliament might produce Presbyterian control and the necessity for major alterations in government. Oliver Cromwell had alienated the Presbyterians by his religious policy, his reliance on military authority,

[93] Robert Baynes to Adam Baynes, October 27, 1659, B.M., Add. MSS 21,425, fol. 168; John Baynes to Adam Baynes, November 3, 1659, *ibid.*, fol. 174.

[94] Viscount Mordaunt to Duke of York, October 31, 1659, *Mordaunt Letter-Book*, p. 83; T. Ross to Colonel Gervase Holles, November 10/20, 1659, H.M.C., *Bath MSS* 2: pp. 139–141.

[95] *The Weekly Intelligencer*, November 23, 1659, p. 227; *The Clarke Papers* 4: pp. 81–82, 121–124.

[96] Viscount Mordaunt to Sir Edward Hyde, October 31, 1659, *Clarendon State Papers* 3: pp. 593–594; Viscount Mordaunt to Charles II, October 31, 1659, *Mordaunt Letter-Book*, pp. 81–83; Viscount Mordaunt to Charles II, November 3, 1659, *ibid.*, pp. 95–96.

[97] Sir Edward Hyde to Viscount Mordaunt, November 14/24, 1659, *ibid.*, pp. 110–111; Sir Edward Hyde to Dr. John Barwick, November 18/28, 1659, *Clarendon State Papers* 3: p. 614.

[98] M. de Bordeaux to Cardinal Mazarin, November 25/December 5, 1659, M. Guizot, *Monk: Or the Fall of the Republic and the Restoration of the Monarchy in England, in 1660*, trans. Andrew R. Scobel (London, 1866), p. 133; hereafter cited as *Monk*.

[99] Alan Broderick to Sir Edward Hyde, December 16, 1659, *Clarendon State Papers* 3: pp. 628–629.

[100] M. de Bordeaux to Cardinal Mazarin, December 5/15, 1659, Guizot, *Monk*, p. 137.

[101] Francesco Giavarina to Doge and Senate, December 10, 1659, *Calendar of State Papers, Venetian* 32: pp. 101–102.

[102] Samuel Morland to Sir Edward Hyde, December 9, 1659, *Calendar of the Clarendon State Papers* 4: p. 478.

[103] J. Vernon to Colonel John Jones, December 12, 1659, *ibid.*, pp. 480–481.

[104] Whitelocke, *Memorials of English Affairs* 4: p. 384.

and his frequent and sharp changes in governmental institutions and policies. As he gradually returned to the traditional form of government, and as time separated Englishmen from 1648, Cromwell gained supporters from the Presbyterian ranks. When Richard almost returned to the historic constitution in 1659, many Presbyterians who had opposed his father supported him. The small core of ardent Presbyterian monarchists, who had protested even against Richard and his government, joined with the secluded Presbyterian members of the Long Parliament and the Royalists against the Rump. The Rump fell, but only to make way for the army council. When the Rump then succeeded in seating itself for a third time, the Presbyterians seemed as far as ever from a rule of law and a free parliament. With the aid of Monck the Presbyterians obtained control of the government by forcing the restoration of the Long Parliament. In this way the Presbyterians, both lay and clerical, came to face the problems from which they had been diverted in 1648. These problems included, of course, the terms under which monarchy and the Stuart family might exist in England and the form or forms through which Englishmen might worship.

The vast majority of the Presbyterian laity, and perhaps of the clergy, under constant prodding from Presbyterian monarchists like Sir George Booth and William Prynne and moderate Royalists like Mordaunt, realized by January, 1660, that a restoration of monarchy and the Stuart line offered the safest and most certain escape from domination by the Commonwealthmen and even from imminent chaos, but the Presbyterians could reach no understanding with Charles II until they were in a position to guarantee Charles a safe and certain return. They were also fully aware that they could best negotiate with Charles II from a position of political or military strength. To achieve this they desired to wrest control of the government from the Rump before anyone or anything else could intervene. Ambassador Bordeaux, watching the situation most carefully and intimate with the leading Presbyterians, informed the French government that

the greater number of those who wish him [Charles II] back do not desire to see him in a position to exercise absolute authority, but rather necessitated to grant them all the conditions they may desire. This capitulation can be made only by a free parliament; this is, therefore, the object aimed at by the Presbyterians, and generally by all the nobility, who are confident that . . . they will restore the monarchy . . . .[1]

In a letter to Cardinal Mazarin, Bordeaux spoke of a "great cabal of the nobles and principal Presbyterians" endeavoring to persuade the London council to demand the full restoration of the Long Parliament. The cabal

was certain that the secluded members would secure sufficient concessions from Charles II.[2]

Bordeaux's summary of the situation is confirmed in reports by the king's agents. Samuel Tuke, a Presbyterian, warned Charles that his friends preferred a parliamentary restoration to one by conquest, and attempted to prepare Charles for fairly stringent conditions.[3] Hartgill Baron wrote Mordaunt on December 29 that the Presbyterians "grow up againe" and that their design was the Newport treaty. "The soberest men here believe," he continued, "these will carry all, at long running, and that a short time will make it."[4]

The Presbyterians had reason to fear, however, that time and national feeling ran against them, for the cause of unconditional restoration was making inroads even in their own ranks. Broderick voiced confidence that the true monarchists constituted the largest party; the "next is the Presbyterians, . . . their numbers declining with the advance of the former; all men grown up since 1656 being of the better sense, beside many worthy converts."[5] The conservative reaction was manifest in the London council election of December 21, 1659. Usually Presbyterian, even under Cromwell, the new council contained not a single alderman who possessed either crown or church lands.[6] Of the Presbyterians elected, Sir William Wild, recorder of the City, and Richard Ford, a wealthy merchant, were now more monarchist than Presbyterian in politics.[7]

Similar evidence could be cited for almost every section of England. Leaderless and out of power, the Presbyterians could not retain any semblance of solidarity. Their interests were varied. Lawyers, merchants, landed gentry, and clergymen possessed different ambitions and problems. Some, notably the lawyers and merchants, needed a strong and stable government which the old monarchy alone seemed to offer, and the lawyers tended to be Erastian on matters of religion. With the tide running strongly toward monarchy, the Presbyterians, as a political party, had to consider the reversionary interest of the potential ruler, Charles II, and a government in being that they could never accept.

With divisions growing among themselves, Monck marching southward toward London, and Charles bartering for troops for an invasion, the Presbyterians recognized that they had either to join with or them-

---

[1] M. de Bordeaux to M. de Brienne, December 19/29, 1659; Guizot, *Monk*, p. 142.

[2] M. de Bordeaux to Cardinal Mazarin, December 19/29, *ibid.*, p. 143.

[3] Samuel Tuke to Charles II, December 23/January 2, 1659/1660, Bodleian Library, Clarendon MSS 68, fol. 6; hereafter shortened to B.L. and Clar. MSS respectively.

[4] Hartgill Baron to Viscount Mordaunt, December 29, 1659, *ibid.*, fol. 27.

[5] Alan Broderick to Sir Edward Hyde, December 21, 1659, *Clarendon State Papers* 3: p. 631.

[6] Dowager Countess of Peterborough to Viscount Mordaunt, December 24, 1659, *Mordaunt Letter-Book*, p. 146.

[7] John Heath to Viscount Mordaunt, December 30, 1659, *ibid.*, pp. 150–151.

selves oust the Rump, if they were to be the architects of the restoration, and architects they hoped to be, though their plans were still mere sketches.

On December 27, the day after the return of the Rump, twenty-one of the secluded members met at the lobby of the commons to seek admission. The Rump, thinking perhaps of Prynne's tactics of the previous May, had posted guards with instructions to deny access, even to the lobby, to the secluded members. The secluded members therefore resorted to a written protest. Despite their weighty and lengthy constitutional arguments, the secluded Presbyterians were compelled to accept the Rump's answer that the question of their admission would be considered on January 5.[8]

The Rump, however, made no pretense of fulfilling its promise. It decided on January 2 to issue writs for elections to fill up the Commons. No one was surprised, therefore, when this action was followed in three days by a vote to discharge the members secluded in 1648 and 1649.[9] Prynne in an anonymous broadside of December 30 had castigated the Rump;[10] now he filled the streets with pamphlets. On January 4 he pointed out that more than two hundred members of the Long Parliament survived, but only forty-three, of whom seven were added after 1648, sat in the Rump. Prynne cited the fact that several counties had not a single representative within the Rump, and made a special plea to Westminster and Middlesex, whose members were all excluded. So criminal was the Rump that the people should use their militia to "Dishouse these Forcible Usurpers, . . . bring them to publick justice," and replace them with the secluded members. Prynne personally denounced Haselrigg, Speaker Lenthall, Salisbury, Pembroke, and Denzil Holles, who had entered the Rump for the first time since 1648, as individuals.[11] Such intemperateness toward the Independents and Holles, a Presbyterian of sorts, eventually worked to the disadvantage of the Presbyterians.

Unrelenting and unmerciful toward his enemies, Prynne knew no fatigue or danger. His *Case of the old Secured, Secluded and Excluded Members* of January 13 contained more than his customary defiance of the Rump; he revealed to the public that on January 4 he and some unnamed persons had met at Arthur Annesley's house in Drury Lane to draw up a declaration of their "Case & unjust antiparliamentary exclusion" and that the Rump sent a captain and forty men to apprehend them.[12] This confession that the secluded members were holding meetings to plan strategy and to issue declarations holds more than passing interest.

Insight into what was taking place may be gained, in part, from Mordaunt's letter to Charles II. This account ran as follows:

to incense the Counties, that unanimously they might appear for a change of the present power, and having such convincing arguments made known to me by Mr. Prynn and Mr. Annesley, I immediately dispatched into the shires their sense, and withal, that it was concurring with your Majesty's instructions given to me, upon your commanding me hither; this, though I failed in part, hoping I should have induced them to declare for a free Parliament, yet in the main it succeeded, they only inserting the additional clause of the secluded Members, and in this I was overborn by Colonel [Edward] Cooke and Mr. [John] Crew . . . .[13]

Clearly, then, many of the hundreds of petitions and declarations printed during the first three months of 1660 were nothing more than copies of the material provided Mordaunt by the secluded Presbyterians, notably Annesley and Prynne. More important, Mordaunt's letter reveals how close was the association between Mordaunt's Royalists and the Presbyterian monarchists. As for policy, this association had resulted in an agreement that the Long Parliament would be fully restored, if possible, before any other course was undertaken. This decision was a significant victory for those Presbyterian politicians who hoped to control the restoration of monarchy to the exclusion of Royalists, but it also limited the opportunity for subsequent maneuvering by those so deeply involved in Mordaunt's plans.

The net result of these activities became evident in the flood of petitions and declarations in behalf of either the secluded members or a new parliament. Perhaps the earliest of these was one from Cornwall dated December 27.[14] In this connection, Miss Coate discovered among the Buller Papers a draft of a letter headed "Letter to P. about ye Declaration of Cornwall," which she concluded was a letter to Prynne. The letter advised Prynne to " 'see all moderation . . . be used to preserve us from violent and unreasonable ingagements and I am persuaded that wee have declared for us the Common sense not only of the west but of other parts of England.' "[15] This perhaps represented the typical attitude of the Presbyterian landed gentry, and it suggests that Prynne carried on a private correspondence with some of his country friends. This activity, and that of Mordaunt, explains the similarity

---

[8] [William Prynne], *A Brief Narrative* . . . (London, 1660); Whitelock, *Memorials of English Affairs* **4**: p. 384.

[9] Whitelock, *Memorials of English Affairs* **4**: pp. 386–387.

[10] W[illiam] P[rynne], *Six Important Quaeres, Propounded to the Re-sitting Rump of the Long Parliament* . . . (n.p., 1659).

[11] [William Prynne], *Seven Additional Quaeres in behalf of the secluded Members* . . . (n.p., 1660), pp. 1–7.

[12] William Prynne, *The Case of the Old Secured, Secluded, and Excluded Members* . . . (London, 1660), p. 7.

[13] Viscount Mordaunt to Charles II, January 26, 1660, *Clarendon State Papers* **3**: p. 660.

[14] [Cornwall Gentry], . . . *The Humble Remonstrance of us Gentlemen, and Free-holders of the County of Cornwall* (n.p., 1660).

[15] Mary Coate, *Cornwall in the Great Civil War and Interregnum, 1642–1660: A Social and Political Study* (Oxford, 1933), p. 310.

of most of the printed petitions and declarations of the first three months of 1660.

In order to keep the movement underway, Prynne and his colleagues deemed it necessary to publish new declarations or tracts every few days. Prynne dispatched two from the press on Jaunary 19, two on January 30, and a fifth on February 12. In the midst of all this work Prynne's circle found both the time and the courage to undertake a bold legal action against those who had prevented their admission into the commons. Sir Gilbert Gerard, secluded member for Middlesex, brought suit for, and obtained, a writ of presentment and indictment against Matthew Allured, Colonel Okey, and a doorkeeper on a charge of assault and of obstructing the commons by force of arms.[16]

It would be a grave mistake to assume that Prynne was the only active writer among the Presbyterians. A staunch Presbyterian tract, the author of which is not known, urged the Rump to become humble and to repent for violating the Solemn League and Covenant. Parliament should "establish Doctrine, Discipline, and Government according to the Word," pass an act of indemnity, and provide for truly tender consciences, but it should beware of those who call themselves the "Godly Party," for they will break all oaths.[17] This was pure Presbyterianism. The London clergy, not to be outdone by their lay brethren, sent forth a tract on January 23 complaining of the dangerous state of religion. Their strongest protest was against the threat of popery. To the London Presbyterians Rome in 1640 had hidden behind the skirts of the Established Church, but had since found refuge among the sectaries, especially the Quakers. While condemning the radicals, they urged a tacit understanding with the Anglicans.[18]

In the weeks immediately preceding Monck's arrival in London the Presbyterians made various proposals to the Royalists. "Some sober Presbyterians, and other good men," suggested through Broderick that all land sales be confirmed and the court of wards abolished. To compensate church and state for these losses, they proposed to set the excise and customs at 2,100,000 pounds annually and to provide for twenty-six bishops at the rate of two thousand pounds a year each, with an allowance of eight thousand pounds a year for their subordinate officials.[19] These terms would have satisfied many of the Presbyterian demands of the Civil War period. The loss of lands by church and state would make both largely dependent on parliament for revenue, and the abolition of wardship would end a long-standing grievance against the crown. The proposals reveal that their sponsors were Presbyterian in politics and Erastian in religion. Unfortunately, the Presbyterians could not negotiate effectually on this or any other basis without control of parliament.

Whether or not the Presbyterians could take power long enough to sponsor and restrain a restoration of monarchy seemed increasingly to depend on a new quantity, unknown to Presbyterians, Royalists, and Rumpers alike, on George Monck marching quietly southward from Scotland. On January 13 Mordaunt wrote: "Monck no flesh understands; all feare. I like not his proceeding."[20] Thirteen days later he wrote a bit more hopefully.[21] The Presbyterian opinion of Monck altered as often as Mordaunt's. On the sixteenth they thought him Presbyterian;[22] yet some time before January 20 the secluded members sent Annesley to sound him out.[23] Major Harley undertook a similar mission, and returned "not without some hopes, but not so full assurance, as not to use further endeavours & to that end Coll. [Edward] Cooke is gone to him from the Party."[24] William Pierrepoint also met Monck enroute, and rode an entire day in his coach.[25] London sent a delegation of Presbyterians,[26] but Monck's promises, if any, were kept in strict secrecy.

Passing through Yorkshire, Monck conferred with Fairfax, who had raised a personal militia, and with others of the area. The meeting followed several weeks of negotiations between Monck and the Yorkshire politicians of the Fairfax circle. According to an account written later by Brian Fairfax, Lord Fairfax sent word to Monck in December that he would join Monck's forces to oppose Lambert and to restore the king. Monck's reply provoked Fairfax to send his cousin Brian to Newcastle to reassure Monck and to restate Fairfax's views, which were also those of Buckingham and Henry Arthington. Brian's consultations with Edward Bowles, the clerical champion of Yorkshire Presbyterianism, suggest that the Presbyterian clergy played an important role in the drafting of

---

[16] Ethyn Williams Kirby, *William Prynne: A Study in Puritanism* (Cambridge, Mass., 1931), pp. 130–131; the author's bibliography of Prynne's writings contains all but a few Prynne items.

[17] Anonymous, *Things Just and Necessary, which the Parliament must do if ever they would Prosper* (n.p., 1660).

[18] Edward Reynolds and others, *A Seasonable Exhortation of Sundry Ministers in London to the People of their Respective Congregations* (London, 1660); carries the names of 63 London ministers.

[19] Alan Broderick to Sir Edward Hyde, January 13, 1660, *Clarendon State Papers* 3: p. 645.

[20] Viscount Mordaunt to Lady Mordaunt, January 13, 1660, *Mordaunt Letter-Book*, p. 155.

[21] Viscount Mordaunt to Lady Mordaunt, January 26, 1660, *ibid.*, p. 176.

[22] Viscount Mordaunt to Charles II, January 16, 1660, *Clarendon State Papers* 3: p. 649.

[23] Alan Broderick to Sir Edward Hyde, January 20, 1660, *ibid.*, p. 654.

[24] [William Rumbold to Sir Edward Hyde], January 27, 1660, B.L., Clar. MSS 68, fol. 204. There is no indication whether this was Edward or Robert Harley, but it was probably Robert.

[25] Colonel Robert Whitley to Sir Edward Nicholas, March 9/19, 1660, *Nicholas Papers* 4: p. 194.

[26] Aldermen Fowke, Vincent, and Bromfield; see Sir Richard Baker, *A Chronicle of the Kings of England . . . . With a continuation by Edward Phillips* (London, 1665), p. 685; hereafter cited as *Chronicle*.

Fairfax's message to Monck.[27] Before Monck called on him at Nun Appleton, Fairfax had organized a county militia to oppose Lambert,[28] and he probably offered Monck these forces. Fairfax probably advised Monck either to admit the secluded members or to provide for a full and representative parliament, and probably to restore Charles under certain conditions.

If the Yorkshire Presbyterians did not state these things in Monck's presence, they did on February 10, when Fairfax, Falconbridge, Sir Henry Cholmeley, and other landed men of the Presbyterian group met together with Sir Horatio Townshend of Norfolk, who perhaps came as a messenger from the king, and Sir Thomas Wharton of Lincoln, who may have been present to cement an understanding between the Wharton Independent group and the Yorkshire Presbyterians. The fact that the York council met simultaneously with the Presbyterian gentry suggests cooperation between the landed and commercial elements of Yorkshire.[29] The views of the Fairfax group were expressed in a petition to Monck, which the Presbyterian clergy of Yorkshire helped to write, and in a letter and declaration to Monck.[30] One element of their policy was expressed in a letter from Colonel Charles Fairfax to Monck in favor of "liberty of conscience to moderate spirits being necessarily included [in any settlement], without which care all the rest will be fruitless." [31] The Yorkshire Presbyterians, lay and clerical, had thus gone on record favoring the recall of the secluded members of the Long Parliament or the election of a new and free parliament, knowing full well that either course would result in the restoration of Charles Stuart. They had also advised against harsh terms for the king and in favor of religious moderation.

Monck's next secret steps suggest that he reached some tentative decisions in Yorkshire as to his future course and that he intended to work closely with the Presbyterians. On January 15 he requested James Sharp to meet him in London. Sharp was not to disclose the reason for his sudden winter journey into England to anyone but Robert Douglas.[32] Sharp had served Monck in Scotland and perhaps in England, and was well acquainted with and respected by the London clergy and Richard Baxter. He would therefore prove valuable in dealing with the Presbyterian clergy. William Morice, Monck's cousin, received a similar summons on January 23.[33] Morice, as a mild Presbyterian and secluded member of the Long Parliament, possessed the same potentialities with the Presbyterian laymen as Sharp with the clergy.

On the same day that he summoned Morice, Monck wrote publicly to his Devon neighbors that several changes had occurred since the outbreak of the Civil War which made the implementation of their declaration of January 14 [34] for the restoration of monarchy difficult, if not impossible. Both church and state had been monarchical prior to the war, Monck declared, but new interests opposed to the old order had since arisen in the Presbyterians, Independents, Anabaptists, and a variety of sects. These interests drew support not only from their religious and political followers but also from the purchasers of crown and church property and those who had bought private property under the Commonwealth and Protectorate governments. Monarchy could not be restored without subverting the existing religious bodies and the socio-economic structure. Nor could the secluded members be restored without jeopardizing the existing situation. The alternative to the restoration of monarchy or to the readmission of all members of the Long Parliament was for the Rump to fill up its vacancies and establish a government broad enough to embrace all interests.[35] In this letter to the Devonshire gentry, one to John Rolle,[36] a Devonshire Presbyterian and secluded member, and the one to Morice, Monck seemed to urge acceptance of the Rump Parliament.[37]

In the light of Monck's subsequent actions, one naturally asks, why did he write such letters? As yet, no documented answer is possible. Probably Monck intended to stand by the Rump Paliament, at least until he was in military control of the region around London. Monck did not commit himself publicly; he merely stated the possible courses and their results.

[27] H.M.C., *Sixth Report, Appendix, Part I* (London, 1877), p. 466; but compare Baker, *Chronicle*, pp. 726–727.

[28] Anonymous, *An Extract of a Letter from York, dated the 31 of Decemb. 1659*, . . . (London, 1659); Robert Baynes to Adam Baynes, January 30, 1660, B.M., Add. MSS 21,425, fol. 201.

[29] Robert Baynes to Adam Baynes, February 11, 1660, *ibid.*, fol. 204; Ant. Devenere (?) to Adam Baynes, February 13, 1660, *ibid.*, fol. 206; Thomas Lord Fairfax, *The Declaration of Thomas, Lord Fairfax, and the rest of the Lords, Knights, Esquires, Citizens, Ministers and Freeholders of the County and City of York* (London, 1660).

[30] Lord Fairfax, Lord Falconbridge, Christopher Clapham, and Barrington Bourchier to General George Monck, February 20, 1660, B.M., Egerton MSS 2618, fol. 60; the declaration was printed as *A Letter and Declaration of the Nobility and Gentry of the County of York, to His Excellency the Lord Generall Monck* (London, 1660).

[31] Colonel Charles Fairfax to George Monck, February 15, 1660, H.M.C., *Report on the Manuscripts of F. W. Leyborne-Popham, Esq. of Littlecote, Co. Wilts.* (London, 1899), p. 151; hereafter cited as *Leyborne-Popham MSS*.

[32] Mr. Auditor Thompson to James Sharp, February 15, 1660, Robert Wodrow, *The History of the Sufferings of the Church of Scotland, from the Restauration to the Revolution* (2 v., Edinburgh, 1721–1722) 1: p. vi; hereafter cited as *Church of Scotland*.

[33] George Monck to William Morice, January 23, 1660, *The Clarke Papers* 4: p. 260; see also Coate, *Cornwall*, pp. 308–309.

[34] Devonshire Gentry, *A Letter from Exeter, Advertizing the State of Affairs there;* . . . (London, 1660).

[35] George Monck, *A Letter of General George Monck's, dated at Leicester 23 Jan. and directed unto Mr. Rolle* . . . (London, 1660).

[36] George Monck to [John] Rolle, January 23, 1660, *The Clarke Papers* 4: pp. 258–259; this was the forwarding letter on the one to the Devonshire Gentry.

[37] See Burnet, *History of His Own Times* 1: p. 156.

This vagueness would permit him to remain uncommitted until he could reach London and assess the political situation for himself. His obscure advice would provoke parties and individuals to declare their positions more clearly.

Whatever Monck's secret intentions may have been, and the evidence suggests a decision to work with the Presbyterians, response to his arguments was predominantly in favor of restoring the secluded members or the election of a totally new and free parliament. One tract, almost certainly by the mildly Presbyterian John Trevor, roundly opposed Monck's paper. Taking an entirely legalistic approach to the subject, Trevor argued that not even a republic could be established by the Rump. Any government illegally established by the Rump, moreover, could not survive long without a broader base than the Rump could provide. The lands might be repurchased, and absolute uniformity in religion was not essential to monarchy.[38] In addition to such arguments as Trevor's, Monck received petitions, printed and oral, and declarations from any number of groups and individuals, most of which advised him to seat the secluded members or call a new parliament. Mordaunt and the Royalists arranged for some of these petitions and declarations,[39] but certainly not all. In Sandwich, for example, the Presbyterian clergy joined with the old Cavaliers in circulating a petition.[40] The Bristol apprentices sent up a document which certainly owed its construction to William Prynne.[41] Each of the many letters, petitions, and declarations contained the names of several prominent Presbyterians and usually of a secluded member or two.[42] The publicly expressed opinion was in favor of a restoration of the Long Parliament or the election of a new and full parliament. It also favored, either explicitly or implicitly, an early restoration of monarchy. Much less was said about the religious establishment.

In view of the loud demands for the restoration of the secluded members, it is surprising that on February 6, three days after his arrival in London, Monck pledged himself to the Rump. He gave no indication that he intended to support either the Presbyterians or the Royalists. If anything, Monck's sly hint to the Rump

that it should conduct elections to fill all vacant seats indicated his willingness to work with the Rump.[43] Three days later the General carried out orders to destroy the gates and fortifications of London, but not without some misgivings.

On February 11 Monck suddenly altered his attitude toward the Rump. He had acted too precipitately in carrying out the Rump's instructions, and the City's reaction to Monck's acts of February 9 and 10 clearly showed the current of popular opinion in and around London, if not throughout the nation. Divisions within the Rump obviously prevented it from taking any bold and constructive action. Oliver St. John and his party wanted a free parliament; Henry Nevill's group wanted a parliament on the Protectorate basis; still others were for a restoration of monarchy.[44] A combination of these circumstances, and signs of disaffection in his army, probably, more than anything else, accounted for Monck's demand of February 11 to the Rump that it immediately conduct elections.[45] This sudden shift caused considerable alarm on the part of the Rump.[46]

The hour for the secluded Presbyterians to act had now arrived. For some time they had been in contact with Sir Anthony Ashley Cooper and John Weaver, whose group, some of whom were religious Presbyterians, in the Rump favored the admission of the secluded members. Cooper, Dr. Thomas Clarges, Monck's brother-in-law, Mrs. Monck, who was a violent Presbyterian, and perhaps a secluded member or two were present at the meeting of February 11 when Monck agreed to break with the Rump. Cooper and Alexander Popham were among those who managed the retirement of Monck from Whitehall into the City.[47] Sharp, who arrived in London on the thirteenth, was sent immediately by Monck to work with Cooper and Weaver.[48] Thus it was that the Presbyterian-inclined members of the Rump were joined with both Monck and the secluded Presbyterians. At this stage Monck apparently followed the leadership and advice of others.

In the face of these new developments, Monck realized that his future lay with a combination of Cooper's group and the secluded Presbyterians. On the night of February 14 a number of the secluded

[38] J[ohn] Trev[or], *The fair Dealer: Or, a Modest Answer to the Sober Letter of His Excellency, the Lord General Monck; . . .* (London, 1660).

[39] Viscount Mordaunt to Sir Robert Moray, January 26, 1660, *Mordaunt Letter-Book,* p. 178.

[40] *The Publick Intelligencer,* No. 214: pp. 1066–1067.

[41] Bristol Apprentices, *A Letter of the Apprentices of the City of Bristol to the Apprentices of the Honourable City of London . . .* (London, 1660).

[42] The Devonshire declaration contained the names of five secluded members, *Mercurius Politicus,* No. 603: pp. 1035–1036. Many of these, first printed as broadsides, were collected and reprinted as *A Happy Handfull, Or Green Hopes in the Blade; in order to a Harvest, of the Several Shires, humbly Petitioning, or heartily Declaring for Peace* (London, 1660).

[43] George Monck, *The Lord General Monck His Speech Delivered by Him in the Parliament on Munday, Feb. 6, 1659* (London, 1660).

[44] Johnston, *Diary of Sir Archibald Johnston,* p. 174; Samuel Pepys, *The Diary of Samuel Pepys,* ed. Henry B. Wheatley (8 v., London, 1923) 1: pp. 44, 72, and 77; hereafter cited as *Diary.*

[45] Ludlow, *Memoirs* 2: p. 220; Baker, *Chronicle,* p. 748; George Monck, *A Letter from The Lord General Monck and the Officers under his Command to the Parliament; in the name of Themselves, and the Souldiers under Them* (London, 1660).

[46] See the exchange of letters between Monck, Haselrigg, and the council of state in *The Clarke Papers* 4: pp. 260–263.

[47] Brown, *The First Earl of Shaftesbury,* pp. 88–89; Ludlow, *Memoirs* 2: p. 222.

[48] James Sharp to [Edinburgh Ministers], February 14, 1660, Wodrow, *Church of Scotland* 1: p. vi.

members met at Monck's quarters with some of the Rump and with some who had voluntarily refused to sit with the Rump. The following day Monck requested Haselrigg, Colonel Herbert Morley, Colonel White, Thomas Scot, St. John, Cooper, Carew Raleigh, and Robert Reynolds to confer with a like number of secluded members at his house on the following Friday.[49]

The meeting of Friday, February 18, was marked by further conflict between the Rumpers and the secluded members, but was followed by an agreement between Monck and the secluded members. Annesley and Haselrigg were particularly antagonistic toward each other, and Haselrigg finally left the conference in anger.[50] So far as is known, nothing was accomplished. Monck and his officers were willing to admit the Presbyterians on the basis of a declaration for a commonwealth, confirmation of the land sales, and dissolution of the Long Parliament on a prearranged date. Clarges, Clobery, and Thomas Gumble, Monck's chaplain, met with some of the secluded members, who insisted on leaving the questions of government and land sales to the next parliament and on calling the House of Lords to sit with the commons of the Long Parliament. Monck agreed in principle, but demanded that the secluded members agree to settle the military forces, pay the land and sea forces, appoint a council of state to settle the governments of Scotland and Ireland, issue writs for a parliament to convene on April 20, and to dissolve the Long Parliament as quickly as possible. The secluded members eventually accepted these terms as the basis for their admission.[51]

At the last moment, however, Monck seemed to veer away from the Presbyterians. According to Cooper's account, Monck recommitted himself to Haselrigg and Scot on the afternoon of February 20. Upon hearing this confirmed by Monck, Cooper quickly gathered together Mrs. Monck, Clarges, Clobery, Ralph Knight, and probably a few more. This group argued with the General until three in the morning before convincing him to summon the secluded members to the commons at nine that same morning. By eight o'clock Cooper and Clarges had collected most of the secluded members in town at Annesley's house, from whence they went to Whitehall.[52] Guarded by a special troop under Cooper's command, the Presbyterians marched into the commons. The Rumpers stood aghast at what they saw, and Samuel Pepys found humor in the fact that Prynne carried a cumbersome basket-hilt sword.[53]

The restored members lost no time in undoing the work of the Rump. Many Rumpers deserted the house, leaving the Presbyterians with a clear majority. On the first day they declared null and void all acts previously passed against them, appointed a committee to search the records for other measures to be annulled, named Monck commander-in-chief, and discharged several of their friends from prison. They also drafted and read twice a bill to create a new council of state of thirty-one members.[54] On the second day the commons committed a bill on taxes and voted for a new parliament to meet on April 25.[55] Thus the restored Presbyterians hastened to carry out their part of the bargain with Monck.

The new council of state was chosen by ballot, with 116 members present, on February 23.[56] It was a mixed group, and not nearly as Presbyterian as has generally been thought. Seven members sat in the Rump from 1648 to 1653. At least eight others had been servants or friends of Oliver Cromwell. Fully a third or more were already corresponding with the exiled Stuart.

In handling the religious question, the restored Long Parliament was constrained to follow a mild Presbyterian course. Calamy and Manton received the honor of officiating on the day of thanksgiving for the restoration of the secluded members.[57] However, it was not until the eighth day that the commons appointed a committee to study the questions of settling ministers in their livings, a confession of faith, and other religious matters.[58] Without solicitation, and obviously without doubt as to the outcome, the London Presbyterian clergy presented their recommendations to the commons on March 1. They recommended suppression of popery, strict observance of the Sabbath, appointment of a committee to approve ministers, a bill to protect ministers in their benefices, adherence to the Westminster Confession of Faith, and the convening of a national assembly of divines.[59] Not a suggestion of compromise with either Independency or Anglicanism appeared in the document, unless an assembly of divines could be termed a conciliatory gesture.

As James Sharp accurately observed, the Presbyterian clergy feared that Charles would return and

[49] George Monck to Sir Arthur Haselrigg, February 15, 1660, *The Clarke Papers* 4: p. 264.

[50] Ludlow, *Memoirs* 2: p. 228; Thomas Rugge, "Mercurius Politicus Redivius," B.M., Add. MSS, 10,116, fol. 61; Brown, *The First Earl of Shaftesbury,* p. 90. The secluded members present were Lewis, Evelyn, Holland, Gerard, Popham, Annesley, Knightley, Crew, Trevor, Harley, Norton, Temple, and Birch, Baker, *Chronicle,* p. 749.

[51] *Ibid.,* pp. 749–750; George Monck, *The Speech and Declaration of His Excellency the Lord General Monck delivered at Whitehall upon Tuesday the 21 of February 1659* . . . (London, 1660).

[52] Brown, *The First Earl of Shaftesbury,* pp. 90–91. Whitelock's version, *Memorials of English Affairs* 4: p. 398, differs from this in that he states that the secluded members decided on

the nineteenth to go to the house on February 21; but see Pepys, *Diary* 1: p. 58.

[53] *Ibid.* 1: p. 60.

[54] *Commons Journals* 7: pp. 846–847.

[55] *Ibid.,* p. 847.

[56] *Ibid.,* p. 849.

[57] *Ibid.,* p. 850.

[58] *Ibid.,* p. 855.

[59] James Sharp to Robert Douglas, March 1, 1660, Wodrow, *Church of Scotland* 1: p. ix; the Presbyterian paper is printed on p. li.

bring "moderate Episcopacy, at the least," with him. "The good Party" moved every stone "to keep the Covenant interest on foot." Yet, as Sharp shrewdly saw, the Presbyterian members of the Long Parliament, more astute politically than the clergy, dared not press the question of a Presbyterian government too heavily for fear of losing the forthcoming election to the Independents or to the Anglican Royalists. Caught between these two possibilities, the Presbyterian clergy in London sought aid from Scotland in the form of a declaration for Presbyterian government throughout all three kingdoms. Sharp's attitude, then and later, was that a union of Presbyterians throughout the three nations was "not yet seasonable." [60] On this point at least Sharp performed a valuable service for the Anglicans by preventing a second Solemn League and Covenant.

The Long Parliament acted just as Sharp had predicted. The Committee for Religion under the chairmanship of Edward Harley first brought in a bill for approbation of ministers and a bill to establish the Westminster Confession. There was nothing dangerous about the bill for approbation, which was read twice and committed. Two chapters of the Westminster Confession were rejected, however, on the first reading of the bill.[61] These rejected chapters, which dealt with censures, synods, and councils, comprised the heart of the Westminster Assembly's work. The amended bill was read three times, a very unusual practice, and passed on March 5. The same day saw the passage of a proclamation against papists and an order for the Solemn League and Covenant to be printed, posted, and read in every parish.[62] Significantly, and contrary to past practice, the commons appointed no clergymen to assist the Committee for Religion until the major religious bills had been passed. Edward Harley requested Calamy, Reynolds, Ashe, Manton, Haviland, and Jacomb on March 5 to consult with the Committee,[63] probably to nominate the ministers commissioned in the bill for approbation of ministers, which passed the house three days later.[64] The bill for setting ministers in their livings and maintenance passed on March 16,[65] rounding out the religious enactments of the Long Parliament. The clergy lost on two counts. There was now little chance that Presbyterian government would be adopted, even by the next parliament, and there definitely would not be a national synod until after the next parliament convened, if then. Undoubtedly these considerations were partly responsible for the early shift of the Presbyterian clergy toward some compromise with episco-

pacy, and the same considerations probably strengthened the Laudians in their determination that there should be no important concessions.

The restoration of the Long Parliament had important political implications. A restoration of the Stuart family was reasonably assured from the moment the secluded members re-entered the commons, but neither Presbyterian nor Royalist could state at that date what the conditions might be. The final terms agreed upon by both parties came as a result of various events stretching from February to May, and, as might not be expected, the religious and political issues were not always joined together. For its short session the Long Parliament was able to influence, but not control, the restoration of Charles.

The Presbyterian cause, largely bound up with that of the Long Parliament, was weakened from the close and long alliance between certain of its followers (such as Sir William Waller, Denzil Holles, and Lord Willoughby) and Charles II. With the passage of time, other leading Presbyterians and persons having influence with them, formed, or attempted to form, personal treaties with the king. Only a few key figures can be discussed here. Manchester, the nominal leader of the Presbyterian politicians and some of the clergy, secretly offered his services to Charles early in January, 1660. Northampton, acting as intermediary, sent one Bray to Hyde with a proffer of Manchester's services on the condition that Manchester be made lord treasurer. Hyde at first thought the offer fraudulent and Bray an imposter,[66] but Mordaunt soon confirmed Manchester's aspirations.[67] Although Manchester failed to come to definite terms before the Restoration, he went over afterwards, receiving the lord chamberlainship.

Cooper, who had ingratiated himself with the Presbyterians from 1659, was a misleading figure to them. He can be called a political Presbyterian with considerable justification, but his religious views, if any, were far from Presbyterian.[68] Nevertheless, Cooper could always carry a large number of Presbyterians with him, especially after his efforts to serve the secluded members proved successful. Cooper was a political opportunist. Hyde realized this when he wrote Willoughby on February 11.[69] Lady Willoughby replied on February 24 that both Waller and Cooper favored a restoration but might become involved in the design to exact harsh conditions.[70] Hyde then assured Lady Willoughby that Waller would favor moderate terms. Of Cooper, he accurately said:

[60] James Sharp to John Smith, March 4, 1660, *ibid.*, pp. ix–x.
[61] *Commons Journals* 7: p. 858; Whitelock, *Memorials of English Affairs* 4: p. 401.
[62] *Commons Journals* 7: p. 862.
[63] Edward Harley to Edmund Calamy, March 5, 1660, H.M.C., *Portland MSS* 3: p. 219.
[64] *Commons Journals* 7: p. 867.
[65] *Ibid.*, p. 880.

[66] Sir Edward Hyde to William Rumbold, January 13/23, 1660, *Clarendon State Papers* 3: p. 657.
[67] Viscount Mordaunt to Sir Robert Moray, January 26, 1660, *Mordaunt Letter-Book*, p. 178.
[68] Burnet, *History of His Own Times* 1: p. 175, called Cooper a deist.
[69] Sir Edward Hyde to Lord Willoughby, February 11/21, 1660, *Calendar of the Clarendon State Papers* 4: pp. 557–558.
[70] Lady Willoughby to Sir Edward Hyde, February 24, 1660, *Clarendon State Papers* 3: p. 689.

I [do not] take him to be a person at all concerned in Presbytery, except in the ambition of it, and when once he intends well, I suppose he will be advised by those who will give him good council, and particularly by my Lord Southampton, whose niece he hath married.[71]

On the basis of this view of Cooper's political character, Charles authorized William Coventry to negotiate with Cooper.[72] On March 9 Lady Mordaunt informed the king that Cooper was "inclinable to a personall treaty."[73] Eight days later Hyde wrote that he was sending Henry Coventry to assist in winning Cooper.[74] Henry Coventry arrived with a letter from Charles II to Cooper,[75] and by April 25 Cooper was an esteemed member of the king's circle.

Annesley, perhaps more influential with the Presbyterians than Cooper, was also enticed to join the king's party. Annesley provided Mordaunt with pamphlets and petitions, and he apparently followed Mordaunt's advice on securing the admission of the secluded members. Annesley's appointment to the council of state, of which he became president, made him an important figure. On February 27 Charles II wrote a personal letter to Annesley.[76] Mordaunt and Annesley became so intimate by March 8 that Annesley was providing Mordaunt with details of the council's actions, for which Mordaunt recommended that Annesley be shown special consideration for his Irish interests.[77] After receiving such news, Ormonde, who was destined to become lord lieutenant of Ireland, wrote Annesley, who took Ormonde's letter "very kindly" and replied.[78] Although Ormonde's letter and Annesley's reply are unavailable, it is reasonable to conclude, in the light of subsequent developments, that Ormonde assured Annesley that he would not suffer any loss in Ireland and perhaps promised to secure him a position in Irish affairs. In any event, Mordaunt left no doubt that Annesley had joined the king's interest.

How many others tied themselves and their followers to Charles in exchange for personal reward or honor? Naturally, not every case can be uncovered; nor can every known instance be cited.[79] A few of the more important examples should be mentioned, however, to indicate the general trend. Colonel John Birch, who

had purchased church lands, asked that his purchases be confirmed.[80] Edward and Robert Harley are two more examples. Edward at one point insisted on the abolition of episcopacy, parliamentary control of the militia, an act of indemnity, and confirmation of land sales.[81] Robert early allied himself with Monck,[82] and both Edward and Robert had satisfied Massey as to their intentions by March 16.[83] The Earl of Clare promised his influence to Charles II.[84] Sir John Northcote and several other Cornish Presbyterians committed themselves by March 9. Sir Harbottle Grimston confessed that he had been "faulty" and expressed a desire "to expiate that crime."[85] Edward Rossiter, Lord Fairfax, Alexander Popham, Lord Willoughby, Sir John Norwich, Sir Thomas Wharton, and others made some engagements with Mordaunt.[86] To this partial list must be added those unnamed persons covered by Sir Thomas Peyton's reference to the secluded members: "The fear I knowe many of your Majesty's partie have of their Presbyterian way is easily qualified by distinguishing the times of what they tooke up at first, and of what they hold now of that perswasion."[87] In other words, a Presbyterian of 1642 was not necessarily to be considered a Presbyterian in 1660. Changes of opinion, concern for property and office, and fear of republicanism took a heavy toll among those who had joined the Presbyterian cause in the Civil War. Age and death had taken away a large number of those who had formed the Presbyterian ranks.

Inside the Long Parliament, some Presbyterians proved beyond question that they eagerly awaited the return of monarchy. The issue which revealed how far some so-called Presbyterians were prepared to go was the new parliament. The picture, as seen by the Venetian minister, was:

Many members would like the writs issued without restrictions or limitations and the elections to be the same. Others desire to impose restrictions both on the electors and on those to be elected. Others again are of opinion that these should be for the latter but not for the former.

One member moved that the peers be called upon to summon a parliament in the king's name and to invite

[71] Sir Edward Hyde to Lady Willoughby, March 3/13, 1660, B.L., Clar. MSS 70, fol. 83.

[72] Sir Edward Hyde to Lady Willoughby, March 17/27, 1660, ibid., fol. 190.

[73] Lady Mordaunt to Charles II, March 9, 1660, ibid., fol. 118.

[74] Sir Edward Hyde to Lady Willoughby, March 17/27, ibid., fol. 190.

[75] Charles II to Sir Anthony Ashley Cooper, March 15/25, 1660, ibid., fol. 159.

[76] Charles II to Arthur Annesley, February 27/March 8, 1660, ibid., fol. 46.

[77] Lady Mordaunt to Charles II, March 9, 1660, ibid., fol. 119.

[78] Viscount Mordaunt to Marquis of Ormonde, March 16, 1660, B.L., Carte MSS 213, fol. 660.

[79] See Calendar of the Clarendon State Papers 4 for any number of letters between the Royalists and the Civil War party.

[80] Edward Massey to Sir Edward Hyde, February 24, 1660, B.L., Clar. MSS 70, fol. 26.

[81] Statement by John Halsall about a conference with Colonel Har[ley], March 1/11, 1660, ibid., fol. 57.

[82] Robert Harley to Edward Harley, March 2, 1660, H.M.C., Portland MSS 3: p. 218.

[83] Edward Massey to Sir Edward Hyde, March 16, 1660, Thurloe State Papers 7: p. 855.

[84] Charles II to [Earl of Clare], March 6/16, 1660; and Sir Edward Hyde to Gervase Holles, March 21/31, 1660, H.M.C., Bath MSS 2: pp. 143 and 144.

[85] [J. Seymour] to Sir Edward Hyde, March 9, 1660, B.L., Clar. MSS 70, fol. 110.

[86] Lady Mordaunt to Charles II, March 9, 1660, ibid., fol. 119.

[87] Sir Thomas Peyton to Charles II, February 19, 1660, ibid., fol. 3.

Charles home without conditions. This motion was opposed by all who had purchased lands or had engaged in the trial of Charles I. Some proposed recalling Richard Cromwell, and others suggested that Monck be named protector. Monck, more than any other, urged electoral restrictions.[88] Edward Stephens told the house that until "the sunne, the moone, the stares were placed in their proper orb" England could not be happy, and made an especially harsh attack on those who had purchased lands.[89] When the method of dissolution was debated on March 8, Prynne "asserted the Kings right in such bold language that . . . he may be stild the Cato of this age."[90] Prynne's speech produced a great silence in the house until Annesley moved that the matter be postponed.[91] Grimston went so far as to address the commons openly in favor of recalling Charles immediately.[92] Such men were not likely to haggle long with Charles Stuart over the conditions of his return.

Although the Presbyterian politicians dashed almost madly into the king's camp, their clerical friends seemed to stand still.[93] Richard Baxter was among the Presbyterian clergy who viewed the restoration of Charles Stuart with suspicion. Baxter had been solicited by his Anabaptist friend William Allen in December to use his influence to effect a compromise between the Rump and the secluded members.[94] Almost a year before Baxter wrote John Swinfen, an ardent Presbyterian layman and secluded member, a lecture praising the Humble Petition and Advice, offering advice on politics, and urging the passage of new laws on religion.[95] Even after the Long Parliament dissolved, Thomas Bampfield, a Presbyterian lawyer from Exeter, engaged Baxter to aid in framing a bill on doctrine, discipline, and worship.[96]

Many of the Presbyterians, especially the clergy, were concerned about their obligations of loyalty to the various oaths and engagements which they had taken since 1642. As believers in a narrow interpretation of Scripture, they felt a moral obligation to adhere to oaths. Upon the admission of the secluded members, the Long Parliament had repealed all engagements except the Solemn League and Covenant, expunged them from the records, and declared that no person was any longer bound by them.[97] If a parliament could repeal Cromwell's engagements, what sanctity would the Covenant have from a future parliament? In addition to working on Bampfield's request for Scriptural proof for Presbyterianism, Baxter prepared to publish his views on the continued validity of oaths and engagements.[98] The publication of such views would certainly revive and strengthen the Covenant interest.

While Baxter worked on his projects, some of the London clergy were no less busy in steering a Presbyterian course. When Sharp arrived in London on February 13, he was welcomed with open arms by Thomas Manton as a friend and fellow believer who would place the Scottish Presbyterians alongside their English friends in a battle for Presbyterianism.[99] The London Presbyterians had taken a rigid Presbyterian position in their petition of March 1 to the Long Parliament. When this address met with a cool reception in the Long Parliament, the ministers began to fear that both monarchy and episcopacy would return, and they begged Sharp to obtain them a firm alliance with their Scottish brethren. This request Sharp failed to honor. Calamy, Ashe, and Taylor employed Sharp as their spokesman with various members of parliament. The clergy feared that, if the Long Parliament surrendered to a free election, they would have no security against episcopacy. On the other hand, they feared that, if the Long Parliament continued to sit, the king and the bishops might come home without any restrictions.[100] Thus the clergy were pinned on the horns of a dilmma. They knew that the Long Parliament intended to dissolve without making adequate provision for Presbyterianism, and they were reasonably certain that the new parliament would be lukewarm at best toward their beliefs.[101]

The Presbyterian clergy, who were dissatisfied with the Long Parliament's failure to make more adequate

[88] Francesco Giavarina to Doge and Senate, March 2/12, 1660, *Calendar of State Papers, Venetian* **32**: pp. 125–126; see also *A second Seasonable Speech made by an Honourable Member of the House of Commons, demonstrating the Necessity of the Kings Restauration by this present Parliament* (London, 1660), which could be Prynne's speech.

[89] Edward Massey to Charles II, March 7, 1660, B.L., Clar. MSS 70, fol. 104.

[90] Thomas Luttrell to Marquis of Ormonde, March 9, 1660, B.L., Carte MSS 213, fol. 645; see also Sir John Grenville to Sir Edward Hyde, March 9, 1660, B.L., Clar. MSS 70, fol. 115.

[91] James Mowbray to Sir Edward Walker, March 9/19, 1660, B.M., Add. MSS 15,750, foll. 55–56. A slightly different account is in Major Wood to Sir Edward Hyde, March 9, 1660, B.L., Clar. MSS 70, fol. 121.

[92] Sir Harbottle Grimston's Speech, B.M., Harl. MSS 1576, foll. 284–285.

[93] Brown, *The First Earl of Shaftesbury*, p. 92, says that more Presbyterians opposed the restoration of Charles than favored it, which might be correct for the clergy but not for the laity.

[94] William Allen to Richard Baxter, December 30, 1659, Baxter MSS, Letters I, No. 29/24.

[95] Richard Baxter to John Swinfen, February 17, [1659], *ibid.*, VI, No. 10.

[96] Thomas Bampfield to Richard Baxter, March 26, 1660, *ibid.*, IV, No. 106/5.

[97] Whitelock, *Memorials of English Affairs* **4**: p. 403.

[98] Earl of Lauderdale to Richard Baxter, March 20, 1660, Baxter MSS, Letters V, No. 301.

[99] James Sharp to [Edinburgh Ministers], February 14, 1660, Wodrow, *Church of Scotland* **1**: p. vi.

[100] James Sharp to Robert Douglas, March 6, 1660, *ibid.*, p. x.

[101] Alderman James Bunce to Sir Edward Hyde, March 16, 1660, *Calendar of the Clarendon State Papers* **4**: p. 606. Bunce said that "Calamy and other Presbyterian ministers have lost themselves through a petition for the secluded members and the Rump," which can only mean that the London clergy made an effort to stop the dissolution.

provision for the Presbyterian doctrine and government, feared that some form of episcopacy would be the upshot. The clergy were also dubious of the king's character, habits, and religion. His father had possessed prelatical, if not popish, tendencies, and his mother was an ardent Roman Catholic. Charles II had already displayed his love of pleasure. His long sojourn abroad among Laudians and Catholics made him even more suspect to the Presbyterians, despite his "forced" subscription to the Solemn League and Covenant.

After Sharp's arrival in London on February 13, he endeavored to lessen the fears of the Presbyterian clergy and to make possible the restoration of episco-pacy.[102] Sharp was, however, a practitioner of du-plicity. He brought Calamy and Ashe together with Monck,[103] and perhaps assisted Sir Thomas Ingram in arranging a meeting between some Anglican and Presbyterian ministers.[104] After observing Sharp's activities, Edward Massey notified Hyde that Sharp was working for the king, not the Presbyterians, and should be rewarded.[105] There seems to be no evidence that the Presbyterians were aware of Sharp's standing with the other side.

The Earl of Lauderdale, who was then Sharp's patron, launched a successful attack against Richard Baxter's recalcitrancy. Baxter and Lauderdale had corresponded rather frequently during Lauderdale's imprisonment at Windsor Castle. Lauderdale won the approval of Baxter as a devout Christian and as a serious scholar because of some translations which he did for Baxter. Lauderdale had sent Sharp to visit Baxter at Kidderminster in October, 1657, probably for the purpose of winning Baxter over to royalism.[106] Baxter's open allegiance to Richard Cromwell brought an end to his correspondence with Lauderdale until February 6, 1660, when Lauderdale reopened their friendship by reporting Sharp's arrival in London.[107]

Soon after the secluded Presbyterians returned to power, they ordered Lauderdale's release from Windsor Castle.

Lauderdale was concerned about Baxter's efforts to keep alive the cause of Presbyterianism and to frustrate the movement toward an unconditional restoration. Although Baxter's letters to Lauderdale seem to be lost, it is obvious from Lauderdale's letter of March 20, 1660, that Baxter informed Lauderdale of his fears and activities in a letter of March 7. Lauderdale did not receive Baxter's letter until March 19, but replied the following day:

essone as I am enabled I shall come incognito to Keder-minster. I long (more than you can) to speake with you even about that controversie which you hint at. It is a vanity for me to pretend that I can satisfy you in any point of controversie; yet in this I am confident I can. Wee are agreed as to the doctrine, and in the application I can say so much, and I am so confident you will trust me in matter of fact & heare my reasons that I shall beseech you not to ingage against the generall received opinion till I can have the happiness to see you. This I say because it is reported in town that you have declared against a gentleman to whom I wish very well. I doe not beleeve it, yet friendship compells me to give you this hint. One hint more let me give you. All secluded members are not of a minde. Some may be changed since you saw them.[108]

The "gentleman" in question was none other than Charles Stuart. The "controversie" consisted of the king's religion and the matter of the Civil War and Cromwellian oaths and engagements. The "hint" about the secluded members was nothing more than a thinly veiled threat that Baxter and his clerical friends had better reconsider their positions or be left completely in the lurch by the restoring fever of the politicians. Just how far Baxter had gone in declaring against Charles Stuart and a restoration of monarchy is not clear.

Baxter's reply of March 24 to Lauderdale's letter of March 20 is missing from the Baxter materials, but it is obvious from Lauderdale's letter of the "Last of March" that Baxter raised so many objections and questions that Lauderdale could answer only the more pressing ones in a letter, promising anew to visit Kidderminster within a fortnight, unless Baxter found it possible to come to London. Lauderdale stressed the fact that the Cromwellian oaths could not abrogate earlier oaths to Charles I and his heirs and pointed out the flaws in the legal positions of Oliver and Richard Cromwell. Lauderdale warned Baxter about the republican Independents by stating that the important question was "whether a sword shall prevaile to the apparent ruine of Churche & state or if England shall returne againe to be governd by Parliaments." England should have no fear of a parliament elected under the

---

[102] James Sharp to Robert Douglas, March 10, 1660, Wodrow, *Church of Scotland* 1: p. xi.

[103] James Sharp to Robert Douglas, March 13, 1660, *ibid.*, pp. xii–xiii.

[104] Sir Thomas Ingram to Charles II, March 13, 1660, B.L., Clar. MSS 70, fol. 153; Robert S. Bosher, *The Making of the Restoration Settlement: The Influence of the Laudians, 1649–1662* (Westminster, 1951), pp. 105–106, gives the impression that these talks did not commence until Dr. George Morley arrived later in the month, but Ingram's letter leaves no doubt that the discussions began prior to Morley's arrival; hereafter cited as *Restoration Settlement*.

[105] Edward Massey to Sir Edward Hyde, March 16, 1660, *Thurloe State Papers* 7: p. 856.

[106] Robert Beake to Richard Baxter, October 16, 1657, Baxter MSS, Letters I, No. 12; Earl of Lauderdale to Richard Baxter, February 16, [1657], Frederick J. Powicke, "Eleven Letters of John Second Earl of Lauderdale (and first Duke), 1616–1682, to the Rev. Richard Baxter (1615–1691)," *Bulletin of the John Rylands Library* 7: p. 85; Earl of Lauderdale to Richard Baxter, October 19, 1657, *ibid.*, pp. 80–83; and Powicke, *Richard Baxter*, p. 137.

[107] Earl of Lauderdale to Richard Baxter, March 17, 1659, Powicke, "Lauderdale Letters," *Bulletin of the John Rylands*

Library 7: p. 104; Earl of Lauderdale to Richard Baxter, February 16, [1660], *ibid.*, pp. 84–85. Powicke misdated the last letter as [1657/58?].

[108] [Earl of Lauderdale] to Richard Baxter, March 20, [1660], Baxter MSS, Letters V, No. 301.

prescribed conditions. As if to assure Baxter of his sincerity, the Earl asserted, "If I know my owne heart I may solemnly profess that the interests of Jesus Christ & the good of his people shall ever sway me beyond the interest of any or of all the men on earth." Baxter was assured most emphatically that Charles and James Stuart could be trusted. Pulling out all stops, Lauderdale appealed to Baxter's ever present feeling of divine purposefulness:

For the Lords sake ingage not in anything which may hinder you from being the great instrument of union in these Churches. If you should smile again at it, I am most confident God will reserve you for that worke.[109]

As if Lauderdale's pleas and arguments might prove insufficient, Dr. William Bates, a prominent London Presbyterian minister, wrote a covering letter in which he warned Baxter that the loss of his services to the party of peace and union would be a grave one. Bates implied that he and his colleagues supported Lauderdale's views.[110]

Baxter now wasted no time in answering the call of Lauderdale and providence to do battle for religious unity. When he arrived in London about April 13,[111] Baxter found the political situation moving forward to a return of monarchy and episcopacy. Some of the Presbyterian ministers had conferred with Monck just before the Long Parliament dissolved, by which time arrangements had been completed for a conference between some Presbyterian and Anglican ministers. Calamy and Ashe were convinced by Monck that the Long Parliament must be dissolved. The early election returns, to be treated in the next chapter, certainly influenced both minister and politician. Everywhere the polls reflected increasing monarchical, and in many cases Anglican, popularity, even among former Presbyterian laymen. Sharp and Lauderdale pressed upon the clerical Presbyterians the necessity to act with haste if they hoped to salvage anything from the situation.

The mission of Lauderdale and Sharp was to prevent any combination or alliance between the Scottish and English Presbyterians. Their strategy was to emphasize the possibility of a compromise between English Presbyterianism and Anglicanism, which embraced the calculated loss of the strict Presbyterians. Massey, who was personally acquainted with Lauderdale, wrote Hyde on March 23 that Lauderdale was already "very busy" with the Presbyterian ministers,[112] which means

that Lauderdale lost no time after arriving in London about March 19. At the same time Sharp was told by the Anglicans "to move nothing in prejudice of the Church of England, and they would do nothing in prejudice" of the Church of Scotland.[113] Slowly and surely Sharp and Lauderdale drove a wedge between the Scottish and English Presbyterians so as to prevent any recurrence of the 1643 alliance.

Another prominent feature of the immediate pre-Restoration period was the constant appeal for a union of Presbyterians and moderate Anglicans against the other Protestant groups. The common plea ran much like the following:

nor is there so great difference between a moderate Episcopal man, and a sober Presbyterian, but that both will jointly meet and kiss each other, for the settlement of the Nation in peace and unity.[114]

The extremists among the Anglicans and Presbyterians received equally strong criticism.[115]

There were men in both the Anglican and Presbyterian parties who devoted themselves seriously to reconciliation. Two such men were John Gauden and Edward Reynolds. Both had been ordained before the Civil War; both had taken the Solemn League and Covenant; and both became bishops after the Restoration. There was no question concerning their dedication to the principle of religious comprehension. Both were active in attempting a compromise between episcopacy and presbytery. It was not a novel project for either. Each had participated in such projects during the Cromwellian period. Gauden spent his life in the shadow of Archishop James Usher, Bishop Ralph Brownrigg, and Dr. Nicholas Bernard, all of whom were noted for their anti-Laudianism. It was Gauden who preached Brownrigg's funeral sermon in December, 1659. On the publication of this sermon Gauden took occasion to add a lengthy section propounding the benefits of modified episcopacy of the Usher variety,[116] a view which commended Gauden to the followers of Baxter. For this and previous displays of moderation Gauden was selected by the City of London to preach a thanksgiving sermon for the restoration of the secluded members. Gauden's selection for this major sermon was an indication of the future path of the London council. The sermon struck at division and animosity, and carefully trod a narrow course between the Anglicanism of Laud and the Presbyterianism of Knox. Gauden held out hope to the moderate

---

[109] [Earl of Lauderdale] to Richard Baxter, March 31, [1660], *ibid.*, I, No. 29/27.

[110] W[illiam] B[ates] to Richard Baxter, March 30, 1660, *ibid.*, IV, No. 29.

[111] Baxter, *Reliquiae Baxterianae,* Pt. II: p. 215, gives April 13, but see James Sharp to Robert Douglas, April 13, 1660, Wodrow, *Church of Scotland* 1: p. xviii; and Powicke, *Richard Baxter,* pp. 189–190.

[112] Edward Massey to Sir Edward Hyde, March 23, 1660, *Thurloe State Papers* 7: p. 867.

[113] James Sharp to Robert Douglas, March 27, 1660, Wodrow, *Church of Scotland* 1: p. xv.

[114] Anonymous, *The Army's Declaration: Being a True Alarum in Answer to a False and fiery one . . .* (n.p., 1660), p. 7.

[115] Anonymous, *Expedients for Publique Peace. Shewing the Necessity of a National Union . . .* (n.p., 1660).

[116] John Gauden, *A Sermon Preached . . . at the Funeral of . . . Dr. Brownrig late Lord Bishop of Exceter . . .* (London, 1660).

Presbyterians for a compromise through discussion in a freely chosen synod of divines.[117] Such expressions of moderation, joined with circumstances over which the Presbyterian clergy had little control, offered the moderate Presbyterians an escape from the intolerance of the Laudians and from the extreme decentralism of the Independents. It proved to be an illusion, but the moderate Anglicans and Presbyterians had little choice.

Another factor which influenced the Presbyterian clergy was the arrival of Dr. George Morley at the end of March as Hyde's personal agent in religious matters. It is therefore pertinent to know precisely the situation upon Morley's entrance. A representative of the old Cavalier party, Alan Broderick, assured Hyde that the Presbyterians were "now apt for good impressions, if gently applied."[118] Dr. John Barwick, an Anglican of the Laudian type, agreed so far as the moderate Presbyterians were concerned, and recommended gaining them which would

digg up the others by the rootes by finding themselves deserted and in that way I hope I have made some progress. . . . As for the grandees of that party they will come in of themselves when they see the tide begin to turne but I fear no sooner.[119]

Miles Barton warned, however, that, while the laity showed great moderation, "the Presbiterian Parsons (not all of them neither) doe spur hard, (& if itt were possible) to drive the people to another rebellion, but they are little listened unto, and lesse believed."[120] Alderman John Robinson, a former Presbyterian destined to become a successful court politician and who knew London and its people better than most people, informed his royal patron that "some of the Presbyterians, who have been formerly forward enough, begin a little to flag now, and fear the settlement of Episcopacy, and that your Majesty will slip in without conditions . . . ."[121] There was general agreement, then, that the clerical party was divided into camps, and three of the four sources mentioned above held that the moderates were ready to think in terms of modified episcopacy. We must also conclude, as did our witnesses, that the Presbyterian shift toward a restoration of monarchy and episcopacy was rather sharp.

In general, subsequent developments support the above conclusions. Yet, "the real Presbyterians" of London requested a meeting with Lauderdale and Sharp on March 31 for the following Monday "to concert Matters against Sectaries and Cavaliers."[122] Two important features of the situation are here revealed. First, the clergy still had faith in the two Scots; and, secondly, they continued to fight both sectary and Anglican at the same time. The intemperateness of some Anglican clergy, subsiding somewhat after Morley's arrival, contributed to the wariness of the Presbyterians.[123]

Whether by design or not, Morley's arrival coincided with the concentrated effort by the Anglicans to win over the more moderate Presbyterians. Morley was summoned before the council of state to answer questions concerning his mission, and received permission to operate without hindrance. Assuming that Morley was frank with the council, it must be concluded that the council did not object to Morley's activities. Within the week Morley reported to his superiors that the Presbyterians seemed "to desire a conference with some of the moderate men of the Episcopal persuasion." Morley attempted to give Hyde the impression that he was not prepared to act on the Presbyterian suggestion until the receipt of "particular directions." Highly elated by the election returns, Morley gave as his opinion "that all that is in difference betwixt us, is to be referred to the decision of a national Synod and free Parliament."[124] The implication was, of course, that any conference of ministers held preceding the Convention Parliament and the return of the king should be for the purpose of mollification, exploration, and delay.

Sharp's account of the situation, almost as vague as Morley's gave a somewhat different impression. He and Lauderdale met as arranged with ten of the Presbyterian divines,

whom they could trust, where Lauderdale, they, and he agreed upon the Necessity of bringing in the King upon Covenant Terms, and taking off the Prejudices that ly upon some Presbyterians against this. There are Endeavours for an Accommodation between the moderate Episcopalian Party, and the Presbyterians: But . . . at our Meeting, Lauderdale and I obtained of those Ministers, *that they should not give a Meeting to the Episcopal Men, till they first met among themselves, and resolved on the Terms they would stick to.*[125]

Sharp's summary makes it obvious that he and Lauderdale were more involved than they admitted to the English Presbyterians. Not every minister could be trusted so they selected those ten most likely to be converted as leaders of the rest. These ten were then convinced to accept a Covenant basis for the religious settlement, but Lauderdale and Sharp's interpretations of the Covenant never called for the total extirpation of

[117] John Gauden, . . . *Slight Healers of Publick Hurts Set Forth in a Sermon Preached in St. Pauls Church, London . . . Feb. 28, 1659* (London, 1660).

[118] Alan Broderick to Sir Edward Hyde, March 30, 1660, *Clarendon State Papers* 3: p. 714.

[119] John Barwick to Sir Edward Hyde, March 30, 1660, B.L., Clar. MSS 71, fol. 109.

[120] Miles Barton to Sir Edward Hyde, March 30, 1660, *ibid.,* fol. 107.

[121] John Robinson to Charles II, March 30, 1660, *Clarendon State Papers* 3: p. 716.

[122] James Sharp to Robert Douglas, March 31, 1660, Wodrow, *Church of Scotland* 1: pp. xvi–xvii.

[123] Bosher, *Restoration Settlement,* pp. 108–110.

[124] Dr. George Morley to Sir Edward Hyde, April 5, 1660, *Clarendon State Papers* 3: p. 722.

[125] James Sharp to Robert Douglas, April 5, 1660, Wodrow, *Church of Scotland* 1: p. xvii; italics added.

episcopacy, merely reformation of some Laudian abuses of it. Sharp's account also suggests that the motions for a conference between the Anglicans and Presbyterians came from the Anglicans but that he and Lauderdale blocked the request until such time as the Presbyterians had prepared a set of proposals. It is also possible, though not subject to confirmation, that they arranged for the Presbyterians not to hold their preparatory conference until after the Convention Parliament met.

This interpretation of the Morley and Sharp letters is substantiated by letters of a later date from Sharp and Barwick. The tone of the Anglican strategy was that suggested by Barwick on April 6. Barwick exhibited no concern about the laity, only of the clergy who "do what they can to uphold their cause." He proposed to employ both mollification and division as devices against the Presbyterians. For this reason Barwick consulted with Lauderdale who "professeth vehemently he is of no faction, but will obey the King's command in any thing." [126] What clearer proof of Lauderdale's dissimulation could exist? Sharp, Lauderdale, and Sir Robert Moray arranged for some French Protestants to send over testimonal letters concerning the king's character and religion which succeeded in satisfying Baxter on those scores. Sharp even prevailed upon five of the clergy to send Charles a thousand pieces of gold as evidence of their affection, though they still refused to agree to the Anglican requests for an "Accommodation" conference.[127]

It was not until about April 13 that the Presbyterians around Lauderdale and Sharp finally agreed to "speak one by one" with the Anglicans. Sharp then informed them that he had been asked to confer with the Anglicans, and the Presbyterian ministers granted Sharp permission to meet with Morley on April 13.[128] Thus Morley, whose authorization to negotiate with the Presbyterians had not reached England as yet, and Sharp brought their furtive affair into the open. Bosher incorrectly interpreted Morley's activities, being misled by Morley's reference to "those that converse with them" into the assumption that Morley wrote as a third party.[129] Actually, the same letter contained the use of the first person. To be exact, however, Morley wrote:

Those that are the chief, and have the most power amongst them, are content to admit of the name Bishop, but not the power, which we think to be inseparable from his office. . . . And whereas they thereupon infer that then the Episcopal Government will be arbitrary and tyrannical, *I tell them* they may be secured from that fear by those Canons and Ecclesiastical Laws whereby he is to govern, and which, if he do transgress, he is answerable for it to a free Synod. With this, *I am confident* Dr. Reynolds is fully satisfied, but Calamy and others are not.

Thus far Morley had gone in conferring with the Presyterians. True, there had been no large conference between the two groups, but only because, as Morley stated, "they do not press for it, so we have no reason to desire it." Furthermore, Morley visited Manchester and obtained a promise that Manchester would "serve the King by disposing the Presbyterians to admit of Episcopacy in such a notion" as Morley described to the Presbyterian clergy.[130] Manchester's promise, made before April 13, left the clergy without a prominent layman to intercede for more than modified episcopacy.

When Morley's instructions from Hyde arrived they authorized Barwick, Morley, and "other discreet Men of the Clergy" to converse and confer with the Presbyterians so as "to reduce them to such a Temper, as is consistent with the good of the Church." Hyde suggested that they assure the Presbyterians of "present good Preferments." [131] In the absence of any detailed reports from the Anglicans or from Sharp one must conclude that little, other than informal discussions, occurred between April 13 and 25. Sharp's only significant letter to Douglas for this period reported that the question of religion would be completely waived in any treaty negotiations and presented subsequently to a synod.[132] Only one conclusion is possible: Lauderdale, Sharp, Morley, Barwick, and Manchester succeeded in convincing the London clergy that no other solution was possible under the circumstances then prevailing.[133] Too, the Presbyterians had received the promise of equal treatment in a free synod called to thresh out all differences to the mutual satisfaction of all.

In the realm of secular politics the dissolution of the Long Parliament was the signal for more concrete negotiations between the king and General Monck. Hyde, contrary to general belief, was not opposed to a formal treaty between the Long Parliment and his master. Only six days after the secluded members returned to power, Hyde instructed Mordaunt to

advise as well with new friends as old, when it may be seasonable to publish the Proclamation from the King. I cannot possibly comprehend how they can call a new Parliament after they have dissolved this; nor why they should not better begin a treaty with the King upon the foot of that which was begun at Uxbridge, for the Treaty

---

[126] John Barwick to Sir Edward Hyde, April 6, 1660, *Clarendon State Papers* 3: p. 723.

[127] James Sharp to Robert Douglas, April 7, 1660, Wodrow, *Church of Scotland* 1: p. xvii; and Powicke, *Richard Baxter*, p. 190.

[128] James Sharp to Robert Douglas, April 12, 1660, Wodrow, *Church of Scotland* 1: p. xviii.

[129] Bosher, *Restoration Settlement*, p. 114.

[130] Dr. George Morley to Sir Edward Hyde, April 13, 1660, *Clarendon State Papers* 3: pp. 727–728; italics added.

[131] Sir Edward Hyde to Dr. John Barwick, April 12/22, 1660, Barwick, *Life of John Barwick*, p. 525.

[132] James Sharp to Robert Douglas, April 19, 1660, Wodrow, *Church of Scotland* 1: p. xviii.

[133] There is some reason to believe that Morice, after conferring with Morley, influenced Baxter; see John Collins, "Mysteria Revelata," H.M.C., *Leyborne-Popham MSS*, p. 228; Baxter, *Reliquiae Baxterianae*, Pt. II: p. 215.

will best settall other things in order, and best provide for the execution of them.[134]

Here, then, was a definite desire to see a treaty negotiated along lines similar to those discussed at Uxbridge. Hyde and the king were, in fact, anxious to publish a royal proclamation or declaration as a step toward formal negotiations between the Long Parliament and Charles II. Hyde continued to advocate this plan as late as March 14.[135] Nor was Sir John Grenville's interview with Monck on March 19 inconsistent with such a policy. Hyde's proposal was defeated by Monck and the Long Parliament jointly, not by Monck alone. The Prynne and Grimston faction in the Long Parliament strongly urged a restoration by the Long Parliament. Monck opposed them, perhaps because of his troops, and only three members actively supported the motion to recall the king before dissolving.[136]

Sir John Grenville's interview with Monck on March 19 was in reaction to the failure of the Long Parliament to negotiate with the king and in line with Monck's personal wishes. Not much is known about the conversation between Grenville and Monck. In fact, one knows only that Monck advised Charles II to grant an amnesty and toleration, to confirm land sales, and to withdraw from Brussels into Holland. Grenville delivered this oral message to the king at Brussels, only revealing it to Mordaunt later.[137] It is inconceivable that Monck had not discussed his advice to Charles with the leading members of the council of state before seeing Grenville. Cooper, Sharp, Annesley, and the Harleys undoubtedly influenced Monck's decision to see Grenville, and probably participated in formulating the message sent Charles.[138]

Sending suggestions and securing their acceptance by the parties concerned were two entirely different operations. There were still many individuals to be won over to a restoration without conditions. A group within the council of state still labored for terms similar to those offered Charles I at the Isle of Wight.[139] Immediately following the dissolution of the Long Parliament the council of state met in secrecy for the purpose of framing propositions to present to the king. Thomas Luttrell, who may have been known more than he disclosed, informed Ormonde that he was confident that "his Majestie will treate upon them."[140] Actually, a struggle was taking place within and without the council of state. A "Junto" of rigid and aspiring Presbyterians, consisting of a small block from the council and some peers, Manchester, Bedford, and Wharton, had been formed.[141] This group approached Bordeaux for French intervention and assistance, but Bordeaux clearly perceived that

the ministers of state hold too conflicting opinions to come to an agreement in so short a time. Some are desirous to follow exactly the treaty of the Isle of Wight, others wish to append additional restrictions thereto, and some are willing to content themselves with the safeguard of the ancient laws of the realm: this last opinion is held in common with the people.[142]

In other words, Bordeaux was of the opinion that the council of state would at the last moment demand little more than general assurances from Charles II and that France should offer no assistance to those who for the moment hoped for something more positive and concrete than vague promises from Charles Stuart.

When Mordaunt returned from Brussels about April 18, he reported that the Presbyterian cabal consisted of Northumberland, Manchester, Fairfax, Holles, Lewis, Pierrepoint, Gerard, and Cooper and that it met every night at Suffolk House. Their strategy was to prevent the old Cavaliers and young peers from entering the House of Lords until they could force the king to repeal every act against the Long Parliament since 1643 and to sign the Isle of Wight treaty, less the preamble, before negotiating further. The cabal also intended to capture all the major offices: Holles as secretary of state, Gerard as treasurer of the navy, Northumberland as admiral, Manchester as treasurer, Pierrepoint as privy seal, and Lewis as president of Wales.[143] Subsequent events proved that most of these

[134] Sir Edward Hyde to Viscount Mordaunt, February 27/ March 8, 1660, B.L., Clar. MSS 70, fol. 50. The proclamation referred to is almost certainly the one in Henry Hyde's hand found in Clar. MSS 71, foll. 359–361.

[135] Sir Edward Hyde to William Rumbold, March 14/24, 1660, *ibid.*, 70, fol. 158.

[136] M. de Bordeaux to M. de Brienne, March 19/29, 1660, Guizot, *Monk*, p. 197.

[137] Edward Hyde, Earl of Clarendon, *The History of the Rebellion and Civil Wars in England begun in the year 1641*, ed. W. Dunn Macray (6 v., Oxford, 1888) **6**: pp. 194–195; hereafter cited as Hyde, *History*; T. H. Lister, *Life and Administration of Edward, First Earl of Clarendon* (3 v., London, 1837– 1838) **1**: pp. 497–498; hereafter cited as *Clarendon*; Carte, *Ormonde* **2**: p. 198; and Leopold von Ranke, *A History of England Principally in the Seventeenth Century* (6 v., Oxford, 1875) **3**: pp. 298–299; hereafter cited as *History of England*.

[138] Baxter, *Reliquiae Baxterianae*, Pt. II: p. 214, said: "The chief Men . . . that turned his Resolution, to bring in the King, were Mr. Clarges and Sir William Morice, his kinsman, and the Petitions, and Affections, of the City of London, principally moved by Mr. Calamy and Mr. Ashe, . . . (with Dr. Bates, Dr. Manton, Dr. Jacomb, and other Ministers of London who concurred): And those were encouraged by the Earl of Manchester, the Lord Hollis, the (late) Earl of Anglesey, and many of the (then) Council of State." Burnet, *History of His Own Times* **1**: p. 178, thought that Cooper, Holles, Annesley, Manchester, and Robartes were chiefly responsible.

[139] Samuel Morland to Charles II, March 19, 1660, *Clarendon State Papers* **3**: p. 703; James Halsall to Sir Edward Hyde, March 23, 1660, B. L., Clar. MSS 71, fol. 28, reported that some wanted parliamentary control of the militia for fifteen years, no negative voice for the king, episcopacy to stand but deprived of its land, and all land sales to be confirmed.

[140] Thomas Luttrell to Marquis of Ormonde, March 27, 1660, B.L., Carte MSS 213, fol. 683.

[141] Henry Slingsby to Sir Edward Hyde, March 23, 1660, *Clarendon State Papers* **3**: p. 705.

[142] M. de Bordeaux to Cardinal Mazarin, April 12/22, 1660, Guizot, *Monk*, pp. 213–214.

[143] Viscount Mordaunt to Sir Edward Hyde, April 19, 1660, *Clarendon State Papers* **3**: pp. 729–730.

men were interested more in office and personal career than anything else. Fairfax, Holles, and Cooper dropped out completely before April 25, and Manchester soon after.

What then was the situation with regard to a treaty with the king? The Long Parliament dissolved without proposing anything. Three days later Monck sent his advisory message to Charles, and the Presbyterian "Junto" busied itself with discussions of terms to submit to the king. The treaty party received its first obvious setback on March 25 when the London council offered its advice on the matter in a petition to the council of state. London, though predominantly Presbyterian, was, like most trading centers, under the control of merchants and lawyers who, desirous of stable conditions and low taxes, did not wish to prolong the political uncertainties. The London council suggested that Charles be requested to grant a general amnesty, to pay off the army, and to refer the religious settlement to an assembly of divines.[144] Gone was the delusion that London, the stronghold of Presbyterianism and banker of the Long Parliament in the Civil War, would stand again on guard against monarchy and episcopacy. After all, the old Cavaliers were promising not to seek revenge against their old enemies.[145]

From March 15 to April 25 a handful in the council of state and three or four Presbyterian peers fought a rearguard action in defense of the Isle of Wight terms, but some important members of the council, particularly Cooper and Annesley, had already been won over to the position occupied by Monck on March 19. Denzil Holles, leader of the parliamentary Presbyterians during the Civil War, had long since made his peace with Hyde, and was so tired of the struggle that he wrote his wife:

I wish with all my heart, I could slipp my neck out of the collar here, for in good truth I am not ambitious of this employment [in the council of state] & will gett out of it as soone as I can.[146]

Probably others of the older generation felt too battleworn to continue long as opponents to the horde of energetic youth loudly acclaiming Charles II.

Although the Presbyterian pulpits might "thunder" against the election results,[147] Dr. Bates' protest against the return of Hyde and others around the king,[148] and the "Junto" members of the council of state beg Monck

to consent to some propositions being sent to Charles, Monck stoutly adhered to his earlier resolution to leave all things to a free parliament,[149] and pictures of the exiled Stuart appeared in prominent places around London.[150] Annesley reported each night to Mordaunt and Geoffrey Palmer on the day's events and decisions in the council of state and at Suffolk House, where he had treacherously become a spy, so that the restoration crowd knew every proposal or pending action of the treaty party.[151]

The council of state finally resolved not to treat with the king prior to the opening of the Convention Parliament, preferring to commit that business to the care of some other body. It was also agreed, though not authorized by the Long Parliament, that the House of Lords as constituted in 1648 should meet on April 25. Thurloe, whose opinion can never be disregarded, felt that the council of state "designed" to frame terms, for presentation to the Convention Parliament, similar to those submitted at Newport "unlesse in some thinges the vigour of some of them be abated, which is inclyned to." There was hope that Charles would appoint a lieutenant of the kingdom to act in his stead. Thurloe's letter to Montagu closed:

By this your Lordship sees how farre matters are advanced, & not only the Council but all other gentlemen already chosen [for parliament] as they come to towne are to be spoke with to engage them in these things. And truly I thinke this is like to be the issue of our affaires if noe interruption happen . . . .[152]

The agreements had to be altered during the last fortnight. "There are," wrote Bordeaux, "none who do not neglect the public advantage in order to attend to their own private interests."[153] This trend may well explain why even Manchester and Northumberland assured Alderman Bunce at the last minute that they intended "to make the propositions easy" for the king.[154] Lambert's escape from the Tower further

[144] The paper is in B.L., Tanner MSS 49, foll. 1–2; see Ranke, *History of England* 3: pp. 295–296, for his summary and discussion.

[145] See for example, *A Declaration of the Nobility and Gentry that adhered to the late King, now residing in and about the City of London* (London, 1660), which was only one of countless such printed declarations.

[146] Denzil Holles to Lady Covert, April 5, 1660, B.M., Add. MSS 32,679, fol. 60.

[147] Lady Willoughby to Sir Edward Hyde, April 20, 1660, *Clarendon State Papers* 3: p. 731.

[148] Dr. George Morley to Sir Edward Hyde, April 18, 1660, B.L., Clar. MSS 71, fol. 295.

[149] Henry Slingsby to Sir Edward Hyde, April 11, 1660, *Clarendon State Papers* 3: p. 726.

[150] Rugge, "Mercurius Politicus Redivius," B.M., Add. MSS 10,116, fol. 87.

[151] Viscount Mordaunt to Sir Edward Hyde, April 19, 1660, *Clarendon State Papers* 3: p. 729.

[152] John Thurloe to Edward Montagu, [ca. April 13, 1660], B.L., Carte MSS 73, fol. 406; the date is from Montagu's endorsement. Compare this letter with Thurloe to George Downing, April 6, 1660, *Thurloe State Papers* 7: pp. 886–887, for the changes that occurred in one week. See also James Sharp to Robert Douglas, April, 1660, Wodrow, *Church of Scotland* 1: p. xix, to the effect that the council had gone through the "most sticking Parts of the Articles to be laid before the Parliament for a Treaty; that of an Indemnity, and Sales and Purchases, which the King will agree to." Baxter, *Reliquiae Baxterianae*, Pt. I: p. 105, believed that the council, because of Annesley, actually voted against a treaty and the Covenant, which is not unlikely.

[153] M. de Bordeaux to Cardinal Mazarin, April 23/May 3, 1660, Guizot, *Monk*, p. 218.

[154] Alderman James Bunce to Charles II, April 24, 1660, B.L., Clar. MSS 72, foll. 17–18.

terrified some and temporarily revived the hopes of the harsh treaty party. On the very eve of the Convention Parliament Mordaunt confidently wrote Charles II that the Northumberland-Manchester cabal "neither have . . . any interest now considerable to doe good or ill." The restoration party, on the other hand, had already arranged for the Declaration of Breda and the accompanying letters to be read on April 25. Morice, at the request of Grenville, was to speak in behalf of the king; Heneage Finch, through the efforts of Mordaunt, was to second Morice's motion. Annesley anxiously pressed the need for expeditious handling of the entire business, lest some accident occur. There is no question that Annesley, and probably others of the council of state, knew the general nature of the king's Declaration and letters, if he had not read them.[155]

Everything was in readiness for the Convention Parliament's action. A sufficient number of the council of state had been brought to accept the views of Monck and the London council as the basis for the restoration. Religion was not to be treated upon. The negotiations, if any, were to deal with indemnity for past actions, settlement of the army, and confirmation of the land transactions. The Presbyterian clergy were to await the action of a promised assembly of divines. Only a contrary-minded coalition within the Convention Parliament could alter the course of events already charted behind the scenes.

V. THE CONVENTION PARLIAMENT

When the Long Parliament dissolved itself on March 16, 1659, it was generally assumed that Charles II would be restored, but few people anticipated the unconditional return of monarchy and episcopacy. Yet on May 29 Charles II re-entered London without formally signing away any of the rights and privileges of either monarchy or episcopacy. The Stuart Restoration definitely was not in accordance with the Presbyterian program of 1648, which had included a proposed treaty between king and parliament. In brief, the Stuart Restoration was essentially unconditional. Why the Presbyterians failed to effect a formal treaty with Charles II, or to curb materially either monarchy or episcopacy, is the subject of this chapter. Since the Convention Parliament was at least technically responsible for the return of Charles II, it is logical to look to the Convention for an answer to the major question, and perhaps some of the lesser ones.

The first important point to consider is the composition of the House of Commons of 1660. Until Miss Louise Fargo Brown's essay of 1907 historians generally took it for granted that the Presbyterians

dominated the Convention commons.[1] Only the year before, however, no less an authority than Professor W. C. Abbott made the traditional assumption,[2] and as recently as 1952 Godfrey Davies asserted his own doubt as to the validity of Miss Brown's conclusion that "the Presbyterians had at no time a clear majority in the lower house of the Convention Parliament."[3] Keith Feiling, historian of the Tory Party, dismissed the issue with the compromising assertion that "the experienced Presbyterian politicians of the Commonwealth" dominated the Convention Parliament.[4] But such conclusions are, as Miss Brown correctly observed,[5] very much out of line with the activities of the Convention, a fact which none of her disputants has seen fit to question.

In examining any election one naturally turns to the precept for the election. There was considerable disagreement among the members of the Long Parliament in 1660 as to the qualifications, if any, to be prescribed for candidates and electors, with a fairly large group in favor of no restrictions beyond the traditional ones.[6] Had Monck not interfered the more impatient members might well have succeeded in setting aside all novel qualifications. At Monck's insistence,[7] however, all men, together with their sons, who had voluntarily participated or aided in the war against the Long Parliament since January, 1642, unless they had since displayed affection to the parliamentary cause and had received parliamentary absolution for their sins, were declared ineligible for election, though not deprived of their parliamentary franchise.[8] Did these restrictions actually exclude many potential candidates? Part of the answer to this question is to be found in an Act of March 12 for settling the militia throughout England

---

[155] Viscount Mordaunt to Charles II, April 24–27, 1660, B.L., Clar. MSS 72, fol. 19; see also Masson, *Life of Milton* 5: p. 666, where this same conclusion is hinted at.

[1] Louise Fargo Brown, "The Religious Factors in the Convention Parliament," *English Historical Review* 22: pp. 51–63; see p. 51 for a summary of views about the composition of the commons.

[2] Wilbur C. Abbott, "The Long Parliament of Charles II," *ibid.* 21: p. 27.

[3] Godfrey Davies, "The General Election of 1660," *Huntington Library Quarterly* 15: p. 211; Brown, "Religious Factors in the Convention Parliament," *English Historical Review* 22: p. 63. Davies in his last work on the subject concluded that "it is probable that the Cavaliers were the more numerous if to this side should be added those who were more Royalist than Presbyterian," *The Restoration of Charles II, 1658–1660* (San Marino, Calif., 1955), p. 333.

[4] Keith Feiling, *A History of the Tory Party, 1640–1714* (Oxford, 1924), p. 98.

[5] Brown, "Religious Factors in the Convention Parliament," *English Historical Review* 22: pp. 51–52.

[6] *Commons Journals* 7: p. 869.

[7] Francesco Giavarina to Doge and Senate, March 2/12, 1660, *Calendar of State Papers, Venetian* 32: pp. 124–127; M. de Bordeaux to M. de Brienne, February 28/March 9, 1660, Baschet Transcripts, Public Record Office, 31/3 (106), foll. 100–102.

[8] *Acts and Ordinances of the Interregnum, 1642–1660*, ed. C. H. Firth and R. S. Rait (3 v., London, 1911) 2: p. 1472.

and Wales.[9] Although the parliamentary families dominated the list of commissioners for each county, Cavaliers and sons of Cavaliers appeared quite frequently, especially for Kent, as militia commissioners. Under any plausible interpretation parliamentary approval to serve on the county militia commission would constitute, or at least suggest, eligibility for election to the commons.

The old Royalists had expected rigid electoral restrictions against them,[10] but, if election activity is any guide, they were not particularly displeased with the qualifications imposed. As for the militia and judicial reorganization carried out by the Long Parliament, the Royalists were anything but unhappy;[11] the only serious complaints came from the more ardent Presbyterians who had been outmaneuvered.[12] Realizing that the eventual settlement would rest with the Convention Parliament, both the old and new Royalists resolved to capture as many seats as possible.[13]

No election is complete without campaign literature. That for the election of 1660 indicated considerable aggressiveness by the Royalists and seeming retrenchment by the Presbyterians. In addition to the countless tracts and declarations of a general nature on politics and religion, there were at least five items which gave advice to electors. Three of these were Cavalier in authorship and content. Rodger L'Estrange anonymously advised against electing lay preachers, selfish and indebted persons, or any who had displayed malice toward Charles I, or had profited from his death.[14] *Considerations . . . to Regulate . . . Elections* was even more Royalist. It condemned the Civil War, the intervention of the Scots and the Solemn League and Covenant, and applauded the Anglicans and Cavaliers. After denouncing the Rumpers in particular, the tract urged electors to overlook all purchasers of crown, church, or delinquent lands; officeholders or others who had made profit from the Civil War; commanders of former or present armies; tax collectors and commissioners. Choose only knights, esquires or gentlemen resident in the county of election, and pay no heed to the prescribed qualifications.[15] This was budding Toryism. *Englands Directions for Members Elections*

was only a trifle milder in advocating the exclusion of the regicides and in advising electors to

> Make none had their hands,
> In Church Livings or lands

their choice for parliament.[16]

Only two major pieces of election literature can be classified as Presbyterian. Samuel Keme, while favoring a restoration of monarchy, made a special plea for men of "Piety before Policy," of "known Integrity and Fidelity to God and Man," of "Verity before Heresy," for "Gospel-Reformation" and for "Unity and Order in Religion."[17] Keme's battle cry had much in common with that of the Puritans of 1640. William Prynne's *Instructions* set forth the need for the election of men favorable to the conclusion of a "speedy honorable, safe, Christian treaty and accord with our long Protestant King and royal posterity, upon moderate, just, righteous, terms and propositions on either side, whereby the bleeding Protestant cause and religion . . . may be promoted and secured . . . ."[18] Thus the campaign tracts were weighted in favor of monarchy and uniformity, though the latter was heavily veiled for practical political reasons. Keme's defense of the zealous reformers of the Westminster Assembly fell outside the main stream of election literature.

Election mongering, however, did not await such advisory writings. It actually began some time before the Long Parliament decided formally on dissolution and an election. Sir Horatio Townshend started his campaign at King's Lynn prior to February 23 by seeking admission as a burgess of that borough,[19] and Andrew Henley commenced his preparatory activities by February 29.[20] Manchester wrote an election letter for Sir Henry Yelverton on March 6,[21] and even Monck anticipated matters by having his secretary, Matthew Lock, solicit a Warwickshire borough seat for Clarges.[22] In view of the report sent Sir Edward Nicholas,[23] these instances serve only to indicate the existence of a

---

[9] *Ibid.*, pp. 1425–1455.

[10] Lady Willoughby to Sir Edward Hyde, February 24, 1660, *Clarendon State Papers* 3: p. 689.

[11] Alan Broderick to Sir Edward Hyde, March 9, 1660, *ibid.*, p. 697; Thomas Luttrell to Marquis of Ormonde, March 2, 1660, B.L., Carte MSS 213, fol. 632.

[12] James Halsall to Sir Edward Hyde, March 23, 1660, B.L., Clar. MSS 71, fol. 28.

[13] Dr. John Barwick to Sir Edward Hyde, February 27, 1660, *ibid.*, 70, foll. 48–49.

[14] [Roger S. L'Estrange], *A Necessary and Seasonable Caution, concerning Elections* (n.p., 1660); see *L'Estrange His Apology*, p. 99, for authorship.

[15] Anonymous, *Certain Considerations . . . Presented to the Free-holders . . . to Regulate their Elections . . .* (London, 1660).

[16] Anonymous, *Englands Directions for Members Elections* (n.p., 1660); this work is entirely verse.

[17] Samuel Keme, *King Solomon's Infallible Expedient for Three Kingdoms Settlement . . .* (London, 1660), pp. 8–10, which was a sermon preached at Gloucester on the Sunday preceding the election there.

[18] [William Prynne], *Seasonable and Healing Instructions Humbly Tendered . . .* (n.p., 1660).

[19] Robert Stewart to Sir Horatio Townshend, February 23, 1660, B.M., Add. MSS 41,656, foll. 12–13.

[20] Andrew Henley to John Chattey, Jr., February 29, 1660, B.M., Sloane MSS 815, fol. 3.

[21] Earl of Manchester to Lord Montagu, March 6, 1660, H.M.C., *Report on the Manuscripts of the Duke of Buccleuch and Queensberry, K.G., K.T., Preserved at Montagu House, Whitehall* (3 v., London, 1899–1926) 1: p. 312; hereafter cited as *Buccleuch and Queensberry MSS*.

[22] Matthew Lock to an unidentified peer, March 6, 1660, B.M., Stowe MSS 185, fol. 144.

[23] Colonel Robert Whitley to Sir Edward Nicholas, March 9/19, 1660, *Nicholas Papers* 4: p. 202.

widespread anxiety to corner seats in anticipation of a dissolution of the Long Parliament and the election of a new body.

In the elections, shire and borough, the Presbyterians displayed far less vigor and organization than the Royalists, and where they clashed openly the Royalist candidate, more often than not, was successful. Unfortunately, not much is known about the issues involved in many of the contests. More is known about the shire elections than the borough contests, and in almost every case religion and Civil War record played important roles. The Essex Royalists and Anglicans carried that county against the Presbyterians.[24] The same thing happened in Cambridgeshire[25] and in Worcestershire, where Baxter and the Presbyterians supported the losers, Foley and Graves.[26] In Surrey the two Onslows were greeted with shouts of "Noe Rumpers, no Presbiterian that will put bad conditions on the King," and lost the election to two secret Anglican Royalists.[27] Sir Horatio Townshend, a Royalist and Anglican, had the nomination of all men returned from Norfolk.[28] Edward Harley, a new Royalist with a Puritan background, had to seek recommendations from the Cavaliers in his Herefordshire candidature;[29] Sir Gilbert Gerard, though he combined with Sir William Waller, lost to Lancelot Lake, son of a delinquent, in Middlesex.[30] Richard Hampden and Richard Winwood, both Cromwellians and the first Baxter's friend, suffered defeat in Buckinghamshire.[31] In each of these shire elections religion and political principles were determining factors.

The foregoing evidence on the shire elections is rather startling, but not nearly as convincing as the complete results. A contemporary report on the election stated that those persons who "assisted Sir George Booth [were] looked on as eminent servants,"[32] by which the writer meant that those who worked for a joint Presbyterian and Royalist uprising in 1658 and 1659 were very popular in 1660. Another letter said that "not any where a Knight of a County chosen, reputed to be of that [Presbyterian] persuasion, without the current desires of the King's party; and when that interest hath been slighted, the Presbyterian hath been most shamefully baffled."[33] A thorough study of the men returned as knights of the shire bears out these statements. Godfrey Davies concluded that of the seventy-eight "who sat for English shires, at least a quarter were Cavaliers or their sons" and "probably ninety percent or more" of the knights would support an unconditional restoration of Charles II.[34] A biographical study reveals that Davies' estimates were inaccurate. His first estimate is too low, and the second too high. At least thirty-four, and probably more, of the seventy-eight English county members were Cavaliers or sons of Cavaliers. To this figure, however, should be added men like Lord Aungier, whose Irish interests and clerical family made him an Anglican and a secret Royalist, and Sir Robert Bindlosse, who, as deputy lieutenant in 1662, diligently pursued dissenters. Perhaps the list of Anglican Royalists should include John Crew, father-in-law of the deistic Edward Montagu and father of a future bishop of Durham. In all, there were at least twelve knights of the shire, in addition to the thirty-four Cavaliers, who were more likely to support Anglicanism than Presbyterianism.[35] The best generalization on the county elections is that wherever Cavaliers or their sons ventured to stand they received support over all other candidates; otherwise the freeholders chose Presbyterian monarchists openly professing an intention to restore monarchy and episcopacy without stringent restrictions. Not a single radical was returned as knight of a shire.

The borough elections are impossible of detailed treatment here, but a few random cases should serve to illustrate the pattern in the boroughs. Townshend's control of Norfolk, through his own and the Howard influence, insured that the borough members of that county were Anglican Cavaliers or extremely mild Presbyterians like Sir John Holland. The Howard influence extended to Suffolk and Surrey from whence many good Royalists were returned.[36] The Kentish

[24] Robert Phillips to Sir Edward Hyde, April 20, 1660, *Clarendon State Papers* 3: p. 731; Sir John Bramston, *The Autobiography of Sir John Bramston*, ed. P. Braybrooke (London, 1845), pp. 114–115; Ralph Josselin, *The Diary of the Rev. Ralph Josselin, 1616–1683,* ed. E. Hockliffe (London, 1908), p. 134.

[25] George Tomlinson to Sir Edward Hyde, April 13, 1660, B.L., Clar. MSS 71, fol. 242.

[26] John Halsall to Sir Edward Hyde, April 6, 1660, *ibid.,* fol. 170.

[27] E. Willoughby to Madam Shaw [Sir Edward Hyde ?], April 6, 1660, H.M.C., *Laing MSS* 1: pp. 310–311; Henry Champion to Hugh Potter, April 12, 1660, H.M.C., *Third Report, Appendix* (London, 1872), p. 89.

[28] Lady Mordaunt to Sir Edward Hyde, April 26–27, 1660, B.L., Clar. MSS 72, fol. 63; this is confirmed by William Doyly to Sir Horatio Townshend, March 20, 1660, B.M., Add. MSS 41,656, fol. 14. Townshend received a slight setback when Lord Richardson, designed for a borough, was elected for the county over Doyly, who then shifted to Great Yarmouth, Miles Barton to Sir Edward Hyde, April 6, 1660, B.L., Clar. MSS 71, fol. 157.

[29] John Halsall to Sir Edward Hyde, April 20, 1660, *ibid.,* fol. 352.

[30] Miles Barton to Sir Edward Hyde, April 6, 1660, *ibid.,* fol. 156; T. C. to Thomas Fry [Sir Edward Hyde?], April 6, 1660, *ibid.,* fol. 174.

[31] Whitelock, *Memorials of English Affairs* 4: p. 406.

[32] Lady Willoughby to Sir Edward Hyde, March 30, 1660, B. L., Clar. MSS 71, fol. 103.

[33] Robert Phillips to Sir Edward Hyde, April 20, 1660, *Clarendon State Papers* 3: p. 731.

[34] Davies, "The General Election of 1660," *Huntington Library Quarterly* 15: pp. 220–221.

[35] The sources employed on this biographical study of the Convention Parliament are too numerous to be cited, but include published biographies, county and local histories, county and borough parliamentary studies, and manuscript materials.

[36] The Howard family claimed control or influence over 18 to 24 seats.

members were predominantly Anglican and Cavalier.[37] Cornwall, on the other hand, returned men who were probably, as Miss Coate concluded, "more Parliamentarian than Royalist, and more Presbyterian than Anglican."[38] A good test of the Presbyterian popularity was the London election where some thirty or forty candidates were nominated. Even in this center of Presbyterianism "none of the most popular presbyterians could get any voyces (in a maner)."[39] In fact, John Robinson, Sir Richard Brown, and Sir William Wild were already good courtiers and destined to prove excellent supporters of the Clarendon government. William Vincent, the other London member, probably followed his brother in forming a profitable alliance with the Duke of York. However, these examples cannot be taken as typical. Local politics, family or property interest, and a host of other factors frequently counted for more than national issues. The confirmed Presbyterians, by and large, were more successful in the boroughs than in the county contests. Market towns and out ports probably returned more Presbyterians than Royalists, but boroughs under the control or influence of landed gentry supported Anglican Royalists more often than not.

Certain features of the election stand forth prominently. One of these was the surprising independence of the freeholders and burgesses in refusing the radicals. Two hundred gentlemen rode into Leicester to warn that borough against returning Haselrigg.[40] Thurloe, though recommended by Monck, was denied at Bridgnorth,[41] and Speaker Lenthall suffered the same fate at the University of Oxford.[42] St. John was rejected by the junior university.[43] Although eleven regicides

were returned, several on contested returns, only one, Richard Ingoldsby, managed to retain his seat.[44] With the exception of a few Rumpers the Convention Parliament was, on the whole, rather conservative. Not a single case of a Presbyterian-Independent combination against a Royalist is known. The usual thing was for the Presbyterians and Independents to enter separate candidates against the Royalists or for the Presbyterians and Royalists to combine against the Independents.

Another important aspect of the election was the electioneering of Monck and Montagu. A comparison of their efforts and successes or failures indicates that Monck definitely was not a tool of Hyde and Charles during the election, that he displayed a lack of political aptitude, and that he was relatively unsuccessful. Monck, as already stated, attempted unsuccessfully to get Clarges, who was seated from Westminster, returned from a Warwickshire borough, Thurloe from Bridgnorth, and Lenthall from the University of Oxford. He also worked unsuccessfully in Dr. Walker's behalf at Droitwich.[45] Despite his personal popularity, which declined considerably by April 25, Monck succeeded in securing the election only of himself from Devonshire and Cambridge, Admiral Penn from Weymouth,[46] and Clarges from Westminster. Not a one of Monck's successes could be termed political. All his failures involved Independents. These facts suggest that Monck did not directly assist either the Presbyterians or the Royalists in the election of 1660.

Montagu's activities exceeded those of Monck, largely because of his control of the Cinque Ports, were more successful, and seem to indicate a greater determination to join with the shift toward an unconditional restoration of both monarchy and episcopacy. Montagu sent Samuel Pepys to Sir Thomas Widdrington to ask that the writs for the Cinque Ports be entrusted by the council of state to his supervision.[47] The writs were then delivered to John Raven.[48] Montagu made a successful effort at Dover for himself,[49] and unsuccessful attempts at Hythe,[50] Sandwich,[51] and Hastings [52] for

[37] John Heath to Sir Edward Hyde, March 30, 1660, B.L., Clar. MSS 71, fol. 105.

[38] Coate, *Cornwall in the Civil War*, p. 313.

[39] Dr. John Barwick to Sir Edward Hyde, March 30, 1660, B.L., Clar. MSS 71, fol. 109; John Heath wrote Hyde on the same day that the London members were "all such as we wish," *ibid.*, fol. 105.

[40] William Morice to Edmund Prideaux, April 5, 1660, Coate, "William Morice and the Restoration of Charles II," *English Historical Review* 33: p. 376.

[41] George Monck to Bridgnorth, April 7, 1660, *Thurloe State Papers* 7: p. 888; Thomas Gilbert to John Thurloe, April 11, 1660, *ibid.*, p. 895.

[42] Davies, "The General Election of 1660," *Huntington Library Quarterly* 15: pp. 222–223, whose account should be corrected in so far as vice-chancellor John Conant is concerned. Conant made an early appeal to Matthew Hale, who indicated a disinclination to serve, before falling back on Lenthall as his candidate; see John Conant to Matthew Hale, April 2, 1660, and Hale's undated reply, *Memoirs of the Life, Character and Writings of Sir Matthew Hale, Knight, Lord Chief Justice of England,* ed. J. B. Williams (London, 1835), pp. 45–48. This is a good point to acknowledge an indebtedness to the essay by Davies and to one by H. N. Mukerjee, "Elections for the Convention and Cavalier Parliaments," *Notes and Queries* 166: pp. 398–403, 417–421, for some references and ideas, though differing with Davies on some conclusions.

[43] William Hetley to Edward Montagu, April 2, 1660, B.L., Carte MSS 73, fol. 400.

[44] The other ten were Wallop, Mildmay, Harrington, Ludlow, Scot, Cawley, Hutchinson, Lassells, Harrison, and Luke Robinson.

[45] Magistrates of Droitwich to George Monck, April 13, 1660, H.M.C., *Leyborne-Popham MSS*, p. 174.

[46] William Wheeler to Edward Montagu, April 5, 1660, B.L., Carte MSS 73, fol. 376.

[47] Pepys, *Diary* 1: p. 90.

[48] John Haven to Hastings, New Romeny, Hythe, Rye, Winchelsea, and Seaford, March 27, 1660, B.L., Carte MSS 73, foll. 362–363.

[49] Thomas Browne to Edward Montagu, March 24, 1660, *ibid.*, foll. 357–358.

[50] Captain Thomas Tiddeman to Edward Montagu, April 2, 1660, *ibid.*, foll. 369–370. Tiddeman, Captain Valentine Tatnell, John Raven, William Wheeler, and Henry Oxeden were his agents.

[51] Mayor and Jurates of Sandwich to Edward Montagu, April 11, 1660, *ibid.*, foll. 393–394.

[52] Pepys, *Diary* 1: p. 90.

his kinsmen Edward and George Montagu. Montagu apparently made no effort to control New Romeny, Rye, Winchelsea, and Seaford where local strength and tradition were probably too great for outsiders. He assisted Robert Montagu, Viscount Mandeville and eldest son of the Earl of Manchester, win the Huntingdonshire election, but lost both Huntingdon borough seats.[53] In three other places, however, Montagu was successful. He helped secure the election of his brother-in-law, Sir Henry Wright, at the post office borough of Harwich;[54] was returned himself for Weymouth where he almost clashed with Monck's recommendation of Admiral Penn;[55] and he surely assisted John Crew, his father-in-law, who was returned as knight of Northamptonshire. In by-elections, three of his kinsmen (George, Edward, and William Montagu) were chosen with his assistance at Dover, Weymouth, and Cambridge. All of Montagu's candidates became supporters of the administration before May 29. Each eventually returned to the Anglican fold. The Montagu family, then, serves as an excellent example of how some men appeared as Presbyterian, Independent, and Anglican without adopting the principles of any group Although it is impossible to estimate the number of such politicians, it is safe to assume that they were many in number. Important, too, is the fact that career politicians and government servants like Montagu were among the most loyal of the returning king's supporters.

All contemporary statements about the election agree that the Presbyterians were utterly dismayed and frustrated by the success of the Cavaliers and those Presbyterians and career politicians almost inseparable from them. As early as March 22 Bordeaux predicted that the parliament would be composed of young men who, "not having been engaged in the war, will not make use of . . . precautions" against monarchy and episcopacy.[56] James Sharp made repeated references to the success of the "Royal Party" and the increasing fear of the "sober Party."[57] Dr. Morley, when he arrived in England toward the end of March, reported much the same impression.[58] Hyde received one report that the Rev. Thomas Case, terrified by the returns, attempted to unite the Presbyterians and the "Phanatick party, for undoubtedly the Chavaleer party now appears too considerable for either of thos factions."[59] On

March 30 an old Cavalier, John Heath, predicted that "three fourths will bee right" so far as the terms of the restoration were concerned.[60] Thurloe, watchful as ever, expressed the opinion that the only hope for the Presbyterians lay in an alliance with the sectarian interests, which he thought not likely to happen.[61] With the electors casting aside some "chief men,"[62] disregarding openly the qualifications,[63] refusing those who were "the most influential and turbulent in the Long Parliament," and returning men of "pacific temperament,"[64] it is not surprising that the Presbyterian pulpits thundered against the elections.[65] Nor is it surprising that the Presbyterian clergy became faint-hearted.[66] The Presbyterians were so alarmed by the early elections that they, with assistance from Monck's wife, persuaded Monck to go to the council of state and insist that orders be sent to each returning official to read the qualifications and the council's proclamation at each polling place.[67] Despite this warning, the electors continued to vote for disqualified persons.

How serious were the Presbyterian reverses? Writing twelve years later, Hyde said that the

. . . Party of the Presbyterians was very numerous in the House of Commons [at first]. . . . But the Spirit of the Time had of itself elected many Members, notwithstanding the Injunctions sent out with the Writs, and expressly contrary to such Injunctions, of a very different Alloy; who together with such as were chosen after his Majesty's return, were numerous enough to obstruct and check any Prevalence of that Party, though not of Power enough to compel them to sober Counsels.[68]

However, Montagu told Pepys on April 26 that he believed that "the Cavaliers have now the upper hand clear of the Presbyterians."[69] John Collins, fourteen years later, wrote that the Royalists "became the more prevalent party" in the commons immediately after the house sat down.[70] It is certain that there were between 100 and 120 well-known, old Royalists

[53] *Ibid.*, p. 84.
[54] *Ibid.*, p. 94.
[55] George Monck to Edward Montagu, April 7, 1660, B.L., Carte MSS 73, foll. 378–379; both Penn and Montagu were elected.
[56] M. de Bordeaux to Cardinal Mazarin, March 22/April 1, 1660, Guizot, *Monk,* p. 199.
[57] James Sharp to Robert Douglas, March 27, 1660, Wodrow, *Church of Scotland* 1: p. xv.
[58] Dr. George Morley to Sir Edward Hyde, April 5, 1660, *Clarendon State Paper* 3: p. 722.
[59] Miles Barton to Sir Edward Hyde, April 6, 1660, B.L., Clar. MSS 71, fol. 156.

[60] John Heath to Sir Edward Hyde, March 30, 1660, *ibid.,* fol. 105.
[61] John Thurloe to George Downing, April 6, 1660, *Thurloe State Papers* 7: p. 887.
[62] Francesco Giavarina to Doge and Senate, April 6/16, 1660, *Calendar of State Papers, Venetian* 32: p. 137.
[63] M. de Bordeaux to Cardinal Mazarin, April 9/19, 1660, Baschet Transcripts, Public Record Office, 31/3 (106), fol. 150.
[64] Francesco Giavarina to Doge and Senate, April 13/23, 1660, *Calendar of State Papers, Venetian* 32: pp. 138–139.
[65] Lady Willoughby to Sir Edward Hyde, April 20, 1660, *Clarendon State Papers* 3: p. 731.
[66] Dr. John Barwick to Sir Edward Hyde, April 6, 1660, *ibid.,* p. 723.
[67] John Collins, "Mysteria Revelata," H.M.C., *Leyborne-Popham MSS,* pp. 202, 229; John Heath to Sir Edward Hyde, March 30, 1660, B.L., Clar. MSS 71, fol. 105. The proclamation was issued on March 28.
[68] Hyde, *Life* 2: p. 139.
[69] Pepys, *Diary* 1: p. 110; Montagu was even more emphatic on April 29, *ibid.,* p. 229.
[70] John Collins, "Mysteria Revelata," H.M.C., *Leyborne-Popham MSS,* p. 229.

returned by April 23,[71] and of the 208 or more political newcomers in the Convention commons probably the majority were both Anglican and Royalist. Forty-eight members were returned after the king's arrival, and these were almost entirely Anglican supporters.[72] The votes and debates indicate Anglican and Royalist equality, if not superiority, from the opening day. By the end of the session the Presbyterians were definitely a minority party.

Despite the foregoing evidence, the myth of a Presbyterian majority in the Convention Parliament still persists in certain circles. Fortunately, a contemporary study of the original membership of the commons has survived. Lord Wharton, who moved from Presbyterianism to Congregationalism between 1642 and 1660, attempted to form a party from the Presbyterian and Independent members. From the original membership Wharton could find only 124 likely supporters of a reformed church and state,[73] and some of these proved to be of entirely different mettle. Allowing for losses and gains and every possible support from the Low Church element, Wharton's project could never have rallied more than 150 adherents. This being true, the reforming element, even on April 25, was inferior in numbers to the Anglican membership of the commons. All in all, Wharton's list confirms all the more vividly what Miss Brown concluded from a study of contemporary statements: at no time, not even on April 25, did the Presbyterians possess a working majority in the Commons. On some issues they might, by a combination with the Independents, the Roman Catholics, or some of the Royalists, appear as a majority element, but on questions touching directly upon religious or political change they never dominated.

The Convention Parliament, contrary to what might have been expected, proceeded to business very casually; yet with an eye always to the inevitable moment when the question of Charles II would have to be considered. Following a time-honored practice, the lower house met first at St. Margaret's Church to hear Dr. Reynolds. One group of Presbyterians, about forty in number, either did not attend the religious service or was more rapid afoot than the Royalist party organized by Mordaunt. Mordaunt's friends had "engaged 4 parts of five" for Edward Turner as speaker, but a group headed by Denzil Holles, Sir William Lewis, William Pierrepoint, and Monck had chosen and seated Sir Harbottle Grimston when Mordaunt's friends arrived in the house.[74] In view of the fact that Grimston was elected before the house was officially called, it must be concluded that the Presbyterians were so aware of their numerical weakness as to resort to unusual methods in the election of a favorable speaker.

The only major business, other than organizing the house, concluded on the opening day was the appointment, at the request of the Lords, of Monday, April 30, as a day of public humiliation and the selection of Calamy, Gauden, and Baxter to preach.[75] Gauden's nomination was well received, but "above 60" negative voices greeted those of Baxter and Calamy.[76] This indicates that a substantial body of Anglican Royalists felt safe in expressing their opinion of Presbyterianism. It also warned the Presbyterians that they faced a rocky road.

Two major developments occurred on the second day. Holles moved that the house examine all election returns. This frightened the Royalists into thinking that the Presbyterians intended to expel all those who failed to qualify under the terms of election, and perhaps Holles hoped to carry out such an eviction. "Neere 100 were put out," but these, for the most part, were from boroughs sending in double or even triple returns and not permanent disqualifications at all.[77] If the Presbyterians intended to eject the Cavaliers they were foiled by the unusual promptness with which the country squires came up to London.[78] On May 5, the earliest date for which there is any attendance figure, 408 members were participating.[79] Far from being sent home, the Royalists captured control of the committee of privileges and elections and chose as chairman Edward Turner, their defeated candidate for the speakership. This action so frustrated the Presbyterian strategy that Sir Thomas Widdrington could not get a second for his motion to abide by the election qualifications, following which Sir William Lewis was sent to assure Dr. Morley that the Presbyterians would

[71] M. de Bordeaux to Cardinal Mazarin, April 23/May 4, 1660, Baschet Transcripts, Public Record Office, 31/3 (107), fol. 7; Ranke, *History of England* 3: p. 304, estimated the old Royalists at 150, which still seems low.

[72] Brown, "Religious Factors in the Convention Parliament," *English Historical Review* 22: p. 55.

[73] Lord Wharton's List of Possible Supporters in the Convention Commons, B.L., Carte MSS 81, foll. 73–78. This list was compiled on the basis of the original returns as printed in an early broadside, which is bound with Wharton's list. The fact that the list is in several hands suggests that it was composed by a group working with or for Wharton.

[74] Viscount Mordaunt to Charles II, April 24–27, B.L., Clar. MSS 72, fol. 19; Viscount Mordaunt to Sir Edward Hyde, April 27, 1660, *ibid.*, fol. 62; Bramston, *The Autobiography of Sir John Bramston*, pp. 116–117.

[75] Sir Edward Dering, "Diary," fol. 1. The author is much indebted to Professor Caroline Robbins of Bryn Mawr College for permission to use her transcript of this manuscript diary, now in the possession of Doreen, Lady Brabourne, London. Unfortunately, Dering was not a very thorough recorder at this point in his political career, even stopping altogether on August 15.

[76] W. Ellesdon to Sir Edward Hyde, April 27, 1660, B.L., Clar. MSS 72, fol. 44.

[77] Dering, "Diary," fol. 2; Viscount Mordaunt to Charles II, April 24–27, 1660, B.L., Clar. MSS 72, foll. 19–20.

[78] Collins, "Mysteria Revelata," H.M.C., *Leyborne-Popham MSS*, p. 229, said that the Presbyterians had hoped to exclude the Cavaliers but failed to control the committee of elections and privileges because of the haste with which the Royalists came up to London.

[79] *Commons Journals* 8: p. 14.

not question the qualifications of any member.[80] The only persons actually discharged were Independents, not Cavaliers. This is further proof, if any is needed, that the Presbyterians had anything but a clear majority at the opening of the Convention Parliament.

The second major business of April 26 concerned the House of Lords. Only twelve of the parliamentary lords of 1648 survived, and it was the hope of Manchester's junto that these might sit alone as a check on the restoration fever of the commons. The conventional story has been that Monck was a party to an agreement to exclude the Cavalier peers and the sons of deceased Cavalier peers but that he broke this pact by refusing to prevent the younger peers from entering the lords on April 26.[81] Once again, the Monck legend seems a bit inconsistent with the facts. Dering's diary refers to this question of the House of Lords as though it was discussed in the commons, and

it was thought, that it was a good step to the Kings admission . . . & the doore being open & no force to restraine them it was thought infallible that all the young Lords would come in, & not be excluded by the opinion of those 12 Lords [who] did first set alone . . . .[82]

One thing is certain: Monck was not consulted by the young peers before they entered the House of Lords. William Powell, knight of Herefordshire, informed his patron, Viscount Scudamore, that Dorset, Middlesex, St. John, Rivers, and Peters went unexpectedly into the lords and then sought out Monck who refused to become involved. "And therefore the Oath of Abjuration being taken by those who were suspected to be Recusants equal freedom is admitted to all Peers."[83] There is also a letter from Strafford, in behalf of himself, Oxford, Bridgewater, and Bolingbroke, to Monck after the young lords had been seated. This handful of old Cavaliers, after learning that Monck was "much displeased with the young Lords that went into the House," attempted to apologize for their youthful confederates.[84] Even Mordaunt agreed with this story when he reported that Manchester voluntarily sent for Southampton and Hertford "to moderate the others."[85] Clearly, then, Monck and the Presbyterians were both tricked by the boldness of the young peers, who could have been ousted only at the risk of civil strife. This was the last thing that Monck and

the Presbyterians wanted, so the Royalists came one step closer to an unconditional restoration.

It was not until Friday, April 27, that the question of the executive was broached. Rather innocently the commons was asked to consider a petition of one Birkhead to be restored to his former office as serjeant of the mace. This petition was soon forgotten when Heneage Finch moved it out of order on the ground that the government was not composed as it had been when the petitioner held his post. This prompted Colonel King, whom Mordaunt had recently converted into a Presbyterian Royalist, to move that the house examine and settle the government but not until after the house could render unto God on Monday, April 30. After King's motion had been seconded by Finch, Turner, Stephens, and Birch, the commons adjourned until Tuesday.[86]

To clarify this adjournment it is necessary to examine some closet politics surrounding Monck's message of March 19 to Charles II. After receiving Monck's advice at Brussels, Charles moved to Breda as suggested. The exiled court then decided to frame the Declaration of Breda of April 4 as the initial basis for negotiations with the Convention Parliament. Hyde later maintained in his *History* that the Declaration differed from Monck's advice because of the early election trends, a statement which is entirely plausible.[87] Monck recommended a general amnesty, confirmation of all land transactions, payment of the army, and general toleration. The Declaration, on the other hand, offered a free pardon to all those not specifically excepted from pardon by parliament, "a liberty to tender consciences" that would not disturb the general peace, a promise to approve any parliamentary action for that purpose, a referral of the land question to parliament, and the payment of Monck's soldiers as parliament should determine.[88] The Declaration, along with letters to Monck, the commons, the lords, the navy, and London,[89] was entrusted to Grenville for delivery. In addition, Charles wrote two warm letters to Morice,[90] and empowered Monck to give Morice the office of secretary of state, which had been vacant since the conversion of the Earl of Bristol to Roman Catholicism.[91] The second letter to Morice made reference to other letters being transmitted to Morice for distribution to Morice's friends, probably West Countrymen.

Grenville's arrival in London cannot be dated precisely. He was at Ostend on April 8 and probably

[80] William Powell to Viscount Scudamore, April 26, 1660, B.M., Add. MSS 11,689, fol. 55; Dr. George Morley to Sir Edward Hyde, April 27, 1660, B.L., Clar. MSS 72, fol. 85.

[81] See Bosher, *Restoration Settlement*, p. 115, for the latest expression of this story.

[82] Dering, "Diary," fol. 2.

[83] William Powell to Viscount Scudamore, April 26, 1660, B.M., Add. MSS 11,689, fol. 55; Bordeaux implied to Mazarin on April 26 that Monck was more or less compelled to consent to their admission, Guizot, *Monk*, pp. 219–220.

[84] Earl of Strafford to George Monck, April 26, 1660, B.M., Egerton MSS 2618, fol. 70.

[85] Viscount Mordaunt to Marquis of Ormonde, April 27, 1660, Carte, *Ormonde Papers* 2: p. 330.

[86] Dering, "Diary," fol. 4; Viscount Mordaunt to Marquis of Ormonde, April 27, 1660, B.L., Carte MSS 30, fol. 582; W. Ellesdon to Sir Edward Hyde, April 27, 1660, B.L., Clar. MSS 72, fol. 44.

[87] Hyde, *History* 6: p. 197.

[88] *Ibid.*, pp. 206–207.

[89] *Ibid.*, pp. 202–210.

[90] Charles II to William Morice, March 17/27 and March 30/April 8, 1660, *Thurloe State Papers* 7: pp. 858–859.

[91] Hyde, *History* 6: p. 202.

remained there until the receipt of Hyde's instructions of the thirteenth.[92] From Mordaunt's letter of April 19 it appears that both he and Grenville returned to London not later than the eighteenth.[93] This gave the Mordaunt-Grenville clique at least six days in which to prepare for the opening of the Convention Parliament. Many of the details of their operations cannot be found in the surviving correspondence, but most of their activities can be pieced together.

The most logical account would have it that Grenville brought unsealed copies of the Declaration and the letters, along with the sealed originals, to present to Monck.[94] This account is consistent with Mordaunt's letter to Charles II and bears up under analysis. The original plan concerted by Mordaunt, Grenville, Morice, Annesley, Finch, and Palmer, probably with Monck's approval, called for the presentation of the king's letters and Declaration on April 25. Morice and Finch were to move and second a proposal to accept the king's message as the means of opening negotiation, but this plan was frustrated by a double return against Morice from Plymouth and the late arrival of his return from Newport. Mordaunt's wing of the intrigue, including Annesley, Finch, and Palmer, wanted to go ahead without Morice, but Grenville and Morice, possessing the vital papers and the support of Monck, prevented any action until Morice could participate.[95]

Knowledge of the king's message and of the plans of the Mordaunt-Grenville group was by no means confined to a small circle. Colonel King and Alderman Bunce knew something of the affair by April 27, when King, at Mordaunt's request, moved to adjourn until the following Tuesday in order that Morice might be placated.[96] Henry and William Coventry were also on the inside,[97] and Philip Warwick's reference to daily meetings suggests that a fairly large group had been informed of the basic strategy.[98]

This delay, the admission of all the peers, the composition of the commons, and the personal treaties cost the Presbyterians dearly. Townshend, who nominated the members from his county, committed all the Norfolk members to Mordaunt. Even Sir George Booth called at Mordaunt's quarters for instructions.[99]

The delay permitted some West Country friends of the king's agents to arrive before the vital business came before the commons.[100] James Halsall had time for further discussions with some doubtful members of the council of state;[101] William Ellesdon lobbied "50 or 60" members.[102] Both Warwick and Barwick agreed that Southampton had won Northumberland and Saye and Sele away from the party in favor of a conditional restoration. These peers now asked only personal rewards and the concessions made by Charles I before the Civil War. Warwick feared, however, that many would contend for Presbyterianism, even though opposed to the principle, in order to block any attempt to ease the political terms that parliament would impose on the king.[103] The Venetian minister reported that even Manchester was "now much tamed and moderate." [104] Everywhere the lay Presbyterians and parliamentary politicians who had voyaged with the Presbyterians were shortening sail as the gathering storm of royalism appeared.

By May 1 nearly everyone felt confident that the restrictions, if any, placed upon either monarchy or episcopacy would be very slight,[105] and the events of that day proved beyond question that both the monarchical state and the episcopal church would be restored in their essential features, at least, if not in the fullness of 1640. The king's messages, having been turned over to Annesley, were finally presented to the House of Commons. Morice then delivered the following "set & elegant" speech:

There are divers persons that would have the King brought in upon Tearmes, others upon noe tearmes at all. To bring in his Majesty without tearmes will not be secure for us, nor safe for him. I feare that it wilbe a griefe soe to bring him in and that wee shall reape little fruit, or benefit by it. Indeed these certainly are in extreames, and they will not hold long, if he come not in by some convenient agreement.

You may perceive by his Majesty's letters and Declaration, that he is as willing to receive tearmes from us, as wee are willing to receive him without tearmes. Lett us therefore not betray the Common Cause, nor give upp our publique interest wherein wee are all soe much concerned. My Motion is that since the King is soe noble in offering us soe much grace & favour that wee returne publique thankes to the King by the same Messenger, and that wee immediately fall upon the worke of drawing upp bills for his Majesty to passe.

---

[92] Sir Edward Hyde to Sir John Grenville, April 13/23, 1660, B.M., Lans. MSS 1054, fol. 71.

[93] Viscount Mordaunt to Sir Edward Hyde, April 19, 1660, *Clarendon State Papers* 3: pp. 729–730; Lister, *Clarendon* 1: p. 502, stated that they returned together.

[94] Lister, *Clarendon* 1: p. 502.

[95] Viscount Mordaunt to Charles II, April 24–27, 1660, B.L., Clar. MSS 72, foll. 19–20.

[96] Viscount Mordaunt to Marquis of Ormonde, April 27, 1660, B.L., Carte MSS 30, fol. 582.

[97] Henry Coventry to [Marquis of Ormonde], April 27, 1660, *ibid.*, fol. 560; this letter may have been addressed to Sir George Lane, not Ormonde.

[98] Philip Warwick to Sir Edward Hyde, April 27, 1660, B.L., Clar. MSS 72, fol. 64.

[99] Lady Mordaunt to Sir Edward Hyde, April 26–27, *ibid.*, fol. 63.

[100] Henry Coventry to [Marquis of Ormonde], April 27, 1660, B.L., Carte MSS 30, fol. 560.

[101] James Halsall to Sir Edward Hyde, April 27, 1660, B.L., Clar. MSS 72, fol. 68.

[102] William Ellesdon to Sir Edward Hyde, April 27, 1660, *ibid.*, foll. 71–72.

[103] Philip Warwick to Sir Edward Hyde, April 27, 1660, *ibid.*, fol. 64; Dr. John Barwick to Sir Edward Hyde, April 27, 1660, *ibid.*, foll. 50–51.

[104] Francesco Giavarina to Doge and Senate, April 27/May 7, 1660, *Calendar of State Papers, Venetian* 32: p. 141.

[105] M. de Bordeaux to Cardinal Mazarin, April 30/May 10, 1660, Guizot, *Monk*, p. 222.

"Mr. Finch and many others spake to the same purpose," was the endorsement added to Morice's speech as sent to Hyde.[106] Presumably, then, Mordaunt, Grenville, Annesley, Finch, Morice, Palmer, Monck, and their friends had decided against any formal treaty with the king and in favor of the terms of the Breda Declaration. They proposed to implement the Declaration by the immediate passage of bills for the king's signature. Initially, this seems to have been the purpose of the commons.

Following Morice's speech, the commons voted, *nemine contradicente,* to prepare a reply to the king expressing their thanks and loyalty and assuring him that they would speedily answer the various proposals made in the Declaration of Breda. For this purpose a committee of seven (Finch, Annesley, Cooper, Monck, Lewis, Morice, and Holles) was appointed to draft the letter. The same committee was dispatched to borrow fifty thousand pounds from the City to send to Charles.[107] That afternoon Annesley reported from a conference with the lords that the peers had voted that the government consisted of king, lords, and commons and that some way should be found to return the king to England. To this proposal the commons readily agreed.[108] Thus the formal procedure of the Stuart Restoration was completed within a few hours.

The problem of agreeing on the specific proposals of the king remained, and for this purpose a committee of forty, together with the long robe, was appointed to consider the king's letter and Declaration and to prepare bills accordingly. In particular, the committee was ordered to draft a bill to abolish all land tenures *in Capite* and the court of wards and liveries, it being agreed that for these ancient, but unpopular, rights the king should receive 100,000 pounds yearly. Heneage Finch, a Royalist and first solicitor general of the restored king, was named chairman of the committee.[109]

Morice's speech in favor of moderate terms and the appointment of a committee to draft bills to implement and supplement the concessions offered by Charles in his Declaration tend to contradict the traditional view that Monck frustrated the effort to impose conditions on the king by a speech in the commons. This story, probably fathered by Bishop Burnet, would have it that Matthew Hale

moved that a committee might be appointed to look into the propositions that had been made, and the concessions that had been offered, by the late king during the war, particularly at the treaty of Newport, that from thence they might digest such propositions as they should think fit to be sent over to the King.[110]

Monck, according to Burnet, replied that there was no need for propositions since Charles had neither army nor navy and that he could not guarantee peace if the settlement was long delayed.[111] However, as just noted, a committee was actually appointed to draft propositions along the lines of the Breda Declaration, together with bills on land tenures and wardship. The truth is that Monck opposed the harsh terms first proposed by a small cabal, who insisted that Charles should annul all his father's declarations against the Long Parliament, honor those of the Long Parliament, and have no control over the privy council or militia for several years;[112] but Monck was far from opposing terms. Morice, who would not have differed much from Monck, quarreled with Edward Harley on May 3 because Harley did not wish to delay the return of Charles by negotiations.[113] Monck and Morice did attempt to separate Hyde from the king's circle, and it was not until May 5 that Monck approved Hyde's return.[114] Even then it required very frank letters from Charles to Monck and Morice to speed Hyde's re-entry.[115]

During May, various elements within the commons endeavored to pass bills to restrict the power and nature of the crown and of episcopacy. Peter Pett, career government official and member of the Rochester shipbuilding family, wrote Montagu on May 1 that the most likely terms would include provision for the Thirty-nine Articles, "a Gospel libertie of conscience," indemnity for real and supposed offenders, and confirmation of "all just & lawfull sales of land."[116] However, Pett's appraisal of the situation failed to take into account several factors. The influence of Monck and Morice was not strong enough to accomplish their objective. The Presbyterian party in the commons was gradually overcome by the restoration zeal of the Anglican Royalists, especially the young Cavaliers, who controlled every important committee.

Not even the voice of Monck could swing the house or the committee which was considering the Declaration of Breda away from extremely easy terms. Some time between May 3 and 8, Monck joined with the treaty Presbyterians in attempting to push through

[106] Speech by William Morice, May 1, 1660, B.L., Clar. MSS 72, foll. 3–5; Dering, "Diary," fol. 6.

[107] *Commons Journals* **8**: p. 4.

[108] *Ibid.*, pp. 7–8.

[109] *Ibid.*, p. 11.

[110] Burnet, *History of His Own Times* **1**: p. 161; see also Carte, *Ormonde* **2**: p. 199; Ranke, *History of England* **3**: p. 305, adopted Burnet's account.

[111] Burnet, *History of His Own Times* **1**: p. 162.

[112] Henry Coventry to Sir Edward Hyde, May 4, 1660, B.L., Clar. MSS 72, fol. 180.

[113] Viscount Mordaunt to Sir Edward Hyde, May 4, 1660, Lister, *Clarendon* **3**: p. 101.

[114] Viscount Mordaunt to Sir Edward Hyde, May 5–7, 1660, B.L., Clar. MSS 72, fol. 234; Alan Broderick to Sir Edward Hyde, May 3, 1660, *ibid.*, fol. 157. Annesley, Cooper, Sir Charles Worsley, and Sir Robert Howard pleaded for three or four weeks with Monck, Mrs. Monck, and the Presbyterians before reducing their opposition to Hyde.

[115] Charles II to George Monck, May 10/20, 1660, B.M., Sloane MSS 1519, foll. 201–203; Charles II to William Morice, May 10/20, 1660, *Thurloe State Papers* **7**: p. 912.

[116] Peter Pett to Edward Montagu, May 1, 1660, B.L., Carte MSS 73, fol. 424.

several propositions.[117]　It is very likely that Monck had the support of some Royalists at first.　Monck's plan called for the following eight concessions from Charles II:

1) All lands purchased by men then in military or naval service should be confirmed for ninety-nine years at a rental of less than one-sixth of their annual value.

2) Church and crown lands, with some exceptions, should be confirmed for sixty years at a rental of one-fifth of their annual income.

3) All other lands should remain with purchasers until the purchase price and six per cent interest should be repaid to the purchasers.

4) Everyone, with the exception of Lisle, Broughton, Holland, Scot, and Cooke should be pardoned.

5) All grants passed since May 22, 1642, under any great seal, other than that of parliament, should be annulled.

6) All acts and ordinances of the Long Parliament submitted to the king should be confirmed, especially the act abolishing the court of wards.

7) The army should be entrusted to Monck for life.

8) The religious establishment should remain as presently prescribed until the king, an assembly of divines, and parliament should settle upon a new one.[118]

These recommendations bear close resemblance to those previously advocated by those Presbyterians desiring a treaty with the king, and indicate how closely Monck was working with them.　In fact, Monck's position in early May was much closer to that of the Presbyterians than it had been at the time of his interview with Grenville.

Despite combined action by Monck and the treaty Presbyterians, it was impossible for them to overcome the parliamentary strength and tactics of the Royalists, particularly the younger members.　The young Royalists, constituting almost one-half of the house, stoutly refused to pass any bills and attempted to ride headstrong over the defeated hopes of the old parliamentarians.　To make matters worse, the old Royalists combined with the old parliamentarians to send old parliamentarians, rather than the ambitious youth, to pay homage to the king.[119]　Action in the commons ground to a halt while the younger Royalists quarreled with their elders about this affront to their court ambitions.[120]　Even worse for the Presbyterians was the absence of some of their ablest and most influential leaders at the very moment when the prospects for Presbyterian legislation were best.　Moreover, public opinion, probably as important in 1660 as at any other point in the century, favored the early return of Charles II, with or without terms.[121]

A combination of the events and factors mentioned above defeated any Presbyterian hope for an ironclad treaty with their returning monarch.　Charles re-entered his dominions under no binding terms.　Only if parliament later insisted, which it did not, on fulfillment of the promises made in the Declaration of Breda would Charles possess less legal power than his father.　As time was to show, it was Charles who, for his own reasons, considered the Declaration of Breda a binding document.　Finch's committee reported bills for indemnity, for the confirmation of sales and judicial proceedings, for settling ministers in their livings, for the voiding of certain grants made since May, 1642, and for the abolition of the court of wards and tenures *in Capite;*[122] but only three bills, the most significant of which legalized the Convention Parliament, were ready for the king's signature on June 1.[123]

Had the Presbyterians been united under capable leadership and had they combined with the Independents and Roman Catholics, they might have succeeded in rushing through restrictive legislation prior to the return of Charles and his exiled courtiers.　Unfortunately, many religious Presbyterians were almost indistinguishable from the Cavaliers on political issues, and still others discarded their Presbyterian proclivities while competing with the Cavaliers for offices and rewards.　The obvious leaders of the political Presbyterians (Annesley, Cooper, Holles, Morice, Edward and Robert Harley, Montagu, and Monck) were soon so closely allied with the court that they felt obligated to assume at least an appearance of neutrality.[124]

Inside the commons the Presbyterians disagreed among themselves and with the Independents and Roman Catholics on almost every issue.　The debates on the indemnity and land bills illustrate very well this point.　Prynne, King, and other Presbyterians desired

[117] Philip Warwick to Sir Edward Hyde, May 9, 1660, B.L., Clar. MSS 72, foll. 288–289.

[118] This paper was transmitted to Hyde, without Monck's knowledge, by Philip Warwick in his letter of May 9, 1660, *ibid.* Lister's inability to date it (*Clarendon* 3: pp. 500–503) arose from the separation of Warwick's letter from its enclosure. Monck's proposals are now found in B.L., Clar. MSS 72, fol. 295.

[119] Alan Broderick to Sir Edward Hyde, May 3, 1660, B.L., Clar. MSS 72, fol. 158.

[120] *Ibid.;* Henry Coventry to Sir Edward Hyde, May 4, 1660, *ibid.,* fol. 180.

[121] See John Mallack to John Willoughby, May 3, 1660, *Trevelyan Papers,* ed. Sir Walter Calverley Trevelyan and Sir Charles Edward Trevelyan (London, 1872), pp. 285–286; Henry Townshend, *Diary of Henry Townshend of Elmley Lovett, 1640–1663,* ed. J. W. Willis Bund (2 v., Worcestershire Historical Society, 1915–1920) 1: p. 36, for examples of public opinion.

[122] *Commons Journals* 8: pp. 11, 19, 38, 40.

[123] See Firth and Rait, *Acts and Ordinances* 3: pp. xxxi–xxxvi; and David Ogg, *England in the Reign of Charles II* (2 v., Oxford, 1934) 1: pp. 152–168, for discussions of Restoration legislation.

[124] Cooper and Annesley, for example, moved in the commons for the restoration of Dr. Matthew Nicholas, brother of Sir Edward, to his mastership of St. Nicholas Hospital near Sarum; Seymour Bowman, "Diary," B.L., Salway Deposit, fol. 3. See Caroline Robbins, "Seymour Bowman, Esq., M.P., Diarist of the Convention of 1660," *Notes and Queries* 183: pp. 56–59, for some valuable notes on the Bowman Diary.

that at least twelve persons should be executed. Prynne made personal attacks on Lenthall and other Commonwealth legal officers.[125] Fairfax, Monck, Morice, and the moderate Royalists joined together to except no more than six regicides from loss of life.[126] The Independents, led by Lenthall, argued that the Presbyterians were as guilty as those who had contributed directly to the death of Charles I.[127] This in turn caused Irby, Bunckley, Northcote, Earle, and a host of other Presbyterians to band together against the Independents,[128] and as the debates progressed this rift between the Presbyterians and the Independents widened and deepened. Finally, on June 18, Prynne's faction proposed that the estates of all persons who helped create and maintain the Instrument of Government be confiscated.[129] This automatically alienated Cooper, Pierrepoint, and many of the lawyers who had assisted Cromwell. The Presbyterians generally voted also for the punishment of Hugh Peters, Philip Nye, and John Goodwin, Congregational ministers.[130]

Despite a personal plea for hasty action by Monck as he took his leave of the commons on June 29,[131] the land bill was lost largely through internecine quarrels among the Presbyterian members. One group of Presbyterians supported Monck's recommendations, while the Prynne group labored against confirming any sales of crown lands.[132] The Presbyterians were, however, in general agreement that the purchases of the Cromwellians should not be confirmed.[133] In the end, the Convention Parliament took almost no action on land sales.[134]

As to Roman Catholics, the Presbyterians assumed a fairly tolerant attitude when considering whether to require an oath of supremacy as a test for indemnity; only Prynne, Morice, and Northcote spoke for the test.[135] But when the question of a double poll tax against Roman Catholics was debated on July 10, the Presbyterians almost without exception supported the proposal. Some wished to impose the same penalty on religious radicals as well.[136] On August 2, Irby went so far as to move that the commons request the king to exclude all Roman Catholics from the lords.[137]

---

125 Humphrey Winch to Major Thomas Henshaw, May 4, 1660, B.L., Carte MSS 30, fol. 657.
126 *Ibid.*; Townshend, *Diary* 1: p. 40.
127 Francis Newport to Sir Richard Leveson, May 15, 1660, H.M.C., *Fifth Report, Appendix, Part I* (London, 1876), p. 150; S. Charlton to Sir Richard Leveson, June 3, 1660, *ibid.*, p. 205.
128 Dering, "Diary," fol. 13.
129 Bowman, "Diary," B.L., Salway Deposit, fol. 4.
130 *Ibid.*, foll. 8–9.
131 *Ibid.*, fol. 33.
132 *Ibid.*, foll. 71–75.
133 *Ibid.*, foll. 123–124.
134 See Joan Thirsk, "The Restoration Land Settlement," *The Journal of Modern History* 26: pp. 315–328, for the most recent attempt to untangle the land question.
135 Bowman, "Diary," B.L., Salway Deposit, foll. 52–55.
136 *Ibid.*, foll. 69–70.
137 *Ibid.*, fol. 116.

Such intolerance toward the Independents and Roman Catholics was political suicide for the Presbyterians, but indicative of their determination then and later to be stalwart opponents of sectarianism and Rome.

In summary, the Presbyterians lost their program at the polling places in the shire and borough elections of 1660. Not even Monck, though he tried, could overcome the numbers and delaying tactics of the Royalists. In April and May the Presbyterians might have rushed their program through the Convention Parliament, but they threw away their opportunity by their quarrels, lack of organization, poor leadership, fear of violence and civil disorder, and impatience to call on Charles. Some, following promises of office and profits, drifted rather than risk everything on a false interpretation of the king's policy. Finally, the Presbyterians unnecessarily alienated both the Independents and the Roman Catholics. These factors produced not only an unconditional political Restoration, but had tremendous influence on the religious settlement as well.

VI. A YEAR OF INDECISION

Although there was a general expectation on April 1, 1660, that a final and satisfactory religious settlement would soon be made, the first year of the Stuart Restoration ended on an indicisive note. On the other hand, many events of great consequence to the final settlement occurred between April, 1660, and April, 1661. During this period, the majority of the leading Presbyterian clergy came to desire membership in a modified version of the Church of England of 1640. They also moved from dependence on parliament to reliance on the promises made to them by Charles II and Hyde, or Clarendon as Hyde was soon known, both of whom grew more and more insistent that the Presbyterians be comprehended within the Anglican Church. Until mid-July there existed considerable uncertainty whether the Convention Parliament or Charles II should hold the initiative in the religious field. The most significant development of the period covered by this chapter was the manner in which the king and the lord chancellor won the confidence and support of the Presbyterians and control of the religious issue by persuasion and prerogative action.

Concrete, rather than general, consideration of the religious problem began with Monck's message of March 19 to Charles II. Monck suggested that general toleration be granted. Six days later the London council urged the council of state to refer the religious controversy to a synod. Charles in the Declaration of Breda adopted Monck's recommendation, thereby discarding the synod idea which had appeared in every earlier declaration or secret proposal from Charles II. Specifically, the king now declared a

liberty to tender consciences, and that no man shall be disquieted, or called in question, for differences of opinion in matters of religion which do not disturb the peace of the kingdom; and that we shall be ready to consent to such an Act of Parliament as, upon mature deliberation, shall be offered to us for the full granting that indulgence.[1]

This section was personally written by Clarendon, and apparently included in the Declaration over the objections of other royal advisers.[2] Clearly evident was the king's desire to make obvious his claim to prerogative power in religious spheres. In all probability he intended by his plan to re-establish the Anglican Church and at the same time to provide for recognized dissent both within and without the Established Church. For the latter purpose parliamentary action would be a necessary adjunct to the exercise of a royal prerogative. Furthermore, the plan probably envisioned the inclusion of the Presbyterians within the Anglican fold by a wide latitude in the ceremonial practices of the Church of England and by some relaxation of the episcopal authority. Here, too, cooperation between the branches of the government would be essential.

Shortly after the Convention Parliament met, probably between May 3 and 8, Monck presented his Restoration scheme to the commons. The General, obviously under Presbyterian pressure and influence, now altered his position of March 19. Instead of general toleration, he recommended that the "exercise of the Protestant religion and ministry . . . continue in the same state as now they are, untill *an Assembly of Divines* of this nation shalbe called by his Majesty, soe that thereby, with the Parliament, the government of the Church may be setled." According to Philip Warwick, Monck originally intended a "Synod or Convocation, but thought fitt to be altered, least, the elections being, according to the legall forme, two in every Archdeaconry, etc., as the clergy now stands, they by number of votes were like to have the advantage."[3] Presumably, Warwick meant that Monck feared that the Anglicans would dominate, as they were to do in 1661, any convocation elected on the historic basis. This was the first expression in the Convention Parliament of the assembly plan.

Monck's paper and the early legislative activitiy in the Convention commons suggest a general agreement that some decision should be reached quickly on religion. By May 8 the commons had pending a bill "for securing the Protestant Religion, and Encouragement and settling of the learned and pious Ministry, and both the Universities in order thereunto, with a due Care of Tender Consciences." The last phrase was added by a house resolution to the measure as reported from the

committee by Finch.[4] According to Broderick, Thomas Bampfield, Baxter's friend from Exeter, and the Presbyterians were to report the bill on May 9.[5]

At this point, however, the legislative program began to falter. On May 9 John Stephens reported a bill "for establishing Ministers settled in Ecclesiastical Livings," which was read a second time on May 16 and committed with instructions for the committee to sit that afternoon.[6] There the matter of livings rested until May 26 when William Prynne reported "an Order touching quieting Possession of Ministers, Schoolmasters, and other Ecclesiastical Persons, in sequestered Living, until they are legally evicted." Prynne's bill was committed and then recommitted two days later with instructions to turn it into a royal proclamation.[7] The result was that no bill on religion got beyond the committee stage prior to the king's return.

The chief reason for the collapse of the legislative program is to be found within the Convention commons. The members of parliament, under the influence of widespread public opinion, decided to subordinate the religious question to that of indemnity. Nearly every letter or diary for the month of May placed indemnity ahead of every other question in importance. So vital was indemnity to an early restoration of monarchy that the commons postponed consideration of religion and other matters on May 12 until the question of indemnity could be settled. Not until June 7, when the indemnity bill was nearing completion, was the committee for religion revived,[8] and by then the forces discussed in the preceding chapter were clearly evident.

Another reason for the legislative inactivity was the attitude of the Presbyterian clergy. To comprehend the Presbyterian clerical policy of May and later, it is necessary to recall the activities of the chief ministers under the two Cromwells. Almost without exception they had attempted to establish something approaching a national church, but, as indicated in Chapter I, they failed because of internal division, lack of agreement with the Independents and Anglicans, and political misfortune. Diverse as was Presbyterian opinion on individual points of doctrine and government, it stood as one on the necessity of a national establishment. Between May, 1659, and March, 1660, the Presbyterian ministers gradually came to realize, almost to a man, that any combination with the religious Independents, if such was possible, would automatically mean sacrificing their principle of a national church and might well open the way to intolerable sects and Roman

[1] Hyde, *History* 6: p. 207.
[2] Nicholas Papers, B.M., Egerton MSS 2542, foll. 328–329. Nicholas made marginal notes on a copy of the Declaration to the effect that Hyde was personally responsible for the preamble and the section on religion.
[3] General Monck's Proposals, [*ca.* May 3–8, 1660], Lister, *Clarendon* 3: pp. 501–502.

[4] *Commons Journals* 8: p. 18; Brown, "The Religious Factors in the Convention Parliament," *English Historical Review* 22: p. 57.
[5] Alan Broderick to Sir Edward Hyde, [May 8, 1660], Calendar of the Clarendon State Papers, V(1), B.L., Clar. MSS 15b, foll. 23–24.
[6] *Commons Journals* 8: pp. 19, 33.
[7] *Ibid.*, p. 47.
[8] *Ibid.*, pp. 25, 58.

Catholicism. This left them with two possible courses: either fight a losing battle for the Civil War system against both Independents and Anglicans, which the politicians and career servants did not sanction, or seek a compromise with episcopacy. After looking backward on the views of Usher, Brownrigg, Bernard, Gauden, and other moderate Anglicans, the Presbyterians were inclined to hope for some modification of the Laudian system.

The events of March and April proved the futility of struggling for a Presbyterian system. As Lauderdale predicted to Baxter, the politicians proved less Presbyterian and more Low Church Anglican than had appeared to be the case during the Civil War when unusual political circumstances precluded any other show of color. Furthermore, a new generation, only vaguely familiar with the religious grievances of 1640 but well acquainted with the chaos which attended the fall of Anglicanism, had come of age. Only a small number of politicians worked actively for a sweeping reformation of the Laudian Church. With many laymen, the religious question was subordinate to such civil matters as indemnity, lands, offices, and honors. Then came heavy defeat at the polls for many of the real Presbyterian laymen. In theory at least, the Presbyterian politicians could yet have combined with the Independents, but this possibility was never fully explored by the Presbyterians after the collapse of Lambert's rising. Nearly all of the clergy moved farther away from the Independents after Baxter's submission to the leadership of Lauderdale and Sharp in April, and the immediate Presbyterian attacks on the Independents in the commons soon rendered impossible any agreement between the two groups for concerted action. Lord Wharton's party disintegrated before it was fully organized. Outside the commons, Sharp and Lauderdale, with Monck's concurrence, prevented any restatement of the Solemn League and Covenant, thereby insuring that the religious establishments of Scotland and England would be considered separately.

With these considerations constantly in mind, the moderate Presbyterians thought they saw some hope in the general promise of modified episcopacy then being held out by many Anglicans. Had not most of the older Anglican clergy tacitly accepted the Presbyterian system? Baxter could find some hope in his successful experiments in Worcestershire. Most of Laud's confederates were now deceased, and the younger Anglicans included men like John Gauden and Nicholas Bernard. Among the Laudians there were confirmed Calvinists like Morley. Gauden had as recently as February 28 preached for church government

not by the Dominion and pomp, luxury and tyranny of bishops, nor yet by the Factious and refractory humours of Presbyters; much less by the schismatick saucinesse of people, who cast off both Bishops and Presbyters; but by the fatherly gravity, prudence, and Eminence of godly and Reverend Bishops; by the brotherly assistance, and son-

like subordination of sober and orderly Presbyters, by the service and obsequiousnesse of humble and diligent Deacons; and by the meek submission of Christian people to the Care, Monition, Counsel, and respective Superiority of every order; as sheep to their chief Shepherds, and their Assistants, or Attendants.[9]

Gauden professed a belief in "Primitive Episcopacy with Presbytery" and a desire for healing propositions. Such remedies, he insisted, "ought [not] to be Secular, but rather Ecclesiastick" in origin;[10] in other words, submit points in dispute to a clerical synod or council.[11] Such moderation appealed to the Presbyterians, especially when they recalled that Gauden's circle owed its rise to Archbishop Usher and Bishop Brownrigg, two apostles of modified episcopacy.[12]

Moreover, that branch of the Presbyterian party led by Edward Reynolds was ready to live in peace with the Anglicans. Reynolds had been the prime mover in publishing *A Seasonable Exhortation* in January. He was a true Puritan, and of the Puritans he had become less involved in controversy than any other. On two occasions in 1657 and 1658 Reynolds preached peace to Cromwell's parliaments.[13] On November 5, 1659, he warned the London council that division had permitted foreign emissaries and strange doctrines to be introduced at the expense of truth and peace.[14] Within a month Reynolds moved closer to peace at any price and told Lord Mayor Thomas Allen of London:

I considered [before preaching to the London Council on December 2, 1659] the sad condition whereunto these nations were reduced, the many and great provocations which we have been guilty of, the miserable commotions and earthquakes, which have not only shaken, but even dissolved our foundations, and made them all out of course. I seriously looked back on the dark and gloomy providences of God amongst us, the untimely death of Princes, the dimidating and dissolving of Parliaments, the frequent expirations and vicissitudes of Governments, the horrid Apostate, Atheisme, Scepticisme, Indifferencey, Prodigies of phrenetick and pernicious Opinions, whereby multitudes have played the wantons with as glorious a light of Orthodox Religion, as any Nation under heaven enjoyed; the defaming of Ministry, decrying of Ordinances, incroaching of many Romish doctrines under a disguize, and other like distempers, whereby we are become a hissing and astonishment to the Nations round about us. In a word, it seemed to me, that the Scene of the Ten Tribes were translated unto these Nations . . . .[15]

Reynolds in his reference to "the Scene of the Ten Tribes" was warning his audience of the disaster lurk-

[9] Gauden, . . . *Slight Healers of Publick Hurts* . . . , p. 78.

[10] *Ibid.*, pp. 79–80.

[11] *Ibid.*, pp. 97–109.

[12] See Chapter I.

[13] Edward Reynolds, *The Works of the Right Reverend Father in God, Edward Reynolds, D.D., Late Lord Bishop of Norwich* (London, 1678–1679), pp. 241–243.

[14] Edward Reynolds, *The Brand Pluck'd out of the Fire* . . . (London, 1659).

[15] Edward Reynolds, *The Misery of a Deserted People* . . . (London, 1659), [pp. 3–5].

ing ahead and advising a retreat into the security and peace of the past.

With the passage of time, Reynolds became even more pointed in his advice to laymen for a restoration of monarchy and for establishing order within the religious state. With each sermon he grew in popularity with the City. He was chosen to preach a sermon of thanksgiving on February 28 for the readmission of the secluded members to the Long Parliament. When printed, the Epistle Dedicatory contained the following exhortation to Lord Mayor Allen:

chuse for this next Parliament, men of Eminency for Piety and Prudence, who may come with healing Spirits, and make it their business to repair our Breaches, and be the Restorers of Paths to dwell in, who may lay to heart the Interest of Christ and his Church, and promote purity of Doctrine and Worship, due Administration of Holy Ordinances, and whatever may conduce to the Power of Godliness . . . .[16]

Perhaps this advice was responsible for the choice of the London members, who were men already active as "Restorers of Paths to dwell in."

Reynolds likewise found favor with the new council of state which chose him to preach before the Convention Parliament on April 25. He selected as his topic "The Author and Subject of Healing" in which he continued his lamentations on the state of the nation and of religion. "Indeed," he said, "we have seen and heard of more evils and confusions, then the hour of a Sermon, or the length of an History can well enumerate."[17] He implored the Convention to show "all possible tenderness and indulgence towards the infirmities, especially the consciences of men of humble and sober, of quiet and peaceable Spirits."[18] At the same time, however, Reynolds urged the establishment of the "True Reformed Religion, an Orthodox, learned and painful Ministry, pure Worship, and the Power of Godliness, suppressing and putting to shame all profane practices."[19] Since modified Presbyterianism was then legally established, it must be assumed that Reynolds recognized the necessity of yielding additional ground to episcopacy, and he certainly desired the restoration of religious order. Reynolds, in reference to most of the Presbyterians, stood at the extreme right of his party.

Baxter, considerably less friendly toward the Anglicans, stood toward the middle, but he did move grudgingly in the direction of compromise. About the time of his conversion to a restoration of monarchy by Lauderdale, Baxter published two works originally intended for the press in December, 1659. One of these, *Catholick Unity*, was a sermon preached in December, 1657, when his unifying zeal was at its peak. Its publication in April, 1660, should have served warning to the Anglicans on what to expect from the Baxter wing of the Presbyterian party. The general tenor of the work is found in the following passage:

Let us first agree in all those points that Papists and Protestants, Calvinists and Lutherans, Arminians and Anabaptists, and Separatists, and all parties that deserve to be called Christians, are agreed in.[20]

This would call for a broad church. Disagreement on nonessentials was unimportant to Baxter who felt:

It is the will of God that the Unity of the Church should not be laid upon indifferent, small, and doubtfull points: but that true Believers who differ in such things should notwithstanding have inward Charity and outward Communion with one another, not Censuring, nor despising, nor dividing from each other upon this account.[21]

Here was the latitude which later made Baxter a friendly correspondent of the Cambridge Platonists, but he made it perfectly clear, even in 1660, that any attempt to settle the "indifferent, small, and doubtfull points" would only result in disagreement and permanent disunity.[22]

The True Catholick, likewise published in April, expanded upon Baxter's earlier remarks and served a clear notice to the Laudians. Taking a leaf from his Worcestershire Association plan, he asserted bluntly that any person who "hath all that is contained but in the ancient Creed, the Lords Prayer and ten Commandments, with Baptisme and the Lords Supper, in his head, and heart, and life, is certainly a member of the Catholick Church."[23] While expressing a desire "to live in the same house" with all parties,[24] he condemned as "uncatholick" any requirement to accept as absolutely essential any convenient "Circumstance of worship."[25] In a postscript Baxter announced that he and Usher had agreed in "half an hour . . . upon the terms which should reconcile the moderate of the Prelatical and Presbyterian way," but warned that he was "never the nearer attaining any such reconciliation" with Laudians like Thomas Pierce, Peter Heylyn, and Henry Hammond.[26] In effect, Baxter drew a line which he said he would never cross. Modified episcopacy of the Usher variety was as far as he offered to go.

It must be assumed that Lauderdale, Sharp, Manchester, and Morley recognized Baxter's reservations and were prepared to accept them for the time being,

---

[16] Edward Reynolds, *The Wall & Glory of Jerusalem . . .* (London, 1660), [p. 7].

[17] Edward Reynolds, *The Author and Subject of Healing in the Church . . .* (London, 1660), pp. 26–27.

[18] *Ibid.*, p. 34.

[19] *Ibid.*, [p. 7].

[20] Richard Baxter, *Catholick Unity: Or the only way to bring us all to be of one Religion* (London, 1660), p. 94.

[21] *Ibid.*, pp. 323–324.

[22] *Ibid.*, pp. 326–329.

[23] Richard Baxter, *The True Catholick. and Catholick Church Described . . .* (London, 1660), p. 19.

[24] *Ibid.*, p. 238.

[25] *Ibid.*, p. 246.

[26] *Ibid.*, pp. 310–311.

hoping, of course, that Baxter could be persuaded to make further concessions to Laudianism. In any event, the Presbyterians and the politicians, Presbyterian and Anglican, accepted and employed Baxter as a leader of the moderate Presbyterians, a position which he rightfully commanded on the strength of his great popularity.

While it is impossible to ascertain the exact positions of other leading moderates directly, it is possible to estimate their general opinions through indirect means. As seen in Chapter IV, Sharp succeeded in bringing several of them together with Morley after April 13. In the absence of any contrary evidence, it is to be assumed that these divines consented to defer the religious settlement to a synod.[27] This assumption is consistent with the tone of Morley's reports to Hyde [28] and with subsequent developments. Open opposition from the rigid Presbyterians did not appear until later.

A more uncertain quantity is what Morley and his confederates promised the Presbyterians. A few general points can be found in the surviving correspond- ence, but it stands to reason that Morley, as well as Sharp and Lauderdale, promised more than Morley dared commit to paper. When pressed by John Davys, a Presbyterian layman, to explain what the Anglicans meant by their printed professions of no ani- mosity toward their former enemies, Morley replied that their declarations clearly meant an intention to

acquisce in what the present Councell of State and future Parliament should determine, as well in order to our Ecclesiasticall as to Civill Concernements without soe much as Disputing or debating. . . . I profess, That if anything shalbe determined either in regard to Civill or Ecclesiasti- call Concernment with which I cannot actively comply I will notwithstanding passively submitt to it, soe fare as not to oppose it directly or indirectly . . . .[29]

This letter, and the printed declarations of peaceful intent and submission to whatever the Convention decided, was designed, on the surface, to allay the fears of the Presbyterians, but it also implied that no Presbyterian could do less than submit passively to the wishes of the Convention Parliament and its successors. The French ambassador, however, knew that Morley was making various commitments, including an offer of liberty of conscience to Quakers;[30] but no mention of this crept into Morley's correspondence with his superiors.

By May 4 the Laudian party in London was suffi- ciently organized to deal with the Presbyterians. Gilbert Sheldon arrived on April 27, and on May 4 the Anglicans (Morley, Barwick, Bishops Wren, Duppa, and Warner, and probably Sheldon and others as well) held a conference.[31] On that day Morley made his longest and most significant report to Hyde which, because of its importance, is here quoted rather fully.

I have bin since comeing to towne with divers of the cheife of the Presbyterian ministers and have reason (or I think) to hope they will be perswaded to admit of & submit to Episcopall government, & to the Practice of the Liturgy in publick, so they may be permitted before & after there sermons & upon occasionall Emergencyes to use such as liturgy formes as they themselves shall think fit without mixing of any thing prejudiciall to the government of the Church & State as they shall be setled. . . . I doe not per- ceive that any of them desires to be a Bishop, at least not at first but some of their freinds tell me that if 3 or 4 of the leading men might be gratifyed with such other preferments as they may hold with theyr charges here in the City (as the Mastership of the Savoy), the Provost- ship of Eaton, or some of the cheif Prebends of Pauls or Westminster) they would be a great meanes to bring over theyr whole Party; which though I hope it be not soe powerfull as absolutely to hinder, yet it is strong enough I feare to give the king much trouble. I foresee the mayne difficulty will be touching theyr Ordinations by Presbyters without Bishops, which we cannot acknowledge to be law- full, nor will they I am affrayed be brought to acknowl- edge to be unlawfull & much lesse to be meere nullities. In this case I have thought of 2 expedients, the one that noe notice be taken whether there have bin any such Ordi- nations or noe but that it be passed over . . .; the other that there may be an Hypotheticall reordination as it will provide so against the nullity of such ordinations, so it will not conclude them to be nullities, but only irregular & uncertaine.

Morley had already submitted both "expedients" to Sheldon and Duppa who approved; another member of the circle, probably Barwick, opposed. Morley's assertion that he promised nothing to the Presbyterians was offset by his own admission that he had told the Presbyterians they would not "repent" of having aided the king.[32] In brief, Morley threw out general and suggestive promises but failed to venture upon many particulars, and he apparently ignored the Presbyterian strength beyond London.

Baxter received much the same impression from an hour long interview with Morley. Hearing that the Anglican Doctor was "a moderate orthodox man, and had often meetings with Dr. Manton and others, whome he encouraged with pacificatory promises," Baxter prevailed upon Morley for an appointment so that he could learn "whether really concord was inten- ded." The man from Kidderminster found that Morley spoke "of moderation in general but came to no particular terms."[33] Nevertheless, Morley gave such

[27] James Sharp to Robert Douglas, April 19, 1660, Wodrow, *Church of Scotland* 1: p. xviii.

[28] Dr. George Morley to Sir Edward Hyde, April 18, 1660, B.L., Clar. MSS 71, foll. 295–296, in which he reported on a satisfactory meeting with Dr. William Bates.

[29] Dr. George Morley to John Davys, April 16, 1660, B.L., Carte MSS 30, fol. 566.

[30] M. de Bordeaux to M. de Brienne, April 23/May 3, 1660, Baschet Transcripts, Public Record Office, 31/3 (107), fol. 2: "Il promet tout à tout le monde, mesme la liberté de conscience aux trembleurs; beaucoup se confient en ses promesses."

[31] Bosher, *Restoration Settlement*, pp. 122–123.

[32] Dr. George Morley to Sir Edward Hyde, May 4, 1660, B.L., Clar. MSS 72, fol. 199.

[33] Baxter, *Reliquiae Baxterianae*, Pt. II: p. 218.

assurances to Reynolds and Calamy that they seemed content "to comply as to Episcopacy and the Liturgy with little alteration." The only difficulty was that these two Presbyterians could make no promises for their brethren.[34] General opinion held that the Presbyterians, except for "some few violent persons," would accept episcopacy.[35]

Immediately, however, the Presbyterians preferred to carry their problems directly to Charles II, and in doing so they virtually assured a postponement of the religious question until Charles had been heard. "After several meetings," the Presbyterians decided to send a delegation to Holland to confer with the king. In addition to delivering a general message, their deputies were to ask the king, "if it be possible," to recommend to the Convention Parliament that it "secure religion in reference to some points."[36] Some eighty ministers were in attendance at Sion College on May 7 when the message to Charles and instructions to the delegation were adopted. This procedure implies that a majority of the London clergy recognized their political weakness and that they placed their trust in the king's authority as early as May. On May 11 Edward Reynolds, Edmund Calamy, William Spurstowe, Thomas Case, and Thomas Manton, and perhaps others, departed from London for Holland; Edward Bowles from Yorkshire went as chaplain to a delegation from the commons to the king.

No record exists of exactly what the Presbyterians hoped to accomplish abroad. One obvious purpose was to establish friendly relations with Charles and his servants. Sharp's letter of May 4 was vague about the real purposes of the mission, and Morley could do nothing more than guess. Morley felt confident that the Presbyterians had, in addition to the general address, "other instructions as namely to treat with & draw into theyr party the Presbyterians of those parts as likewise to offer some Propositions to his Majesty concerning a Synod & other particulars." Anticipating that the ministers intended to ask for a proclamation against atheism and immorality, Morley urged Hyde to prevail on the king to issue such a pronouncement before being pressed by the enemy.[37] Otherwise, nothing is known of their instructions or secret purposes, if they had any.

If the Presbyterian plans included, as they perhaps did, a general synod for the three nations, together with representatives of the foreign Protestant groups, this project was foredoomed by the activities of James Sharp and company. Hyde and Charles approved

such a plan in 1649, and it was not completely dropped until the Declaration of Breda. In April, the London Presbyterians, as discussed more fully in Chapter IV, endeavored to concert with the Scottish Presbyterians through Sharp, and the Scots, through the same medium, attempted to reopen their Covenant interest in England.[38] Sharp fought successfully, probably with Lauderdale's support, to frustrate both sides. Proof that the English Presbyterians did not readily relinquish their idea for a general synod is contained in an anonymous pamphlet of April 27. The author, or authors, proposed an assembly of "English, Scots, French and Dutch, Protestant Ministers, Episcopalians, Presbyterians, and Congregational persons." The breadth of the proposed synod, as well as the work's references to Archbishop Usher, suggests very strongly that the pamphlet owed its authorship to someone from Baxter's circle.[39] The suggestion of a comprehensive assembly was soon crushed by Morley and Sharp. Mordaunt wrote Charles on May 9:

Doctor Morley desires me humbly to beg of your Majestie in case the Parliament presse a Synod of the three Nations and the assistance of the Foraigne Divines that your Majestie please not to consent to it, being the Scotts have assured him they will not interpose, and as to the Foraigne Divines he beseeches your Majestie to engage them to perswade the Presbyterians heere to submit to such a present government as your Majestie shall setle by Bishops.[40]

Since no other notable Scots were in England, Morley's informants must have been Sharp and Lauderdale, with whom he was frequently in conference. Sharp and Lauderdale also undoubtedly influenced Monck's message to the commons calling on them to settle religion by an assembly of English divines.

Sharp's hurried visit to Holland in May probably had the same purpose. As soon as he learned that the Presbyterians intended to send a deputation to Charles, the Scot hastily departed from London on May 4. To Douglas and the Resolutionists, Sharp wrote that he was going to Holland as their agent,[41] but to his friend James Wood, Sharp wrote on the same day:

I have been two dayes agone surprysed with a desire from my L. Generall to carrye a message from him to the King; the requests of some of our freinds in the Citty have prevailed with mee to yeeld, especially since the message doeth concerne the interest of religion as it is professed by honest men heer.[42]

[34] Viscount Mordaunt to Charles II, May 9, 1660, B.L., Clar. MSS 72, fol. 284. This letter was written at Morley's request.
[35] William Hinton to Sir Edward Hyde, May 2, 1660, *ibid.,* fol. 139.
[36] James Sharp to Robert Douglas, May 4, 1660, Wodrow, *Church of Scotland* 1: p. xxii.
[37] Dr. George Morley to Sir Edward Hyde, May 10, 1660, B.L., Clar. MSS 72, fol. 316.

[38] Robert Baillie to James Sharp, April 16, 1660, *Letters and Journals of Robert Baillie* 3: pp. 400–401.
[39] Anonymous, *Council Humbly Propounded for the speedy Settlement of these long Disturbed Nations . . .* (London, 1660), pp. 3–5.
[40] Viscount Mordaunt to Charles II, May 9, 1660, B.L., Clar. MSS 72, fol. 284.
[41] James Sharp to Robert Douglas, May 4, 1660, Wodrow, *Church of Scotland* 1: p. xxi.
[42] James Sharp to James Wood, May 4, 1660, *The Lauderdale Papers,* ed. Osmund Airy (3 v., London, 1884–1885) 1: p. 25.

It is more than likely, however, that Sharp went to Holland for the purpose of presenting his arguments against the comprehensive synod plan. In fact, it is doubtful whether he went as a serious messenger from Monck, since Monck sent his brother-in-law, Thomas Clarges, on the same ship. Secondly, Sharp carried a letter of recommendation from Sir John Grenville, who was certainly no friend to Presbyterianism.[43] Finally, Sharp was hardly in Holland before he admonished the Scots once again to stay out of English affairs.[44] Unquestionably, his hasty trip was related to the Presyterian decision to send a delegation to see the king. It is very doubtful, however, whether he went as a friend of the English, or the Scottish, Presbyterians.

Odd as it máy seem, the Presbyterian delegation received as much support from Sir Thomas Wharton as from any other source. However, it should be observed that the Whartons operated from the premise that nothing could be gained for their Congregational friends until the Presbyterians were pacified. Sir Thomas set forth his principles in a letter of May 2 to Ormonde:

Nothing is more likely to bring and confirm our uninterrupted peace, then the not countenancing ministers to stand severely upon things that are not absolutely necessary, and not to discountenance those that are realy pious, and no disturbers, but promoters of publicke peace in Church and State, though possibly they do not concurre in every circumstance of ceremony, or discipline.[45]

Wharton assumed that episcopacy would be restored, but recommended that toleration be granted both inside and outside the establishment. John Dury, who later conformed despite his Congregational proclivity, urged much the same policy.[46]

Every letter, including those of Morley cited above, to Charles or Hyde commented on the pacificatory spirit and moderate demands of the Presbyterian delegation. Philip Warwick described them as "noe killing enemies to the Churchs Essence in Episcopacy & Liturgy, though they'd divest her of her Ornaments." He obviously thought reconciliation between Anglican and Presbyterian likely.[47] Sir Thomas Wharton wrote a very long letter in their behalf, which he sent via Case, to Ormonde. "Their reception," he advised, "with Civility and afection may very much conduce to the Kings reall service. For they are men who have

an exceeding great influens uppon the most considerable persons in London, and indeed over all England." Wharton described Reynolds as "a very learned, pious, moderate man"; Calamy as well received by the "Kings divines"; and Case as a man who had preached for the king's benefit. Of the rest Wharton knew little except that he heard "well of them" and that they were for a "moderated Episcopacy." Bowles was pictured as a "very wise man, understanding men and buysines more then any . . . of his calling," and his design was "to bring Episcopall men and Presbyterians to such a condensation in things which are not absolutely necessary, as that ther might be no jarrings, but all agree for publicke good and peace." [48] Morley's opinion of Bowles was much the same. He described Bowles as "the Patriarch" of northern England and governor of Fairfax, and felt that Bowles differed with the Anglicans more for interest's sake than because of conscience. Morley's attitude toward Bowles and the Presbyterians in general was reflected in his recommendation that Bowles be gained "at any reasonable rate; for in gaining him, you gain all the Presbyterians both lay and clergy of the north." He also recommended that Bodbuck of Lancashire, who accompanied Sir George Booth to Holland, be gained for the same reason.[49]

Charles and his advisers showed the Presbyterians every cordiality. At a formal session with the king, the ministers, after delivering their written address, reminded Charles of their past services. They also "professed they were no enemies to moderate Episcopacy but desired that such things might not be pressed upon them in God's worship which, in their judgment who used them, were acknowledged to be matters indifferent, and by others were held unlawful." The king spoke "very kindly" to them, and reminded them of the promises made in the Declaration of Breda. Then followed, according to Hyde, a series of informal meetings in which the Presbyterians pressed Charles to abstain from using the Book of Common Prayer and to dispense with the surplice. There is no reason to question Hyde's statement that the king rejected these pleas, but it is very doubtful that he did so "with some warmth," [50] for such would have been impolitic at that time.

The Presbyterians were, in fact, highly elated by the fruits of their labors. They were convinced of the king's moderation and his respect for them.[51] Baxter said that the king's "encouraging promises of peace" caused some of the delegation to have "high expecta-

---

[43] Sir John Grenville to Sir Edward Hyde, May 4, 1660, *Clarendon State Papers* 3: pp. 741–742.

[44] James Sharp to Robert Douglas, May 9, 1660, Wodrow, *Church of Scotland* 1: pp. xxvi-xxviii.

[45] Sir Thomas Wharton to Marquis of Ormonde, May 2, 1660, B.L. Carte MSS 214, fol. 91.

[46] John Dury to Sir Edward Hyde, May 6, 1660, Calendar of Clarendon State Papers, V(1), B.L., Clar. MSS 15b, fol. 19; Dury's plan dated August 20, 1660, is in the B.M., Harl. MSS 7023, fol. 73.

[47] Sir Philip Warwick to Sir Edward Hyde, May 9, 1660, B.L., Clar. MSS 72, fol. 288.

[48] Sir Thomas Wharton to Marquis of Ormonde, May 10, 1660, B.L., Carte MSS 214, fol. 155. Bosher, relying on the inaccurate and incomplete version printed by Carte, *Ormonde Papers* 2: pp. 337–339, made the mistake of calling Wharton a "Royalist agent," *Restoration Settlement*, p. 128.

[49] Dr. George Morley to Sir Edward Hyde, May 11, 1660, B.L., Clar. MSS 72, fol. 357.

[50] Hyde, *History* 6: pp. 231–232.

[51] Wodrow, *Church of Scotland* 1: p. xxxi, note.

tions." [52] A newspaper reported that the delegation met informally and socially with the exiled Anglicans in Holland.[53] The general opinion in England was that the Presbyterians returned satisfied that Charles would settle both church and state to their satisfaction.[54]

The deputation returned from Holland with the conviction that Charles would insure their comprehension within a national church, though they were uncertain about how far episcopacy would be moderated. Toleration outside the Established Church apparently was never discussed with the king, for the Presbyterians had rejected that possibility before leaving London. The irreconcilable Presbyterians, who favored Presbyterianism over any degree of episcopacy and toleration over comprehension, attempted to join with the Independents early in May, but the Independents, placing their fate on the king's offer of a general toleration, rejected all overtures which might compromise their special position.[55] Thus from the middle of May the Presbyterian hopes rested on comprehension, and the Independents sought toleration.

On June 1, the Presbyterian cause had a good, if not brilliant, prospect for success. The ministers had received promises of royal moderation and of comprehension within the national establishment, and on June 1 Charles gave them further reason for confidence when he proclaimed, at the request of the Convention Parliament, that no incumbent, lay or clerical, could be forced from his estate "without an order of Parliament or legal eviction." [56] This decree seemed to place everything in abeyance until such time as a definitive agreement could be made. What the terms of the final settlement would be no one, not even the king, knew, but the king's actions pointed to a compromise which the Presbyterians might accept.

The London Presbyterians, thus temporarily secured in their livings, began meeting immediately at Sion College. This procedure was in complete harmony with the king's policy, and probably had his warm sanction. Charles certainly made no effort to discourage the Presbyterian conferences. On June 2, the ministers debated a proposal to petition king and parliament for the continuation of their Confession of Faith, their form of government, and the Westminster Directory until a parliament "shall provide otherwise." A majoritiy of the sixty ministers voted that the question be referred to a committee with instructions that it not be considered until the following week. The ostensible reason for the delay was to await the results of a conference between six Presbyterians and six moderate Anglicans then scheduled for the following Monday. Sharp's report to Douglas, from whence this information is obtained, is most illuminating. He found "the Presbyterian Cause wholly given up and lost." There were "many nominal [but] few real Presbyterians," and "such who seemed before to be for Presbytery would be content of a moderate episcopacy," by which they meant Usher's plan, an amended liturgy, and abolition of the canonical prescription of the surplice, the cross in baptism, and kneeling at the Lord's Supper. Only a "few" rigid Presbyterians, mostly in London and Lancashire, opposed comprehension on these terms. The dominant group within the Presbyterian party feared, as did the Low Church Anglicans, that the Laudians or the Erastians, either separately or conjunctly, might carry any convocation, because of pluralism, against any combination of the moderate groups.[57]

The Anglican leaders began to "shift all Offers from an Accomodation and [to] resolve to set up their Way," when it became apparent that the Presbyterians were divided, not only among the clergy, but also in the commons. Initially, the struggle within the Sion College conference revolved around the Solemn League and Covenant, but this question served only as a cloak for more fundamental differences. A London and a northern group, encouraged by some members of the commons, circulated petitions in favor of the Solemn League and Covenant. The northern petitioners contended that the Scots were promising to join again with their English brethren in seeking universal adoption of the Scottish system. The moderate clergy in London, with the support of their friends in the privy council and in the London council, joined together to defeat the London radicals, which, of course, merely added more fuel to the already raging fire.[58]

Another factor which contributed to the Laudian haughtiness was the Royalist resentment against the favors which were being showered upon their old enemies by the king. "Tis not to be imagined," read one letter, "how many are dissatisfied; innumerable flocks of people hovering here to see how they may light upon places and preferments; the Court and royal party grudging at every favour to the presbiterian, and they on the other side thinking they have not enough." Monck was especially abused for securing the appointment of Manchester, Holles, Pierrepoint,

[52] Baxter, *Reliquiae Baxterianae*, Pt. II: p. 218.
[53] *Mercuricus Publicus*, No. 22, p. 341.
[54] Townshend, *Diary* 1: pp. 143–144.
[55] Bosher, *Restoration Settlement*, pp. 116–117.
[56] *Lords Journals* 11: p. 46.

[57] James Sharp to Robert Douglas, June 2, 1660, Wodrow, *Church of Scotland* 1: pp. xxvii–xxviii.
[58] James Sharp to Robert Douglas, June 10, 1660, *ibid.*, pp. xxxiii–xxxiv; James Sharp to Robert Douglas, June 14, 1660, *ibid.*, p. xxxvii; Dr. Thomas Smith to Daniel Fleming, June 11, 1660, H.M.C., *The Manuscripts of S. H. LeFleming, Esq., of Rydal Hall* (London, 1890), p. 26. The London petition was later printed by Zachary Crofton in his *Berith Anti-Baal, Or, Zach. Croftons Appearance Before the Prelate-Justice of Peace . . .* (London, 1660[1661]), [pp. 12–14], with the allegation that it was stopped by "some State Stratagems and Court complement, and over prudent cowardize of some, who contrary to the due order of all Assemblies, would never let it be reported."

Cooper, and Morice to the privy council.[59] Another complained that those

who gaped for preferment and offices . . . fail of their account, for they were divided between the old servitors abroad and the new cavaliers at home long ago . . . ; and at present all gratifications and favours are the Presbiters' portion; if any of the King's party get anything it is inconsiderable.[60]

Disappointed seekers after office could and did become opponents of court policies, especially when those policies seemed to help the Presbyterians.

The animosity and jealousy was increased by divisions within and between the Royalist and Presbyterian groups about the Roman Catholic party of the Queen Mother. Henrietta Maria had been at odds with her first son and his immediate circle for many years. The Louvre Royalists, as her following was frequently called, contained not only Roman Catholics but Presbyterians, principally Scots, and Anglicans alienated from the king's circle for personal and political reasons. For many years this conglomerate collection had been friendly to the Presbyterians, whom they wished to court for political and religious reasons. Early in 1660, a group of Presbyterian politicians, and perhaps some clergy, hostile to Hyde and Ormonde, came to support the Louvre Royalists. This consideration, more than anything else, caused Monck and the Presbyterians to advise Charles to stay away from France. More than once, however, the French ambassador mentioned that a number of Presbyterians were of the Louvre party.[61] These factors made politics, civil and religious, more complicated than most writers have been willing to admit. This complexity, together with recurrent reports of plots, contributed much to the cautious policy of both the court and the moderate Presbyterians who were not anxious for civil disturbance or a gain by the Louvre Royalists.

Notwithstanding divisions within the Presbyterian ranks, and in spite of an air of indifference among the Anglican leaders, Charles, by taking matters into his own hands, and away from the Convention Parliament, preserved a surprising degree of harmony with the Presbyterians. One means by which this was accomplished was the early appointment of Reynolds, Spurstowe, Woodbridge, Wallis, Manton, Bates, Calamy, Ashe, Case, and Baxter as chaplains royal. At least four of these preached before the king during the summer, and these were permitted considerable freedom as to forms and ceremonies.

More important, however, was the manner in which the king forced the Anglicans to negotiate with the moderate Presbyterians. A preliminary meeting has already been mentioned, following which the Anglicans became cold to the Presbyterians. Shortly, however, Charles "propounded to Dr. Reynolds and Calamy for the Presbyterian party to choose 10 others to join with them, and to Dr. Gawden and Mr. Bale for the Episcopall side to take 10 likewise to their assistance and decide the business of Church Government, and the King to be Moderator."[62] Actually, this procedure was suggested to the court by Baxter who employed Broghill as his messenger.[63] As a result of this proposal the Presbyterians met several times with the king, usually at Manchester's house. Reynolds, Calamy, Manton, Baxter, and Ashe were the usual representatives. They immediately disavowed any association with the fanatics and the plots, and expressed hope that the king's policy would lead to a union of the orthodox believers. Baxter, in a lengthy expostulation, listed three points as prerequisites to their acceptance of episcopacy:

1. By making only things necessary to be the terms of union.
2. And by the true exercise of church discipline against sin.
3. And not casting out the faithful ministers that must exercise it, nor obtruding unworthy men upon the people.

Charles gave them "as gracious an answer" as they expected; he also expressed his "gladness" to find the Presbyterians so open to agreement. He also assured them that he would do

his part to bring them together; and that it must not be by bringing one party over to the other, but by abating somewhat on both sides, and meeting in the midway; and that if it were not accomplished it should be along of [the clergy], and not him: Nay, that he was resolved to see it brought to pass, and that he would draw them together himself.

The king requested the ministers to draw up a set of proposals on church government, and assured them, probably after being pressed on the point, that he would order the Anglicans to do the same. The king's self-professed purpose was "to advise with a few of each side, for his own satisfaction," before convening an assembly of divines. The meetings were entirely successful; the ministers left the meeting of June 26 fully satisfied with the king's promises and demands.[64]

---

[59] Guicciardine Ayloffe to Sir Richard Leveson, June 5, 1660, H.M.C., *Fifth Report, Appendix, Part I*, p. 184.

[60] Thomas Gower to Sir Richard Leveson, June 14, 1660, *ibid.*, p. 194.

[61] M. de Bordeaux to M. de Brienne, April 23/May 3, 1660, Baschet Transcripts, Public Record Office, 31/3 (107), foll. 1–5; M. de Bordeaux to Cardinal Mazarin, April 23/May 3, 1660, *ibid.*, foll. 6–8; M. de Bordeaux to Cardinal Mazarin, April 26/May 6, 1660, *ibid.*, foll. 13–14.

[62] Stephen Charlton to Sir Richard Leveson, June 16, 1660, H.M.C., *Fifth Report, Appendix, Part I*, p. 168.

[63] Baxter, *Reliquiae Baxterianae*, Pt. II: p. 230. See *Notes Which Passed at Meetings of the Privy Council Between Charles II and the Earl of Clarendon, 1660–1667, together with a few Letters, Reproduced in Fac-simile from the Originals in the Bodleian Library*, ed. W. D. Macray (London, 1896), p. 8, for what appears to be an exchange of notes between Charles and Hyde on Broghill's mission.

[64] Baxter, *Reliquiae Baxterianae*, Pt. II: pp. 230–232; James Sharp to Robert Douglas, June 28, 1660, Wodrow, *Church of*

Having arrived at a general understanding with the king, the Presbyterians returned to their consultations at Sion College. The daily sessions were open to all Presbyterian ministers, but not all the London clergy attended. Those who did were joined from time to time by visitors from the country. Baxter's treatment of the debates is very enlightening:

> we found the great inconvenience of too many actors . . . for that which seemed the most convenient expression to me, seemed inconvenient to another, and we that all agreed in matter, had much ado to agree in words.[65]

This was quite an admission from one who loved disputation. The debates proved once again that the ministers were "not all in one mind." They eventually agreed to propose Usher's reduced episcopacy, to accept a liturgy, and to request freedom from certain ceremonies,[66] but even Baxter confessed that no one was especially pleased with the paper which they submitted to Charles II on July 10.

On July 10, the Presbyterian delegation orally requested the king to give them an early decision, to declare publicly "his pleasure for the Suspension of Proceedings upon the Act of Uniformity, against Nonconformists in Case of Liturgy and Ceremonies," until concord was reached, to require no new oaths pending a settlement, to permit no entry into a living where the former incumbent was dead, and to keep out all scandalous ministers. The king met the Presbyterian requests graciously and cordially, assuring them that, while the Anglicans were not then present, he would soon call the two parties together. In the meanwhile, Charles declared he would compel the Anglicans to turn in their concessions.[67] By this date, July 10, the Laudians were "bowing a little." The declared intention of Charles to issue a declaration in favor of moderate episcopacy, an amended liturgy, and dispensation of the ceremonies had caused the Laudians to retrace some of their steps.[68]

It so happened that this stage in the negotiations coincided with a crisis in the commons as to whether the Convention Parliament or the king should be responsible for determining the religious settlement. Charles preferred to effect a settlement by prerogative action, but certain elements in the commons desired the finality of legislation. In order to understand this struggle, it is necessary to return to May 1.

The moderate Presbyterians from May 1 had placed their fate in the hands of Charles II, but the old Covenant interest, preserved by encouragement from Scotland,[69] placed its trust in the Convention Parliament, as did the vindictive element among the Anglican Royalists. On June 21, Sharp remarked that the "Parliament complain of his Majesty's Moderation, and that he does not press the settling all *sicut ante.*" [70] "The fire between the Presbytery and the Episcopacy," predicted one writer, "is not yet extinguished; for Jack the Levite labours to confound Aaron the *jure divino* priest." [71] Even while Charles II labored to pacify the clergy, tempers were beginning to flare. A petition circulated in Worcestershire desired a return to the religious system of James I and Charles I.[72] Vindictive Laudians like Dr. Thomas Pierce preached openly and boldly for the system of their martyred leader.[73]

Encouraged by disappointed courtiers, country squires, and many of the Anglican clergy, the young members of the commons threatened in June and July to upset the plans of Charles and the moderate ministers. In a sense, however, much of the trouble stemmed from unfortunate events outside the Convention Parliament. John Gailhard, a confirmed Presbyterian, opened fire against the Anglicans and those erstwhile Presbyterians who had gone over to the Anglican party early in 1660.[74] John Gauden unwittingly aroused the Covenanters, whom he hoped to convert, when he published a tract setting forth arguments why the Solemn League and Covenant did not bind its earlier supporters to an eradication of episcopacy.[75] Although moderate and conciliatory on most points, Gauden's arguments had the sole, and presumably unintended, effect of arousing the irreconcilable Presbyterians to open attacks on episcopacy.[76] A further irritant was Robert Mossom's plea for the restoration of the sequestered Anglicans.[77]

Scotland 1: pp. xli–xlii. Sharp said that Charles stated that bishops would be restored, and the ministers replied they were "not enemies to regulated Episcopacy." At this point, according to Sharp, Charles "bid" the Presbyterians to hand in their concessions, and "promised that none of them should be pressed to conformity until a synod determined that point, and that all who had entered into livings whose incumbents are dead, should be continued, and others, before they were outed, should be provided for."

[65] Baxter, *Reliquiae Baxterianae,* Pt. II: p. 232; Edward Reynolds confirmed this in his *Divine Efficacy without Humane Power* . . . (London, 1660), [pp. 4–5].

[66] James Sharp to Robert Douglas, July 7, 1660, Wodrow, *Church of Scotland* 1: p. xlv.

[67] Baxter, *Reliquiae Baxterianae,* Pt. II: pp. 232–241.

[68] James Sharp to Robert Douglas, July 10, 1660, Wodrow, *Church of Scotland* 1: p. xlv.

[69] Robert Baillie to Earl of Lauderdale, June 16, 1660, *Letters and Journals of Robert Baillie* 3: pp. 405–407; Robert Baillie to George Hutchinson, August 13, 1660, *ibid.*, pp. 408–409.

[70] James Sharp to Robert Douglas, June 21, 1660, Wodrow, *Church of Scotland* 1: p. xxxix.

[71] William Smith to John Langley, June 23, 1660, H.M.C., *Fifth Report, Appendix, Part I,* p. 173.

[72] Townshend, *Diary* 2: pp. 274–275.

[73] Bosher, *Restoration Settlement,* pp. 154–156.

[74] John Gailhard, *The Controversy between Episcopacy and Presbytery Stated and Discussed* (London, 1660).

[75] John Gauden, . . . *The Loosing of St. Peters Bonds;* . . . (London, 1660).

[76] Anonymous, *The Anatomy of Dr. Gauden's Idolized Nonsence and Blasphemy, in his Pretended Analysis* . . . (London, 1660) was the first of many attacks on Gauden.

[77] Robert Mossom, *An Apology in the behalf of the Sequestered Clergy; Presented to the High Court of Parliament* (London, 1660).

The religious quarrel finally moved into the Commons on June 30 as the result of the publication of a form of worship to be used in connection with the nation-wide thanksgiving service for the king's return. Pub-lished anonymously and without the printer's name, the pamphlet bore the inscription "Set forth by Author-ity" and borrowed heavily from the Book of Common Prayer.[78] The Presbyterians in the House of Commons were, as Andrew Newport put it, "scandalized." [79] In the course of the debate, several old proclamations on religion, which dated back to the reign of James I, and a book on the Covenant came under discussion. The immediate solution was to send the thanksgiving forms to a committee for investigation as to author-ship and printer,[80] but this decision merely postponed the inevitable battle over religion.

As the indemnity bill neared its completion, the question of religion replaced it as the most stirring issue in the House of Commons.[81] On July 2, after a delay of two months, Thomas Bampfield moved that his bill on religion be taken under consideration.[82] When the bill was read four days later, every speaker urged its committal either to a grand or to a special committee. Several members spoke for a synod or assembly of divines; Throgmorton condemned Presby-terianism and praised bishops.[83]

With the preliminaries out of the way, the house settled down to business in earnest on July 9 at a grand committee. That the Anglicans dominated the committee is apparent from the fact that Charlton sat as chairman. The entire debate, lasting until ten P.M., concerned one paragraph of the bill. Since the bill has not survived, its other provisions are unknown. The paragraph under debate read:

That the one Christian Protestant faith contained in the scriptures of the old and new Testament and the outward administration of the government of the Church and the public worship of God as they stand established by the laws of the land, and no other shall be publicly professed and maintained within the Kingdom of England and the Do-minion of Wales and the Territories thereunto belonging.[84]

Noticeably absent from the paragraph was any reference to the Thirty-nine Articles. The Puritans had always disapproved of certain of the Thirty-nine Articles, insisting on some statement similar to that submitted

by Bampfield, who probably obtained the contents from Baxter. Battle ensued when Sir Trevor Williams moved that the Thirty-nine Articles be substituted for the Old and New Testaments. This motion auto-matically found support from the friends of Laudianism. A less intolerant group of Anglicans led by Sir Heneage Finch, the solicitor general, and Geoffrey Palmer, the attorney general, seemed agreeable to rephrasing the paragraph so as to produce a compromise. There were also two major divisions within the Presbyterian membership. Every Presbyterian speaker favored the bill as brought in, but Matthew Hale, Prynne, and Swinfen indicated a willingness to accept conditionally the Thirty-nine Articles. The latter group proposed that parliament determine a broad doctrine similar to that under consideration and leave discipline to a synod. Holles, Annesley, and Cooper, who were closer to the court than the other nonconformists, supported the synod proposal; they also joined with Swinfen and Hale in moving an adjournment.

After several hours it became apparent that no decision could be reached. The committee sat an hour in the dark before candles were permitted. Even these were twice blown out. Light was finally "pre-served though with great disorder," and at ten P.M. the committee voted to ask the house to petition the king to summon "a select number of divines to treat concerning this debate." [85]

For some unascertainable reason the committee did not pursue the policy adopted on July 9. Instead, the house went into grand committee again on July 16 when the debate was more acrimonious than on the previous Monday. Sir John Northcote began the session with an attack against deans and chapters, but not bishops, for doing nothing except eating, drinking, and playing. Prynne soon followed with the state-ment that he "could not be for bishops unless they derive their power from the king and not own them-selves to be *jure divino*," which was in line with the Erastian sentiments of many of the Presbyterian lay-men. As on the ninth, the real issue concerned the Anglican effort to turn the bill into a statement of both doctrine and discipline by substituting the Thirty-nine Articles for the Old and New Testaments. Fore-seeing the dangers inherent in the Anglican proposals, Sir Thomas Widdrington, Thomas Grove, Edward Stephens, Sir John Temple, Walter Young, Bunckley, Swinfen, Samuel Gott, Prynne, Sir Gilbert Gerard, Colonel Shapcote, Sir Thomas Wharton, Sir Walter Earle, and others, all Presbyterians or Independents working with them, fought to divide the question into doctrine and discipline. They offered to vote on doc-trine, but argued that it was not proper to interfere with the king's negotiations about discipline, ceremonies,

[78] Anonymous, *A Form of Prayer with Thanksgiving to be used on 28 June 1660 for his Majesty's Happy Return* (London, 1660).

[79] Andrew Newport to Sir Richard Leveson, June 30, 1660, H.M.C., *Fifth Report, Appendix, Part I*, p. 154.

[80] Bowman, "Diary," B.L., Salway Deposit, foll. 35–37.

[81] Thomas Gower to Sir Richard Leveson, June 30, 1660, H.M.C., *Fifth Report, Appendix, Part I*, p. 194, predicted that this would happen.

[82] Bowman, "Diary," B.L., Salway Deposit, fol. 41.

[83] *Ibid.*, foll. 55–56; according to Sharp (letter to Robert Douglas, July 7, 1660, Wodrow, *Church of Scotland* 1: p. xlv), Bampfield was "hissed down" when he spoke against episcopacy, but Bowman failed to record any speech by Bampfield.

[84] Townshend, *Diary* 1: p. 55.

[85] Bowman, "Diary," B.L., Salway Deposit, foll. 64–48. Bosher, *Restoration Settlement*, p. 169, note 1, relying on the incomplete version printed by W. Cobbett, was in error in as-signing the information in this paragraph to July 16.

and forms of worship. The strength and obstructionist tactics of the Anglicans prevented any vote on the motion. The Presbyterians then followed the lead of Cooper, Irby, Knightley, Sir Edmund Jennings, Hugh Boscawen, and Holles in voting for a postponment. Cooper accurately observed that religion was "too much intermixed with interest." Many of the Anglicans, hoping for a thorough victory over the Presbyterians and an end to the king's negotiations, opposed this motion, but Finch and Williams supported Cooper's motion to adjourn the committee "for 3 months and this debate [to be] laid aside." This was accordingly voted at ten P.M. when the committee voted a second time to refer "the debate concerning the settlement of religion to the king and to such divines as he shall please to choose." [86]

Although the grand committee had twice expressed itself on the proposed measure, Charlton, as chairman, delayed three days before reporting to the house. Following Charlton's report from the grand committee, Northcote, Holles, King, Swinfen, Stephens, and Booth attempted to amend the committee's resolution by providing that the committee might be reconvened by order of the house prior to October 23. However, the committee's recommendation, supported by Annesley, was adopted. [87]

This decision pleased very few. A majority of the Anglican members obviously wanted to confirm the religious establishment which had existed prior to 1643. The Anglicans close to the court were willing to pass Bampfield's statement of doctrine but only if it was modified in the direction of Anglicanism. When modification proved impossible, the Anglicans of the court faction voted with the moderate Presbyterians to refer the matter to the king and an assembly of ministers. Except for one or two ill-chosen remarks, the Presbyterian speeches were for the adoption of a broad doctrine by parliament. They were quite content to leave the details of the religious settlement to the king and an assembly of divines. Outnumbered in the committee and in the house, the Presbyterians dared not press for a vote on the question of doctrine "for so they had lost it." [88]

Even while the House of Commons debated religious measures, many of the Anglicans, especially the Laudians, forced their way back into their old livings by various means. As these embittered priests returned to their flocks, they restored the Prayer Book to its ancient position in the service. [89] These actions stirred the Presbyterian ministers to even greater activity in behalf of themselves and their followers. On July 21, "sundry poor Ministers" in sequestered livings presented a petition to the commons through Colonel King. The petitioners desired that a stop be put to all proceedings at law for their ejection. Although the diarist of the Convention Parliament recorded no speeches on whether the petition should be read, the house, with Earle and Irby as tellers for the majority and Vincent and Rich for the minority, voted 125 to 106 in favor of receiving the petition, following which Finch and Holles urged the commons to take it into consideration on July 25. The house agreed by ordering the committee working on the bill to settle ministers to bring in a bill to grant the wishes of the petitioners. [90] Both matters were postponed until July 27, when Prynne reported from committee a "Bill for settling Ministers in Ecclesiastical Benefices, Livings, and Promotions." [91] While Prynne and Swinfen favored an immediate second reading, Annesley, Holles, and Gerard joined with the Anglicans in delaying further action. [92]

When the bill was read for the second time on July 30, it became obvious once again that the Presbyterians were far from possessing control of the commons. Furthermore, they failed to organize their arguments. Prynne and Gewen incited the Independents by attacking "one Bond a preacher that writ a book to justify the king's murder." Swinfen spoke at length against pluralism and for a continuation of all incumbents until Michaelmas without any additional imposition as to discipline. Bampfield predicted that forced subscription to the Thirty-nine Articles would drive 95 per cent of the ministers to nonconformity. Knightley and Lewis voiced the Presbyterian fears when they moved on July 31 to leave discipline to the king's consideration. [93]

For more than a month the bill moved to and from committee. On the afternoon of July 31, it was voted to exclude all "ignorant and insufficient" ministers as well as any who had contributed in "any way" to the death of Charles I. This vote was followed by a debate lasting until after seven o'clock on whether to subject to sequestration all ministers who had refused to administer the sacrament by act or by preaching or writing. [94] The Anglicans carried this point on the next afternoon 83 to 82 by the chairman's untying vote. [95] On August 4 the committee approved a motion,

[86] Bowman, "Diary," B.L., Salway Deposit, foll. 79–87. Bosher, *Restoration Settlement*, p. 169, made the grave mistake of calling Widdrington, Grove, and Stephens Anglicans. Widdrington was a Presbyterian in religion and sufficiently anti-monarchical to be one of Cromwell's favorites; Thomas Grove was Baxter's friend; and Stephens was a Presbyterian monarchist.

[87] Bowman, "Diary," B.L., Salway Deposit, foll. 90–91.

[88] Townshend, *Diary* **1**: p. 55; Francesco Giavarina to Doge and Senate, July 20/30, 1660, *Calendar of State Papers, Venetian* **32**: p. 176.

[89] Stoughton, *History of Religion* **3**: pp. 89–93; Bosher, *Restoration Settlement*, pp. 159–164.

[90] Bowman, "Diary," B.L., Salway Deposit, foll. 92–93; *Commons Journals* **8**: p. 97.

[91] *Commons Journals* **8**: pp. 102, 104.

[92] Bowman, "Diary," B.L., Salway Deposit, fol. 98.

[93] *Ibid.*, foll. 105–110.

[94] *Ibid.*, foll. 112–113.

[95] *Ibid.*, fol. 115.

apparently without serious debate, to continue all ministers ordained prior to December 25, 1659, by bishops, by bishops and presbyters, or by presbyters alone.[96]

On August 7, shortly after Broderick informed the commons that Charles had ordered the bishops to increase all vicarages to one hundred pounds, the committee voted that no minister should hold two livings, that no scandalous clergyman should be confirmed or restored, that the payment of fifths to sequestered Anglicans should be confined to those holding specific orders for them, and that no consideration should be given to the subject of dilapidations.[97] A bill for better observance of the Sabbath was introduced four days later, as well as one against profane swearing.[98] Then on the fourteenth Finch moved to commit Prynne's bill for settling ministers and to add a proviso stating that "no ordinations by presbyters shall be a president for the future." Although the Presbyterians applauded Finch's moderation in the matter of ceremonies, they objected to his defense of pluralities and his motion that no minister should have benefit of Prynne's bill who did not conform to the government of the church by Christmas. Prynne interpreted Finch's speech as favoring compulsory reordination of all ministers not previously ordained by bishops.[99]

Debate on Prynne's bill for settling ministers was postponed four times between August 14 and 20, but Prynne later asserted that the Anglican members moved on August 15 and 17 to expel all clergymen from their livings unless they submitted to reordination within one month.[100] Another Anglican amendment was defeated on August 21. By a vote of 148 to 127 the commons rejected an Anglican proposal to exclude any minister who objected to administering communion to any person of good morals.[101] On August 22 and 23 the commons approved a motion to abolish pluralism and one to exempt incumbents from further payments of fifths to sequestered clergy.[102] The following day they voted to authorize the expulsion of any incumbent who proved himself scandalous. On August 24, an amendment to require that beneficed clergymen take the oaths of allegiance and supremacy passed without a division.[103]

A more controversial question involved the ecclesiastical grants which had passed under the great seal since May. On August 24, a proviso to protect these grants was introduced. After considerable debate, the house voted, 140 to 83, three days later to appoint a committee to examine all such grants. On this question the Presbyterians split into two groups. One group supported the motion, but King and Gerard acted as tellers for the minority.[104] This split in the Presbyterian ranks was caused by the grants of confirmation made to certain Presbyterian ministers, and the dispossession of others by grants to Anglicans. In this connection, a petition for "divers distressed ministers" was presented immediately after the foregoing vote, and referred to the committee appointed to study grants.[105]

Because of an impending adjournment, Prynne's bill for settling ministers went through its final stages rather rapidly.[106] It is more than likely that the court influenced the commons. The absence of any divisions between August 26 and September 13 on the multitude of proposed amendments suggests that some of the Anglicans joined with the Presbyterians and Independents to accept the status quo until the king could conclude his conference with the divines. In addressing both houses on September 13, Hyde said that Charles II "passed this Act very willingly." [107]

The passage of Prynne's bill for settling ministers had three major results. It permitted a large number of Anglicans to return to their former livings, but it confirmed most of the Presbyterians and many of the Independents. Episcopal ordination was no longer a qualification. However, the most important consequence of the Act was that it eased the anxiety of the Presbyterians to a point where Charles could resume his negotiations with the Presbyterians and Anglicans. The adjournment of the Convention Parliament gave the king an opportunity to employ prerogative measures without parliamentary interference.

It will be recalled that the Presbyterians handed in their demands and concessions on July 10 and that Charles then promised to issue a declaration favoring moderate episcopacy, an amended liturgy, and dispensation of certain ceremonies. Some days later the surviving bishops rejected almost every point raised by the Presbyterians. In the words of Baxter, the bishops' paper was one of "bitter oppositions, by way of confutation to our former proposals." [108] In his study, Bosher concluded as charitably as possible that the bishops' reply "refused any essential modifications of the old system, but emphasized the comprehensiveness which could be enjoyed within it." [109] The Presbyterians had proposed, and the Anglicans had rejected. On the surface compromise seemed hopeless.

Immediately, the Presbyterians prepared and de-

[96] *Ibid.*, fol. 121.

[97] *Ibid.*, foll. 125–126.

[98] *Ibid.*, fol. 132.

[99] *Ibid.*, foll. 136–137.

[100] William Prynne, *The Unbishoping of Timothy and Titus, and of the Angel of the Church of Ephesus* (2nd ed., London, 1660), p. 27.

[101] *Commons Journals* **8**: p. 129.

[102] *Ibid.*, pp. 130–131.

[103] *Ibid.*, p. 136.

[104] *Ibid.*, pp. 136, 138. Bosher's treatment, *Restoration Settlement*, pp. 175–176, of this measure is confused.

[105] *Commons Journals* **8**: pp. 138, 140.

[106] *Ibid.*, pp. 148, 149, 159, 161.

[107] *Ibid.*, p. 173.

[108] Baxter, *Reliquiae Baxterianae*, Pt. II: pp. 242–247.

[109] Bosher, *Restoration Settlement*, p. 167.

livered a long defense of their proposals, though several of Baxter's colleagues wished to surrender in despair to the apparent intransigence of the Laudians. The Presbyterian rejoinder concluded as follows:

We perceive your Counsels against Peace are not likely to be frustrated: Your Desires concerning us are like to be accomplished. You are like to be gratified with our Silence and Ejection, and the Excommunication and Consequent suffering of Dissenters.

Baxter's own attitude, in which he found solace until his death, was that the Presyterians should endeavor anything and everything acceptable to their principles which offered "the least possibility of a better issue." Posterity should be convinced that the Anglicans, if the negotiations failed, obstinately refused to act in a Christian and brotherly manner and that the Presbyterians were "ready to do anything for Peace, except to sin and damn our Souls." It appeared to Baxter that the Laudians were taking unfair advantage of the Presbyterians' abhorrence of violence.[110]

The negotiations temporarily ceased at this point, and the Presbyterians resumed their war on Laudianism. An anonymous tract discussed at length why a general reformation was necessary. Addressed to the Convention Parliament, it was endorsed as "By divers Ministers of sundry Counties in England."[111] In addition to providing the usual arguments, the work stated categorically that "where Kings have not curbed the violence of Bishops, they have ever sharply persecuted all that threw off Popery; which Persecutions usually produced Confusions in the Commonwealth." To prevent these dangers and to reform the national religion, parliament should adopt the pattern set under Edward VI and summon "some of the most moderate and able persons of every different party to assist therein."[112] In the realm of practical politics, then, the Presbyterian author, or authors, was willing to leave the details of the religious settlement to a synod summoned either by parliament or by the king. The sentiments expressed in this work were those of the confirmed Presbyterians, not of the moderate group who had already dropped the idea of a general synod for an Anglican-Presbyterian assembly of limited membership. This is not to say, however, that the ardent Presbyterians were not influenced in their decision by their lack of support within the Convention commons.[113]

Between August and November numerous attacks were made on the Anglican position. Zachary Crofton, speaking for the rigid Presbyterians, took an uncompromising position in his defense of a Covenant reformation.[114] Sensing that the final battle drew near, Prynne republished his *Unbishoping of Timothy and Titus* with new arguments pertinent to the changed situation. His purpose was to prove from Scriptural and historical materials that episcopacy owed its development to accident and convenience rather than divine decree. To the aging lawyer it was illogical at best for the Laudians to "UNCHURCH all Presbyterian Protestant Churches both at home and abroad, and NUL both their Ministry and Sacraments" while accepting as valid all Roman Catholic ordinations and sacraments.[115]

From the point of view of civil government alone, Prynne's conclusions held tremendous interest for those clerics and laymen, including Charles II, who were concerned with preserving as much of the royal prerogative as possible. Every statute since Henry VIII, according to Prynne, proved that the

... Archbishops, Bishops, Archdeacons, and other Ecclesiastical persons of this Realm, have no manner of jurisdiction ecclesiastical, but by, under and from the Kings Royal Majesty: to whom by holy Scripture all authority and power is wholy given, to hear and determine all manner of causes Ecclesiasticall, and to correct vice and sin whatsoever, and to all such persons as his Majesty shall appoint thereunto: That all authority and Jurisdiction spiritual and temporal is derived and deducted from the Kings Majesty, as supream head of the Church and Realm of England . . . .[116]

This statutory constitution, as well as the Scriptural, had been violated prior to 1640 by prelates of Laud's school. The necessary corrective lay in a plan similar to that tacitly accepted by Charles I at the Isle of Wight. In other words, restore the episcopal office to its apostolic state by reducing the authority of the bishop to a negative voice over ordination and similar matters and by divesting the bishop of his temporal properties and positions so that he might have sufficient time to exercise his spiritual functions properly.[117] This was nothing more than Usher's plan supported by Erastian and Scriptural proof.

Much of Prynne's earlier zeal for religious reform had diminished by 1660; he was now prepared to accept what was called primitive episcopacy. Earlier Prynne advocated rigidity; now he urged all "Bishops, Prelates, Presbyters, Independents and Sects whatsoever to lay aside all unnecessary contests about Precedency, Church government, superfluous Ceremonies and Formalities." Religious unity was so desirable and so essential that each and every Christian should

submit to that Model of Church government, (with just liberty to truly tender consciences in points not fundamental & consistent with publick peace) which we all hope will

---

[110] Baxter, *Reliquiae Baxterianae*, Pt. II: pp. 248–259.

[111] [Cornelius Burgess], *Reasons Shewing the Necessity of Reformation . . .* (London, 1660).

[112] *Ibid.*, [pp. 3, 4]. This suggests that the tract was written prior to July 9.

[113] These conclusions are well substantiated by a letter of August 10 from Calamy, Ashe, and Manton to Robert Douglas, Wodrow, *Church of Scotland* 1: p. liv.

[114] Zachary Crofton, . . . *The Fastning of St. Peters Fetters* . . . (London, 1660).

[115] Prynne, "Epistle to the Reader," *Unbishoping of Timothy and Titus*, pp. 27–28.

[116] Prynne, "Epistle Dedicatory," *ibid.*, p. 2.

[117] Prynne, "Epistle to the Reader," *ibid.*, pp. 28–30.

ere long be setled by his Majesties pious endeavours, and Royal Authority (according to the Ministers and Commons House Addresses to His Majesty in pursuance of his own Royal Letters and Declaration from Breda) with the Advice of moderate, learned and pious Divines of all formerly dissenting parties and both Houses of Parliament, for the future tranquilty and prosperity both of our Churches and Kingdoms.[118]

Prynne, Baxter, and Burgess were far from being the only spokesmen for the adoption of reformed episcopacy. On August 21, *A Declaration of the Presbyterians* urged the acceptance of Usher's plan, and appealed for the recognition of the king's prerogative.[119] Matthew Poole preached for evangelical worship on August 26. In a preface to the published sermon, Poole attacked the Laudians as intolerant and as disobediant to the expressed desires of Charles II.[120] A few days later Matthew Meade announced that he would rather surrender his ministry than trouble his conscience or dishonor God by administering his office in any manner open to question.[121] Giles Firmin served the same warning to the nation on September 29,[122] accusing the Laudians of acting contrary to the will of the king and warning the bishops that their policy would fill prisons but not pulpits and pews.[123] Valuable assistance was rendered the Presbyterians by the arguments of William Wickins,[124] who later conformed, and of John Tombes,[125] that strange olio of Anabaptist, Presbyterian, and Congregational belief.

Thus between January and October, 1660, the leading members of the Presbyterian party came to place more confidence in the prerogative power of the monarch over the religious state. Only in the king could they see any salvation for their Puritanism. In stating their prinicples so fully and so uncompromisingly, however, they reduced considerably their opportunities for negotiation. As late as September, there was almost no indication that the leading Anglicans, other than Gauden and perhaps Morley, even contemplated compromising the system established under Edward VI and Elizabeth I and improved by Laud. The future looked very bleak to the Presbyterians, unless, by some miracle, Charles would throw his entire weight against the negative position of the bishops and their supporters.

Although he had not been in direct communication with the Presbyterian ministers for some weeks, Charles suddenly informed Baxter's group that he "would put all that he thought meet to grant into the form of a Declaration," which would be submitted to them for comment. On September 4, a preliminary draft of the declaration was delivered to the ministers.[126] Nine days later Hyde, speaking for his master, announced the king's plan to the Convention Parliament in the following statement:

What pains [his Majesty] hath taken to compose [religious differences], after several discourses with learned and pious men of different persuasions, you will shortly see by a declaration he will publish upon that occasion; by which you will see his great indulgence to those who can have any pretension from conscience to differ from their brethren.[127]

There was no mention of parliamentary sanction being invited at any subsequent date; this declaration was to originate from the king as supreme governor of the ecclesiastical establishment, and apparently was intended from the first as definitive on the question of church government. Secretary Nicholas suggested this interpretation on November 1 when he wrote Sir Henry Bennet:

"Tuesday next the Parliament meets again, of which we may hope the better success, since the King hath removed the main bone of division, by taking into his own hand, and [by] his Declaration determining, the great point of church government." [128]

Although the draft declaration of September 4 made numerous concessions to the Presbyterians, it left so many of their objections unanswered that Baxter commented that "it would not serve to heal our Differences" unless much was altered. Baxter, unfortunately, was chosen to prepare the Presbyterian reply. Even Calamy and Reynolds were "troubled at the Plainness of it and thought it would not be endured," and at the insistence of Manchester, Holles, Annesley, Calamy, and Reynolds many passages were stricken or drastically revised before Baxter's paper was submitted to Hyde. It contained five major exceptions: (1) suffragan bishops should be appointed in the large dioceses, (2) bishops should not ordain or discipline without the assistance of their presbyters, (3) confirmation should be administered only with the advice and consent of the local parish minister, (4) a more drastic revision of the Book of Common Prayer should be made, and alternate forms of service should be authorized, and (5) kneeling at communion, along with other ceremonial practices, should be optional.

[118] *Ibid.,* pp. 31–32.
[119] Anonymous, *A Declaration of the Presbiterians; Concerning his Maiesties Royal Person, And the Government of the Church of England . . .* (London, 1660).
[120] Matthew Poole, *Evangelical Worship is Spiritual Worship . . .* (London, 1660).
[121] Matthew Meade, *Spiritual Wisdom improved against Temptation . . .* (London, 1660).
[122] G[iles] F[irmin], *Presbyterial Ordination Vindicated . . .* (London, 1660), p. 29.
[123] *Ibid.,* pp. [4], 22.
[124] William Wickins, *The Kingdoms Remembrancer . . .* (London, 1660).
[125] John Tombes, *A Supplement to the Serious Consideration of the Oath of the Kings Supremacy* (London, 1660).
[126] Baxter, *Reliquiae Baxterianae,* Pt. II: pp. 259–264, for the original draft; James Sharp knew something of this plan somewhat earlier (James Sharp to Robert Baillie, September 5, 1660, *Letters and Journals of Robert Baillie* 3: pp. 409–411).
[127] *Commons Journals* 8: p. 174.
[128] Quoted by Bosher, *Restoration Settlement,* p. 185.

They also stated that many passages were objectionable, and should be altered or omitted.[129]

With a total impasse in the offing, the Presbyterians requested that a conference be arranged. Morley, Henchman, and Cosin met with Baxter, Reynolds, and Calamy, but, according to Baxter, only "roving discourses" occurred. Neither side made any concessions.[130]

Once again Hyde and Charles intervened to save their policy. They asked the Presbyterians to submit specific alterations to the draft of September 4. Following the submission of this paper, Hyde summoned a formal conference for October 22 at his residence, Worcester House. Reynolds, Calamy, Ashe, Wallis, Manton, Spurstowe, and Baxter represented their party. Sheldon, Morley, Henchman, Cosin, Gauden, Barwick, Hacket, and Gunning spoke for the Anglicans. Monck, now Duke of Albemarle, Ormonde, Manchester, Annesley, Holles, and other members of the court attended. "The business of the day was not to dispute, but as the Chancellor read over the Declaration, each party was to speak to what they disliked, and the King to determine how it should be." [131]

Despite the presence of the royal arbitrator, members of both parties, but especially Baxter and Morley, engaged in long and heated debates. The most controversial points concerned ordination and reordination and the efficacy of prelacy. On both these questions Morley and Gunning clashed bitterly with Baxter and Calamy; [132] when the Presbyterians insisted on reducing the bishop's authority to a negative voice, Cosin objected to the king that this would " 'unbishop your bishops.' " [133] After making due allowances for Baxter's prejudices, it is quite obvious from his account that the bishops were not at all friendly to the king's policy or his concessions to the Presbyterians.

Toward the end of the session, Hyde introduced, at the request of the Independents and Anabaptists, a proposed addition to the declaration to the following effect: "That others also be permitted to meet for Religious Worship so be it, they do it not to the Disturbance of the Peace; and that no Justice of Peace or Officer disturb them." This was carrying the royal prerogative onto dangerous ground. Might not Roman Catholics be thus granted toleration? According to Baxter, each side knew that Hyde's proposal meant a "Toleration of Papists and Socinians," but would say nothing. Finally, Baxter, despite a warning from Wallis "to let the Bishops speak" first, said,

As we humbly thank your Majesty for your indulgence to ourselves, so we distinguish the tolerable Parties from the intolerable: for the former we humbly crave great lenity

and favour; but for the latter—such as Papists and Socinians—for our parts, we cannot make their Toleration our Request.

Charles in some irritation replied "That there were Laws enough against the Papists." Throwing all caution to the wind, Baxter undiplomatically snapped back "that we understood the Question to be, whether those Laws should be executed on them, or not." He was now suspicious of the king's intentions with regard to Roman Catholics, and continued so as long as he lived. Worse yet, this debate gave some truth to the charges that the Presbyterians wanted freedom for themselves only, thereby further alienating the Independents and Roman Catholics, whose support was vital to the success of the king's policy.[134]

The conference also sowed seeds of discord within the Presbyterian ranks. As he left Worcester House, Baxter severely reprimanded Annesley for being too favorable toward prelacy. Manchester, Holles, and Annesley, who had more worldly considerations in mind, argued at length with the ministers to yield more ground to the Anglicans lest they lose everything. Ashe apparently sided with the laymen, for Baxter later admitted that Ashe was too eager to compromise. Even Calamy vetoed Baxter's suggestion that they issue a paper setting forth the differences between the reconciling element and their more rigid brethren.[135]

It is no wonder, then, that Baxter went from Worcester House "dejected, as being fully satisfied that the form of Government in that Declaration would not be satisfactory." [136] Yet Andrew Newport reported on the following day that the two groups "agreed in all matters and very suddenly. A declaration of Church government will be set out." [137] Newport was definitely in error on at least one point; no agreement had been reached on the vital question of reordination. Many difficulties of phraseology had yet to be resolved.[138]

In a final effort to bring the two groups to an understanding, Charles appointed Morley, Henchman, Calamy, and Reynolds to meet for the purpose of putting together a revised version of his draft declaration. Holles and Annesley were to decide any differences. Morley entered upon this project with the hopes that the fruits of their labor would give "abundant satisfaction to the honest and peaceably minded men of both partys, and make them cease to bee parties any longer, but unanimously to joyne against the common enemy of Papists." [139]

The finished version of His Majesty's Declaration

[129] Baxter, *Reliquiae Baxterianae*, Pt. II: pp. 265–276, where Baxter's draft and the completed reply are printed.

[130] *Ibid.*, p. 274.

[131] *Ibid.*, pp. 274–276.

[132] *Ibid.*, pp. 278–279.

[133] Quoted by Bosher, *Restoration Settlement*, p. 186.

[134] Baxter, *Reliquiae Baxterianae*, Pt. II: p. 277.

[135] *Ibid.*, p. 278. Baxter was willing to throw over men like Crofton, but Calamy reasoned that Baxter's plan "might offend the Presbyterian Brethren, who expected more of us."

[136] *Ibid.*

[137] Andrew Newport to Sir Richard Leveson, October 23, 1660, H.M.C., *Fifth Report, Appendix, Part I*, p. 157.

[138] Dr. George Morley to Sir John Lauder, October 23, 1660, Lister, *Clarendon* 3: pp. 110–111.

[139] *Ibid.*; Baxter, *Reliquiae Baxterianae*, Pt. II: pp. 277–278.

Concerning Ecclesiastical Affairs, dated October 25, is ample testimony that the two Anglicans submitted to the wishes of their ruler and accepted most of the Presbyterian demands. The only other explanation for its concessions would be that Charles and Hyde rewrote the draft, but the absence of any Anglican protest suggests that Morley and Henchman followed instructions from the court in smoothing out their differences with Calamy and Reynolds. Of course, it is possible that Hyde made further changes in the text before he submitted it to Charles II.

Like all royal proclamations, the Declaration assumed that the king possessed authority over its subject. It also contended throughout that there was a "Church established" by laws as yet in legal force; no indication was given that any of the Civil War and Commonwealth legislation remained in force. The Declaration further assumed that the ecclesiastical power, even in the early days of Christianity, was "always subordinate and subject to the civil." It might be added that this degree of Erastianism marked every subsequent pronouncement of Charles II on religion. Charles studiously avoided any direct attack on the basic principle of episcopacy, which would have been fatal.

Every deviation allowed by the Declaration was, then, in the nature of a concession to the tender consciences referred to in the Declaration of Breda, which was to be a constant theme in the king's utterances for some time to come. Rather than give validity to the Presbyterian arguments, Charles implied that these concessions were necessitated by a fear for the safety of both church and state. He did hint, however, that greater latitude was essential to "the advancement and propagation of the Protestant Religion," if not to its very preservation. The Declaration was further justified by reference to the king's obligation since the Declaration of Breda to permit Presbyterians to worship and minister within the Established Church. It had been the king's intention to summon a "synod of divines" to agree on and to propose a "proper remedy for all those differences and dissatisfactions which had or should arise in matters of religion," but the "over-passionate and turbulent way of proceeding, and the impatience . . . in many for some speedy determination" made it desirable to postpone such a synod until it might meet "without passion or prejudice." The Declaration was a *modus vivendi*, but the king may well have hoped that it would come to be accepted as an enduring settlement. Subsequent developments suggest that Charles in 1660–1661 endeavored to impose a royal settlement in the guise of a temporary arrangement.

The concessions were of great moment. The Declaration seemed to offer hope that Puritanism might yet live. Charles promised to appoint suffragan bishops in the dioceses. Bishops were not to exercise any disciplinary power without the advice and consent of the presbyters. The authority of chancellors, commissaries, and similar officials was abolished. Six ministers, three chosen by the bishop and three by the presbyters, were to assist the archdeacon in the performance of his duties. The presbyters of each diocese were to assist the bishop, dean, and cathedral chapter in ordination and in every exercise of ecclesiastical jurisdiction. Confirmation should be with the consent of the parish minister, who was also granted great discretion over admission to communion. In order to prevent the recurrence of arbitrariness or invention, the king declared that "No bishop shall exercise any arbitrary power, or do or impose anything upon the clergy or the people but what is according to the known laws of the land." Revision of the Prayer Book and the composition of alternate forms would, it was promised, be entrusted to "an equal number of learned divines of both persuasions," but until that time no minister should be compelled to use those passages to which he might object. Charles likewise authorized the Presbyterians to dispense with any ceremonial practice which they found offensive. More specifically, he exempted them from kneeling at communion, from using the cross in baptism, from bowing at the name Jesus, and from wearing the surplice. No longer were ministers, or students at Oxford or Cambridge, required to subscribe to the canons or to take the oath of canonical obedience. The only requirements were the oaths of allegiance and supremacy and the acceptance of the doctrinal portions of the Thirty-nine Articles.[140]

Despite the king's liberality, the Declaration met with less favor than Charles probably expected. Although Baxter admitted that it contained such terms as "any sober honest Minister might submit to," he and the other chaplains failed to render any formal thanks to the king.[141] In fairness to them, however, it should be stated that they thanked Charles informally on October 22 and that they attended a meeting of the London clergy where they urged acceptance of the Declaration. "Most of the Ministers were satisfied," but the aged Arthur Jackson and the rebellious Zachary Crofton refused to sign the London address to the king because they still desired the absolute removal of bishops and archbishops. Signed by nearly all the London ministers, the London address requested, in addition to the concessions already made, that reordination and the wearing of the surplice in colleges might not be imposed.[142] Sixty Lancashire ministers, including the most prominent of that shire, told the king that his Declaration was a "very apt and excellent expedient for union and settlement," suggesting that it be improved and continued so as to provide for

---

[140] *Lords Journals* **11**: pp. 179–182.
[141] Baxter, *Reliquiae Baxterianae*, Pt. II: p. 284.
[142] *Ibid.*, pp. 284–285, where the London address is printed.

"union and accord of all sober men though of different judgments." [143]

There is ample evidence that a number of the Presbyterians were still dissatisfied. Giles Firmin wrote Baxter on November 14:

I doe not thinke things are there [in the Declaration] in all points as you would, but as you can. I beleeve you have found difficult worke to goe so farre & it is mercy that the King (all things considered) is so moderate as hee is.

Firmin was especially doubtful about the section on the Prayer Book and the retention of episcopacy. He was equally apprehensive about "what the Parliament will doe or a synod." [144] Robert Baillie and his friends complained that their English brethren had been "befooled and bewitched," [145] and probably influenced some English Presbyterians against the Declaration.

If Baxter's autobiographical account is placed in its proper perspective and weighed against other evidence, it becomes clear that the ten chaplains who negotiated the Declaration, as well as their immediate circle, accepted the Declaration as an honest effort to create order and peace. Baxter's later opinion of the Declaration was that "it was necessary that moderate things should be proposed and promised; and no way was so fit as by a Declaration, which being no law is a temporary thing, giving place to laws." [146] However, on October 25 he hurried to inform Hyde that if the Declaration were made into law he would join in procuring the consent of others, and there is some evidence that Hyde promised to work for a statutory enactment.[147] Calamy and "some other ministers" lobbied for a confirmatory law, and "sometimes they had some hope from the Lord Chancellor and others." [148] Even the Anglicans complained that the Presbyterians "of late build much upon the Chancellor's favour." [149]

Further evidence of the welcome accorded the Declaration by the moderate Presbyterians is found in the serious consideration which they at first gave to offers of preferment. Through Colonel Birch, Hyde made repeated offers to Baxter, Calamy, and Reynolds throughout the summer and autumn of 1660 of the bishoprics of Hereford, Lichfield, and Norwich respectively. He made a personal appeal to Baxter on October 25. Baxter was tempted to accept on October 25, but raised the question of whether he could "serve the Church best in that way, or in some other." Two days later, after further importunity from Hyde and after consultations with his friends, Baxter declined the bishopric. It is to his credit that he refused before the Convention Parliament reconvened. Baxter's refusal was not based on any personal pique. Rather, it was based on a sincere conviction that acceptance of a bishopric would prove detrimental to the cause of peace and on a personal desire to remain more closely associated with his Kidderminster flock. The old Puritan felt that a rural deanship would be more "suitable to us, in that it hath no Sallery or Maintenance, nor Coercive Power," than a bishopric. Nevertheless, he urged Hyde to appoint more than three Presbyterian bishops, recommending sixteen names for his consideration. For himself Baxter requested only means by which he might remain at Kidderminster as vicar or even as curate.[150]

Reynolds accepted Norwich on September 9, though the formal nomination to the cathedral chapter was not sent until September 30.[151] Calamy almost accepted Lichfield, but was dissuaded by his wife and Matthew Newcomen, his brother-in-law.[152] Manton, Bates, and Bowles were offered the deanships of Rochester, Lichfield, and York respectively, but they refused after some delay.[153] There is also some evidence that Dr. Richard Gilpin was considered for the bishopric of Carlisle.[154] The refusal of preferment by all but Reynolds contributed much to the eventual defeat of the compromise outlined in the king's various declarations. The presence of three or four Presbyterian bishops alongside Reynolds and the moderate Anglican bishops on the episcopal bench in the House of Lords would have given the plan for modified episcopacy great strength. It would have given the Presbyterians an excellent opportunity to elect their friends to the convocation of 1661 and to influence the parliamentary elections of 1661. It would have led to general acceptance of the king's policy among the Presbyterian clergy and their retention within the Established Church.

The decision of the Presbyterians to decline preferment probably owed much to the reception of the Declaration Concerning Ecclesiastical Affairs in the commons when it reconvened on November 6. With

[143] Printed in *Oliver Heywood's Life of John Angier of Denton together with Angier's Diary, and Extracts from his 'An Helpe to Better Hearts'; also Samuel Angier's Diary*, ed. Ernest Axon (Manchester, 1937), pp. 24–27.

[144] Giles Firmin to Richard Baxter, November 14, 1660, Baxter MSS, Letters IV, No. 150.

[145] Robert Baillie to George Hutcheson, November 5, 1660, *Letters and Journals of Robert Baillie* 3: pp. 414–415. Baillie was inclined to write Ashe and Samuel Clarke "to doe their best for a strong petition from the Presbyterian ministers and Citie against Episcopacie and Liturgie," but it is not known whether he wrote prior to the London address of November 16.

[146] Baxter, *Reliquiae Baxterianae*, Pt. II: p. 287.

[147] *Ibid.*

[148] *Ibid.*, p. 284.

[149] Thomas Gower to John Langley, November 24, 1660, H.M.C., *Fifth Report, Appendix, Part I*, p. 196.

[150] Baxter, *Reliquiae Baxterianae*, Pt. II: pp. 281–283, where the letter is printed.

[151] *Calendar of State Papers, Domestic, 1660*, p. 262; *Calendar of State Papers, Domestic, Addenda, 1660–1685*, p. 13. Morley at this time thought all three would accept, Baxter, *Reliquiae Baxterianae*, Pt. II: p. 274.

[152] Baxter, *Reliquiae Baxterianae*, Pt. II: p. 281; Kennett's Collections, LXXXIX, B.M., Lans. MSS 1023, fol. 428.

[153] Baxter, *Reliquiae Baxterianae*, Pt. II: pp. 283–284.

[154] Stoughton, *History of Religion* 3: p. 120.

the Presbyterians Irby, Bampfield, and Stephens taking the initiative, the house voted to thank the king for his Declaration. Irby also moved that it be confirmed by law, but this proposal was first referred to a committee.[155] After several postponements, the committee finally reported a bill on November 28. Several of the Anglicans attacked the Declaration with abandon. The Presbyterian speeches without exception favored the bill. In doing so, the Presbyterians ran the great risk of alienating the king completely, as the Declaration clearly indicated his intention to let matters drift. The four court spokesmen, Broderick, Morice, Finch, and Maynard, all urged the desirability of delay. When the house divided on the question whether to read the bill a second time, the Presbyterians lost by a vote of 183 to 157.[156]

A number of factors were responsible for the failure of the Presbyterians on this motion. Even at best, the Presbyterians in the commons no more than equalled the Anglicans, and on this particular vote they were opposed by "some of the old Commonwealth Party," or Independents, who resented the fact that their clergy had been slighted in the discussions between the Presbyterians and Anglicans.[157] Morice's stand on the bill suggests that he, although a Presbyterian, opposed the measure because it was contrary to his master's wishes, but one cannot help but wonder why the court did not follow the customary procedure of defeating an unwanted measure in committee. The Roman Catholic members no doubt saw the dangers inherent in any parliamentary action on religion. Finally, one must agree with Secretary Nicholas that the bill suffered from the " 'the violent passions of its promoters.' "[158]

When the Convention Parliament dissolved on December 24, it left the Presbyterians holding onto the slim protection afforded them by the Act for Confirming Ministers in Livings. This much had been written into law. For greater things the ministers sought comfort, which vanished as the winter progressed, in the Declaration of Breda and the Declaration Concerning Ecclesiastical Affairs. If the word and promise of a king proved valueless or ineffectual, the Presbyterians could look forward to complete exposure to the vindictiveness of their enemies.[159]

By the end of 1660 some 695 ministers, not all of whom were Presbyterians, were ejected from their livings. Of these, 290 were removed to make way for the sequestered Anglicans. The rest were in some way disqualified for protection under the Act of 1660. Of those ejected in 1660, at least 59 found other livings from whence they were ejected in 1662.[160] Throughout the kingdom angry and hungry laymen and clergymen paid no heed whatsoever to the Declaration of October 25. Justices specifically instructed juries to find against ministers who failed to read the Common Prayer.[161] When such cases came to the attention of Charles II and the lord chancellor they were corrected at once.[162] The Earl of Bedford aided his Presbyterian friends,[163] and Albemarle and Manchester were equally helpful.[164] Unfortunately, not every endangered minister could locate an influential cleric or layman to serve as his watchful patron at court. The court did not choose to arouse the wrath of the Anglican squire and his parish minister by issuing a general directive to supplement the Declaration. To make matters worse for themselves, many of the Presbyterians, including Bates and Manton, seemed to flaunt the Anglicans by making a display of their refusal to use most, if not all, of the Anglican services and ceremonies.[165]

Everywhere the tide of Anglicanism ran so strongly against the comprehension plan envisaged by the king's pronouncements that little short of complete Presbyterian submission to the principles of Laud would have soothed the vindictive squires and their clerical friends. To them Presbyterianism had become the symbol of rebellion, of Scotland, of London, and of change. To the disappointed politician it appeared that the Presbyterians were taking over the court and the multitude of offices which it might bestow. Of what value was a Stuart Restoration if the Civil War and Commonwealth interests continued in possession of lands and offices? These jealousies and hatreds were heightened by recurrent reports of plots against the king, and, although the Presbyterians were not directly involved in any insurrection, they were constantly under suspicion.[166]

Under these conditions, it is not altogether surprising that the Presbyterian writers became active again.

155 William Cobbett, *Parliamentary History of England* (36 v., London, 1806–1820) 4: pp. 141–142.
156 *Ibid.*, pp. 152–154.
157 Thomas Gower to John Langley, November 29, 1660, H.M.C., *Fifth Report, Appendix, Part I*, p. 196. Baxter, *Reliquiae Baxterianae,* Pt. II: p. 379, observed on this point that "the Chief of the Congregational (or Independent) Party, took it ill that we took not them with us in our Treaty."
158 Quoted by Bosher, *Restoration Settlement*, p. 198.
159 Andrew Marvell wrote the Corporation of Hull on November 9 that "We must henceforth rely onely upon his Majesty's goodnesse, who . . . hath hitherto been more ready to give than we to receive," *The Complete Works in Verse and Prose of Andrew Marvell, M. P.,* ed. Alexander B. Grosart (4 v., London, 1872–1875) 2: p. 26.

160 Matthews, *Calamy Revised,* p. xiii.
161 Bosher, *Restoration Settlement,* pp. 201–204. Many individual cases are noted by Matthews, *Calamy Revised.*
162 Baxter, *Reliquiae Baxterianae,* Pt. II: p. 286.
163 William Blagrave to John Thornton, January 20, 1661, B.L., Rawlinson Letters 109, fol. 12.
164 "The Life of Master John Shaw," *Yorkshire Diaries and Autobiographies in the Seventeenth and Eighteenth Centuries,* ed. Charles Jackson (Surtees Society, 1877), p. 155.
165 Bosher, *Restoration Settlement,* pp. 207–208.
166 Wilbur C. Abbott, "English Conspiracy and Dissent, 1660–1674," *American Historical Review* 15: pp. 503–528, 696–722, is excellent on the interrelationship between conspiracy and legislation.

They had sufficient provocation from the Laudians.[167] In November, 1660, a lengthy statement of the Presbyterian attitude appeared. Its author was fully aware of the various obstacles confronting his party, but he was especially concerned about the results of any convocation.[168]

However, the real disputants were men like Crofton and Firmin who stoutly refused to follow the leadership of the Baxter group. Crofton feared that most of the Presbyterians would prove to be of the Baxter following and that the Covenant cause might be compromised. He attacked Gauden, whom he considered the most dangerous of the Anglicans.[169] In March, 1661, Crofton published a tract on the Covenant which was so outspoken that it, together with his sermons, led to his arrest.[170] Thomas Bolde, of whom little is known,[171] was even more bitter in his *Rhetorick Restrained*. He charged Gauden with sedition for his published comments on the Declaration of October, and very foolishly insisted that Charles was obligated by his Scottish oath of 1650 "to use [the Westminster] Directory in his Family, to maintain it in Scotland, and to endeavour to establish it in his other Dominions." [172] Such references to the Solemn League and Covenant aroused old animosities not yet dead, eventually resulting in the public burning of the Covenant by the Cavalier Parliament.

Two other controversies, those concerning liturgy and ordination, captured the attention of the rigid Presbyterians. Charles recognized the difficulties involved in both questions, and purposely glided over them in the Declaration Concerning Ecclesiastical Affairs. In an obvious attempt to reform some of the Presbyterians, Gauden published *Considerations Touching the Liturgy* in which he employed some ill-chosen phrases. He charged that some ministers objected to the liturgy for fear of endangering their "reputation among some people" and that they thereby "Sacrifice their judgments . . . to their Credits," and cited Baxter as favorable to the old liturgy.[173] This work was partly responsible for the tracts by Bolde and Crofton already discussed. It also provoked Giles Firmin to undertake a more complete expression of the rigid Presbyterian attitude toward the Prayer Book.[174] Crofton soon

reviewed all the arguments against reordination, as well as episcopal ordination, and served notice that he would lay down his ministry rather than submit to a second ordination. He also launched a vicious attack on those of his brethren who had submitted to a first or second ordination since May, 1660.[175]

All in all, the developments prior to the convening of the Cavalier Parliament proved beyond any doubt that the Presbyterian clergy were far from unified. Some, like Reynolds, submitted to the partially restored church prior to October 25, and there was an apparent increase in such surrenders after that date.[176] A second group, by no means uniform in opinion and of indeterminate size, joined the ten chaplains in pressing for a comprehensive church along the lines laid down or promised in the Declaration of Breda and in the Declaration Concerning Ecclesiastical Affairs. The third major faction, which was probably smaller than the second,[177] displayed complete dissatisfaction with the two Declarations and with the policy being followed by the Baxter group.

Despite the state of indecision existing at the end of the first year of the Stuart Restoration, much had happened since April, 1660. From April 4, 1660, Charles II was on record as favoring some religious concessions to the Presbyterians. This commitment became stronger during the course of the year. With each step the king came into greater opposition from the Anglicans. It was with great difficulty that Charles carried the negotiations between the Presbyterians and Anglicans far enough to issue his Declaration Concerning Ecclesiastical Affairs, which further committed the court to a policy of comprehending the Presbyterians within the Established Church, by royal dispensation if need be. This development, probably not anticipated by Charles and his advisers in April, was necessitated by the failure of the Presbyterians to win control of the Convention Parliament and by the king's desire to retain a substantial degree of personal authority over church affairs. As the time for a new parliament approached all parties girded themselves for an anticipated assault on the king's position and on the livings still held by the nonconformists.[178]

VII. THE ACT OF UNIFORMITY

The second year of the Stuart Restoration opened with the final religious settlement much in doubt. The king had gone on record in his Declaration Con-

---

[167] See John Douch, *Englands Jubilee* . . . (London, 1660); and John Sudbury, *A Sermon Preached at the Consecration of . . . Gilbert Lord Bishop of London* . . . (London, 1660).

[168] Anonymous, *Complaints Concerning Corruptions and Grievances in Church-Government* (n.p., 1660).

[169] Crofton, *The Fastning of St. Peters Fetters.*

[170] Crofton, *Berith Anti-Baal;* J. A. Dodd, "Troubles in a City Parish under the Protectorate," *English Historical Review* **10**: pp. 41–54, for biographical details.

[171] Matthews, *Calamy Revised*, p. 63.

[172] Thomas Bolde, *Rhetorick Restrained* . . . (London, 1660). Crofton encouraged Bolde to write this work.

[173] John Gauden, *Considerations Touching the Liturgy of the Church of England* . . . (London, 1660), pp. 5, 33.

[174] G[iles] F[irmin], *The Liturgical Considerator Considered* . . . (London, 1661). This work carries a preface by Crofton.

[175] Zachary Crofton, *A Serious Review of Presbyters Reordination* . . . (London, 1661).

[176] Burnet, *History of His Own Times* **1**: p. 236; Matthews, *Calamy Revised*, lists those who later renounced their ordination.

[177] Louise Fargo Brown, "The Reconcilers and the Restoration, 1660–1662," *Essays in Modern English History in Honor of Wilbur Cortez Abbott* (Cambridge, Mass., 1941), pp. 64–65, estimated the Crofton group as the largest single block.

[178] But see Baxter's summary, *Reliquiae Baxterianae*, Pt. II: p. 286.

cerning Ecclesiastical Affairs of October 25, 1660, as favoring a policy of comprehending the Presbyterians within a vastly modified Anglican Church, but each succeeding month saw both the king and the Presbyterians losing ground to the intransigency of the Laudians, who favored the Laudian conformity. The Savoy Conference, which was summoned to revise the Book of Common Prayer and to propose alternate forms for the use of the Presbyterians, terminated in complete failure. The Cavalier Parliament and the convocation of 1661, which were dominated by Anglicans, began at once to undermine the policy of the king and the hopes of the Presbyterians. A parliamentary attempt of 1661 to compel all ministers to accept a Laudian settlement or to surrender their offices to Anglicans was defeated by the king when he adjourned the parliament, but a similar effort in the second session of the Cavalier Parliament resulted in the Act of Uniformity of 1662, under which the nonconformists were ejected on August 24, 1662. In a final effort to save the nonconformists from persecution, Charles II resorted to a prerogative dispensation of the Act, but even this was denied him by the Anglican commons. By March 16, 1663, the Presbyterians had come to prefer their ejection of the previous August to the king's indulgence plan, and by the same date Charles and Clarendon had realized the futility of their efforts.

The king's strategy of 1661 was a logical continuation of his efforts which produced the Declaration Concerning Ecclesiastical Affairs of the previous October. It will be recalled that the Declaration promised that a conference of Presbyterians and Anglicans would be summoned for the purpose of revising the Prayer Book and of proposing alternate forms of worship for the use of the Presbyterians. On April 8, 1661, twelve representatives, plus alternates, of each party assembled in the Master's Lodgings at the Savoy in the Strand, London. For four months the two groups debated what changes, if any, should be made in the Prayer Book and whether additional forms of worship should be authorized.

Most of the known significant material on this fatal conference has been available in print since the publication of Baxter's autobiography in 1696. Despite periodic searches for additional evidence on the Savoy Conference, historians have not been able to add much to the detailed narrative provided by Baxter.[1] Since the detailed story gains nothing by retelling, no attempt is made here to rephrase what is already well known.

It is desirable, however, to call attention to several features of the Savoy Conference which are often overlooked and which bear significantly on the re-

ligious settlement of 1662. Calamy and Reynolds, who made the Presbyterian nominations, included Baxter in the list of representatives over his objections. Baxter and others were not entirely pleased with the selections of Calamy and Reynolds. Several of the Presbyterians attended very rarely, and some not at all. Dr. Horton never attended; Dr. Tuckney and Dr. Lightfoot only once or twice; Woodbridge went no more than three times. Among those who participated there was considerable disagreement. Samuel Clarke brought in a long paper which was thrown out. Many of Baxter's exceptions to the Prayer Book were discarded. Long before the conference ended, Reynolds deserted the Presbyterians and took a seat with the bishops.[2] Matthew Newcomen left in despair prior to May 21 when he urged Baxter to aid in the compilation of a "History of the Nonconformists."[3] Baxter dominated his party to the disadvantage of their cause. The absence or early departure of his colleagues can only mean that they recognized the futility of further argument or that they disapproved of his tactics,[4] and the latter possibility is not a strong one. It is inconceivable that the bishops did not take the Presbyterian apathy, doubts, and dissensions into account when they rejected nearly all the Presbyterian papers. In the end both sides agreed to report to Charles in the following pathetic tone:

that we were all agreed on the ends for the Churches welfare, Unity, and Peace, and for his Majesty's Happiness and Contentment; but, after all our debates, were disagreed of the Means.[5]

Although the failure of the Savoy Conference affected adversely the king's policy of comprehension and the hopes of the Presbyterians, it was by no means solely responsible for the final settlement. Even while the Savoy Conference was in progress, it became increasingly apparent that the success of the conference would not save the king's policy or the Presbyterians. The real causes for the expulsion of the Presbyterians in 1662 are to be found in the convocation of 1661 and the Cavalier Parliament.

Charles II summoned the convocation with some reluctance. In fact, he delayed the writs from February 15, when the parliamentary writs were issued, until April 10, and even then issued them only because of pressure from the Anglicans.[6] The elections proved that the court's fears had been justified, for the Presbyterians constituted a definitely minority party within

---

[1] See Stoughton, *History of Religion* 3: pp. 154–192; Powicke, *Richard Baxter*, pp. 198–204; Bosher, *Restoration Settlement*, pp. 226–230.

[2] See Baxter, *Reliquiae Baxterianae*, Pt. II: pp. 303–368, for the papers and arguments.
[3] M[atthew] N[ewcomen] to Richard Baxter, May 21, 1661, Baxter MSS, Letters V, No. 281.
[4] Dr. Henry Ferne to [Sir Thomas Osborne], July 29, 1661, B.M., Add. MSS 28,053, foll. 1–2; Bosher, *Restoration Settlement*, p. 229.
[5] Baxter, *Reliquiae Baxterianae*, Pt. II: p. 357.
[6] Bosher, *Restoration Settlement*, pp. 213–214.

the convocation. "Wee have also," reported Edward Bowles from the province of York, "chosen here or rather they, for few that are called Presbyterians concerned themselves in the election and the choice is accordingly. But our clerkes only say Amen to Canterbury province, so that is not much materiall."[7] The story was much the same in Canterbury. Baxter and Calamy were chosen by the London clergy, but Bishop Sheldon "excused" them. Baxter's summary of the elections makes it clear that the Presbyterians were partly responsible for their defeat:

Those ministers . . . ordained without Diocesans were in many counties denied any voices in the election of Clerks for the Convocation. By all which means, and by the scruples of abundance of ministers who thought it unlawful to have anything to do with the choosing of such a kind of assembly, the Diocesan party wholly carried it in the choice.[8]

For several weeks Charles prevented this Anglican convocation from upsetting the Savoy Conference by withholding the necessary authorization to transact business. On June 7 Charles authorized the convocation "to consult of matters relating to the settlement of the Church" and twelve days later to revise the canons. Even then he warned the leading figures of the convocation against taking any significant action.[9] Nevertheless, convocation stood poised for action as soon as circumstances would permit.[10]

When the Cavalier Parliament convened on May 8 it, too, was Anglican in composition.[11] This fact became very apparent when the commons prescribed that each member receive the sacrament according to the Anglican form or be disqualified.[12] This was followed by the more drastic measure of May 17 commanding the public burning of the Solemn League and Covenant by the common hangman.[13] On May 30 a bill was brought in to restore the bishops to their bench in the lords, and on June 14 it was sent to the lords, where it received final approval four days later.[14]

The commons also disregarded the concurrent sessions of the Savoy Conference and the king's policy, as laid down in his Declaration Concerning Ecclesiastical Affairs, by attempting to wrest control of the religious settlement from him. On June 25, while the Savoy Conference was still considering the liturgy, the Commons appointed a committee to review all legislation on liturgy for the purpose of bringing in a "compendious Bill to supply any defect in the former laws, and to provide for an effectual conformity to the Liturgy of the Church for the time to come." The same committee was also instructed to study the question of ecclesiastical courts and "to prepare a Bill for Settling the same."[15] On July 27, the latter bill received the approval of the lords. It restored all the ordinary ecclesiastical courts suspended by the Declaration of the previous October, but eliminated the court of high commission, the ex officio oath, and the canons of 1641, which had troubled Anglicans as well as Puritans.[16]

A more direct attack on the royal policy was contained in the Bill of Uniformity, which passed the commons on July 9.[17] When Charles II adjourned the Cavalier Parliament on July 30, the lords, despite pleas from the lower house, had taken no action on the Bill of Uniformity.[18] A plausible explanation for the failure of the lords to act on the measure is that the king and his lord chancellor intervened to prevent the Cavalier Parliament from further upsetting their policy of comprehension and toleration.

The general political situation was much altered, however, when the Cavalier Parliament met for its second session on November 20. The Savoy Conference had ended in failure; rumors of nonconformist plots circulated throughout the kingdom; the Presbyterians were once again associated with rebellion in the minds of many.[19] As resentment against nonconformity spread, important Presbyterian laymen broke with the Presbyterian ministers.[20] These developments, concern about financial and other measures, and the Anglican feeling displayed by the commons in the first session led the king to alter his tactics but not his objective. In his address of November 20, Charles admitted that the religious problems had proved "too hard" and surrendered the initiative to the Cavalier Parliament.[21]

The commons lost no time in taking control of the religious question. Sir Thomas Meres read a "Bill for confirming the Act of the last assembly concerning Ministers."[22] The bill in question was that

---

[7] Edward Bowles to Richard Baxter, May 11, 1661, Baxter MSS, Letters IV, No. 128.

[8] Baxter, *Reliquiae Baxterianae*, Pt. II: p. 333.

[9] Dr. Henry Ferne to [Sir Thomas Osborne], July 29, 1661, B.M., Add. MSS 28,053, foll. 1–2.

[10] For summary treatments of the convocation see Bosher, *Restoration Settlement*, pp. 213–216, 230–231, 244–249; and Stoughton, *History of Religion* 3: pp. 147–192.

[11] See Wilbur C. Abbott, "The Long Parliament of Charles II," *English Historical Review* 21: pp. 21–56, 254–285, for a good discussion of this parliament.

[12] *Commons Journals* 8: p. 247; Andrew Newport to Sir Richard Leveson, May 30, 1661, H.M.C., *Fifth Report, Appendix, Part I*, p. 160.

[13] *Commons Journals* 8: p. 254; Andrew Newport to Sir Richard Leveson, May 18, 1661, H.M.C., *Fifth Report, Appendix, Part I*, p. 160. The vote on this question was 228 to 103.

[14] *Commons Journals* 8: pp. 261, 263, 266–267, 268, 270; *Lords Journals* 11: pp. 279, 281, 283.

[15] *Commons Journals* 8: pp. 279–280.

[16] *Ibid.*, p. 300; *Lords Journals* 11: p. 323.

[17] *Commons Journals* 8: pp. 285, 288–289, 295–296.

[18] *Lords Journals* 11: pp. 305, 308.

[19] Sir Edward Nicholas to Earl of Clarendon, September 13, 1661, B.L., Clar. MSS 75, fol. 191.

[20] Sir Richard Brown, Lord Mayor of London, made a point of displaying his desertion of the Presbyterian ministers; see Dr. Thomas Smith's letters of May 20 and July 9, 1661, to Daniel Fleming, H.M.C., *Le Fleming MSS*, pp. 27–28.

[21] *Lords Journals* 11: pp. 332–333.

[22] *Commons Journals* 8: pp. 321–322.

authored by Prynne. Both Charles II and Clarendon had publicly praised Prynne's measure, which was enacted in 1660, and the court may have been behind the motion to confirm it. When finally passed by the commons on January 8, 1662, Meres's bill carried fifteen amendments which completely negated the intent of the original bill. The most important amendment provided that only those ministers who were in episcopal orders by March 25, 1662, and who administered communion according to the Book of Common Prayer might be retained in their livings.[23] Everyone realized, of course, that the amended bill would mean the removal of nearly all the Presbyterian ministers. For three weeks the lords, definitely under pressure from the court, refused to discuss the bill. On January 29, following an admonition from the lower house, the lords read the bill a second time. A motion was made at once to replace this bill with one to confirm without change the Act of 1660, which had specifically provided for the retention of those ministers not episcopally ordained and for the omission or modification of various sections of the Book of Common Prayer, but this motion failed on a tie vote. Five days later, however, the lords reversed their vote, and passed a bill to confirm the Act of 1660 without change.[24]

The sole reason for this reversal was the court's influence, exercised through the lord chancellor during the debates of a committee of the whole House of Lords on February 3. The only full account, which is well substantiated by less complete sources, is contained in Dr. Peter Pett's letter of February 8 to Archbishop John Bramhall of Ireland:

There have been great animosities lately, and heats in the House of Lords about the bill for the confirmation of ministers that passed in the last Parliament of England. . . . At first all the Bishops in the House of Lords were against it, and most of the Protestant Lords Temporal. But my Lord Chancellor was resolved to oblige the Presbyterians by keeping the Act from being repealed, and at last got seven of the Bishops to join with him, five of which I have not forgot the names of, and they were the Bishops of London, Norwich, Exeter, Lincoln, Worcester. The Duke of York was likewise brought over by his father-in-law, and the Earl of Bristol was vehement in the thing, and all the Popish Lords.

From this letter, then, it is clear that the official policy still favored comprehension and the retention of the Presbyterians in their livings, that at first the bishops uniformly opposed any compromise law but that pressure from the court changed the votes of Sheldon, Reynolds, Gauden, Sanderson, and Morley, and that the Catholic lords supported Clarendon and the Presbyterian lords.

How strongly did Clarendon and Charles feel about their policy? The answer to this question is also found in Pett's letter:

Some of the Commons going to the King the day before, to desire him to express himself positively against the confirmation of ministers, he said he had promised them at Breda the continuance in their livings; whereupon they said that the Commons might possibly, many of them, be tempted not to pass the Bill intended for the enlarging of his revenue, if his Majesty would favour the confirmation of the Presbyterian ministers: to whom the King answered that if he had not wherewith to subsist two days, he would trust God Almighty's Providence rather than break his word.

Thus, by defying the commons, Charles ran the risk of no additional revenue. The Presbyterians were so elated that they sent Calamy, Baxter, and Bates on February 3 to thank the lord chancellor. Not so the unhappy commons who refused to accept the revised bill.[25]

Having lost the parliamentary battle over the bill to confirm the Presbyterians in their livings, the king and his chancellor next attempted to accomplish the same purpose by amending the Bill of Uniformity. The lords took up the measure on January 14, 1662. Read a second time on January 17, the measure was referred to a committee, with instructions to delay action until the submission of the revised Book of Common Prayer.[26] When the Book was finally approved by the lords on March 17, they returned to the Bill of Uniformity.[27] Clarendon at once informed the lords that he wished to present a "proviso recommended by the King, to be inserted in this Bill of Uniformity." [28] The royal proviso spoke of the king's personal obligation to fulfill the promises which he made at Breda for a "liberty to tender Consciences" and of his desire for such an "indulgence as may consist with the good and peace of the Kingdome," for he "would not have a greater severity exercised towards them then what is necessary for the publique benefit and welfare." The proviso proposed to grant the king authority to retain any minister who was possessed of a living on May 29, 1660, by exempting him from wearing the surplice and from signing with the cross in baptism, so long as the minister employed another clergyman to baptize those persons who desired the Anglican ceremony. Nor was an exempted minister

[23] Ibid., pp. 325–326, 330–334, 341.
[24] Lords Journals 11: pp. 364, 372–373, 376.

[25] Dr. Peter Pett to Archbishop John Bramhall, February 8, 1662, The Rawdon Papers, ed. Edward Berwick (London, 1819), pp. 136–139. See also John Parker, Bishop of Elphin, to Archbishop John Bramhall, February 15, 1662, H.M.C., Report on the Manuscripts of the late Reginald Rawdon Hastings, Esq. of the Manor House, Ashby De La Zouch (4 v., London, 1928–1947) 4: p. 126; hereafter cited as Hastings MSS; and Henry Gregory, "The Returne & Restauration of King Charls the Second," B.M., Add. MSS 19,526, fol. 48; and Commons Journals 8: p. 367.
[26] Lords Journals 11: pp. 363, 366, 383, 390, 406, 407, 408. Convocation completed the revision on December 20, 1661, but the Book was not ready for the privy council until February 24, Privy Council Register, Public Record Office, PC 2/55, foll. 549, 552, 554. See Bosher, Restoration Settlement, pp. 244–249, for a summary of the revisions.
[27] Lords Journals 11: pp. 392–393.
[28] Ibid., p. 409.

to write or to speak against the liturgy, rites, or ceremonies of the Church of England.[29] Although the desired indulgence concerned only two relatively minor points, the entire proviso was so vaguely worded that any statute embodying it would have enabled the king to create a nonconformist branch of the Church of England by letters of dispensation to individual ministers, which was exactly what Clarendon had attempted to do wholesale by amending the bill to confirm ministers.

Although passed by the lords on April 9 with only slight modification,[30] the king's proviso did not go unchallenged in the lords. In fact, the lord chancellor never encountered more opposition than on this occasion. According to Secretary Morice, whose account should be reliable, especially when confirmed by other sources, the proviso was read without opposition, but on the second day the Earl of Bristol instigated "sum heates . . . as great as ever were in 41, 42, or 43." Bristol centered his objections around the technical point that it was unparliamentary for the king to take notice of any activity in the lords and the charge that the king had never seen the document in question. This hit directly at all the king's advisers. Therefore, Ormonde, Southampton, and York, along with most of the house, rose in defense of Clarendon, themselves, the king, and the measure. Bristol's real objection became obvious on the third day when he proposed to empower the king to dispense with the hearing of the Common Prayer, and thus to give relief to the Roman Catholics if he chose. Even Cosin, who had supported Bristol on the previous day, spoke against this vague but threatening proposition. On the second and third days of debate, Bristol and Clarendon hurled threats at each other, and on one occasion Bristol delivered a sharp lecture in the Duke of York's direction.[31] Clarendon had the support of Sheldon, Morley, Gauden, Reynolds, the Presbyterian lords, and his own court peers; Bristol, Cosin, "some other bishops and lay peers" formed the opposition.[32] The evidence points to the conclusion that Clarendon carried the king's measure by only a slight margin and after doing serious damage to the court party in the lords.

This conclusion is sustained by the failure of the lord chancellor to carry an amendment concerning the Covenant which was of almost equal importance to

the court and to the Presbyterians. A clause requiring that each minister renounce the Covenant was already in the Bill of Uniformity when Clarendon moved on April 4 that the reference to the Covenant be "expunged out of the Act." This motion led to the creation of a committee of bishops to study the Covenant and to report whether it contained anything that should not be renounced. The bishops having reported contrary to the lord chancellor's wishes that there was nothing of value in the Covenant, the lords voted 39 to 26 against Clarendon's proposal.[33] Morley, Clarendon's only real friend among the bishops, attempted to soften the provision against the Covenant by an explanatory clause, but even this was defeated. The only important amendment, besides the dispensing claims, which Clarendon and his party managed to pass, was one to authorize the king to provide an allowance of fifths to any minister ejected under the Bill of Uniformity.[34]

The debates and votes proved beyond doubt that the court could not force all its policy of comprehension through the lords. Extreme pressure from the court and anti-Bristol feeling provided Clarendon with the votes of seven bishops and some lay peers on the king's proviso, but it failed to block condemnation of the Covenant. It is altogether possible that Clarendon and his supporters, including the Presbyterians, were attempting to prolong the debates on religion until such time as the revenue and other measures could be enacted and parliament adjourned.[35] If so, the attempt was frustrated by deliberate delays in the House of Commons on the revenue and other essential measures.

On April 10 the Bill of Uniformity with the dispensing and fifths clauses and a multitude of small amendments went back to the commons, where it remained for twenty days. The *Journals* record six divisions on the measure during these twenty days. On each occasion the Anglicans won by margins ranging from three to thirty-five. In view of the larger margins in the first session and earlier in the second session on similar measures, it must be concluded that Clarendon and the court were exerting tremendous pressure in behalf of the amendments made by the lords. Charlton, who led in the conference for the lower house, stated as clearly as he dared that the commons would not tolerate any lessening of the uniformity and conformity required in their Bill of Uniformity, the wishes of the king and lord chancellor notwithstanding.[36] The Venetian resident in London had pre-

[29] Printed in H.M.C., *Seventh Report, Appendix* (London, 1878), pp. 162–163, along with the alterations made in the Lords. A draft copy in Clarendon's hand is in the B.L., Clar. MSS 76, fol. 162.

[30] *Lords Journals* 11: p. 425.

[31] Sir William Morice to Sir George Downing, March 21, 1662, B.M., Add. MSS 22,919, fol. 203.

[32] Dr. Edward Lake to Archbishop John Bramhall, April 4, 1662, H.M.C., *Hastings MSS* 4: pp. 129–130; Dr. Peter Pett to Archbishop John Bramhall, March 21, 1662, *The Rawdon Papers*, pp. 140–144; Sir Edward Seymour to Lady Anne Seymour, March 22, 1662, H.M.C., *Fifteenth Report, Appendix, Part VII*, p. 94; Francesco Giavarina to Doge and Senate, March 21/31, 1662, *Calendar of State Papers, Venetian* 33: pp. 124–125.

[33] Dr. Edward Lake to Archbishop John Bramhall, April 4, 1662, H.M.C., *Hastings MSS* 4: pp. 129–130.

[34] *Lords Journals* 11: pp. 421–425; Morley's explanatory clause is printed in H.M.C., *Tenth Report, Appendix, Part VI* (London, 1885), p. 177, and the fifths proviso appears on p. 163.

[35] Dr. Edward Lake found this view to be generally held; see his letter of April 4, 1662, to Archbishop John Bramhall, H.M.C., *Hastings MSS* 4: pp. 129–130.

[36] *Commons Journals* 8: pp. 402–417; *Lords Journals* 11: pp. 446–450.

dicted this stand on March 21 when he said that the king's proviso would never pass the commons "on account of the animosity of the majority there against the Presbyterians and of their rancour against the Chancellor, for which reason they would always oppose any deliberation which they knew him to favour." [37]

Faced with such determination on the part of the commons, and concerned about the outcome of revenue and other measures, the court submitted to the wishes of the commons. On May 19, Charles II gave his consent to the Act of Uniformity. Clarendon's speech on that occasion hinted very strongly that the king was not surrendering his policy and that he would find other means of keeping the Presbyterians within the Church of England.[38]

The king's known intentions toward the Presbyterians, and the political and religious ambitions of various individuals and groups, produced an immediate resumption of the attempts to provide some relief for the nonconformists. Clarendon's failure to soften the terms of the Act of Uniformity afforded his enemies an opportunity to drive a wedge between the king and the chancellor and perhaps to gain the support of the nonconformists by proposing means by which the king might achieve his policy of comprehension and toleration. The debates in the lords had already produced a quarrel between Clarendon and Bristol and a division of the bishops into parties. Behind Bristol's difference with Clarendon was a Roman Catholic desire to obtain relief for Catholic and Protestant nonconformists simultaneously, for otherwise the Protestant dissenters would probably oppose any relaxation of the laws against Roman Catholics. As early as May 20 Bristol was described as "every day more and more adored by people as judging him to grow dayly more the King's favorite." Already, Bristol had "not very privately" lectured Charles on the state of the kingdom, attributing all the discontent and inadequate supply to Clarendon. Charles failed to reprove Bristol for his liberty of speech or to defend his chancellor. Dr. Peter Pett believed that Sir Henry Bennet, "no good friend of the Chancellor," had become a favorite and that the Presbyterians were "angry with the Chancellor for not having done so much." [39] Before the parliamentary adjournment, the Dutch minister remarked that Charles II dared not leave the Cavalier Parliament in session in his absence for fear of an attack on Clarendon.[15]

At least four different proposals for relaxing or evading the Act of Uniformity grew out of this state of discontent and political intrigue between May 1 and August 24, 1662. The first of these was drafted about May 1 by John Gauden, who felt inadequately rewarded by Clarendon and who was sympathetic to the nonconformists, for Bristol's use. This plan was first announced to Bristol in a letter of May 1:

... I have declared my latitude and indulgence to all sober Dissenters from the settled Religion of the Nation. It is but a scheme rough drawn as yet: a better hand may so polish and complete it, as it will fit not only the public interest of peace, but the private of men's consciences and those different persuasions, which they desire to enjoy without trouble, while they give no offence or perturbation to the public.[41]

Gauden contended that rigid enforcement of the Act of Uniformity might be disastrous, if not impossible. His plan called for both legislative and prerogative action, for he would not "propose any generall indulgence or tolleration much less against Law or otherwise then limited by a Law." His meaning is obscured, however, by the statement that the king should "determine & impose what shall bee thought by him fitt." Gauden apparently meant that certain portions of the Act of Uniformity would require alteration and that a permissive act should be passed granting the king certain powers but restricting the extent and direction to which those powers might be exercised. The Presbyterians should be comprehended by repealing the prohibition against the Covenant, the assent and consent clause in the subscription required of ministers, and the requirement of reordination; by dispensing with the wearing of the surplice in parish benefices; and by permitting ministers to employ others to administer the baptismal and sacramental rites to parishioners desiring Anglican forms. Independents and "other Sectaries," but not Presbyterians, should be allowed conventicles under specific license from the king.[42] Bristol, who was very much at Whitehall, probably conveyed the general principles, if not a copy, of Gauden's scheme to the king.

The second proposal touching upon the Act of Uniformity came from Sir Henry Bennet and differed radically from the other three in that it did not provide for an immediate evasion of the Act. Alarmed by the general discontent of the nonconformists and of the taxpayers and by the growing instability of Clarendon's government, Charles sought advice from Bennet, who

---

[37] Francesco Giavarina to Doge and Senate, March 21/31, 1662, *Calendar of State Papers, Venetian* 33: pp. 124–125.

[38] *Lords Journals* 11: pp. 471, 476.

[39] Dr. Peter Pett to Archbishop John Bramhall, May 20, 1662, *The Rawdon Papers*, pp. 163–165.

[40] De Wiguefort's Despatch, May 15, 1662, *Calendar of State Papers, Domestic, 1661–1662*, p. 372. See Feiling, *History of the Tory Party*, pp. 97–134, for a discussion of Clarendon's political difficulties.

[41] John Gauden, Bishop of Exeter, to Earl of Bristol, May 1, 1662, *Clarendon State Papers* 3: Appendix, pp. xcvi–c.

[42] [John Gauden?], "What measure ought to bee taken in Religion with relation to ye present junction of Affaires in England," B.M., Stowe MSS 180, foll. 61–62. This document contains all the general features mentioned in Gauden's letter to Bristol, and there is a striking similarity between the handwriting of the document and that of Gauden. In view of the fact that Bristol and Sir Richard Temple were working together some months later on an identical project, it is assumed that Gauden's paper went to Bristol and from Bristol to Temple, with Charles II being informed by Bristol. If the Stowe document was not written by Gauden, we are faced with five, rather than four, proposals.

held no important post, at some date prior to June 8. Charles was already considering a new declaration on religion, authored probably by Clarendon, when he consulted Bennet. The latter advised the king to enforce the Act of Uniformity until his government was stronger. The new militia act must be executed and, perhaps, additional standing forces raised. Once these things were accomplished, the king might safely declare that he would ask parliament to mitigate the Act of Uniformity.[43] Bennet's approach to the problem was eventually adopted by the king, but only after other schemes had failed.

Clarendon was the author of the third and fourth plans for easing the terms of the Act of Uniformity. The chancellor was almost certainly reacting to the activities of his enemies and to the discontent of the Presbyterians, but it is doubtful whether these factors did more than hasten Clarendon's proposals. Clarendon displayed considerable anguish when he attempted to persuade Baxter to reconsider his decision of May 25 to surrender his pulpit.[44] When a group of Presbyterians petitioned the king on June 2 for relief, Clarendon agreed to intervene with Charles for an indulgence.[45] Six days later the privy council summoned the judges of the Westminster courts and all available bishops to a meeting on the Act at Hampton Court on June 10. In the presence of Archbishop Juxon, Bishops Sheldon and Duppa, Chief Justice Bridgeman, Attorney General Palmer, Albemarle, Ormonde, Morice, Nicholas, and Charles II, Clarendon gave his support to a plan for the suspension of the Act for three months. The bishops, however, opposed this proposal, and the lawyers gave the opinion that Charles could not legally suspend the Act.[46]

In the fourth scheme for evading the Act of Uniformity, Clarendon and his followers turned from the idea of a general suspension of the law to a plan of indulgence to individual ministers. Clarendon and Albemarle, under instructions from Charles II, invited Manton, Bates, Calamy, and "some few more" to petition for individual letters of dispensation.[47] Their petition was unofficially presented to the king on August 20 while he and Clarendon dined with Albemarle at the Cockpit.[48] Charles assured the ministers that he would readily grant individual relief if he could discover a means of preventing bishops and patrons from exercising their legal right under the Act of presenting to benefices held by nonconformists. The king also encouraged the Presbyterians to retain their pulpits as long as possible.

Charles and Clarendon then attempted to secure the approval of the lawyers and the bishops. At some point between August 20 and 27 the question of a limited indulgence was submitted to the lawyers, who apparently sanctioned the technicalities involved but warned that the plan's success would require at least the tacit support of the bishops.[50] The Presbyterian petition of August 20 was then submitted to the privy council on August 27, three days after the Act was executed by the bishops, which ordered all the bishops in London to appear before the council on August 28. Unfortunately for the Presbyterians and the court, all the bishops except Sheldon and Seth Ward, who was too ill to attend the meeting, had gone into the country for the purpose of filling the pulpits being vacated by the nonconformists. Realizing that public opinion, the Act of Uniformity, the Cavalier Parliament, and a majority of his fellow bishops supported uniformity and conformity, Sheldon absolutely refused to participate in any evasion, however slight, of the letter of the Act of Uniformity. Clarendon quarreled bitterly with Sheldon and the Duke of York, whose Catholic inclinations and growing detachment from his father-in-law, led him to support Sheldon on this occasion.[51]

[43] Sir Henry Bennet to Charles II, n.d., Lister, *Clarendon* 3: pp. 198–201. Lister felt that the document was submitted between May 19 and August 24, but probably closer to the first than the second date. It seems more accurate to say that the letter was written prior to the decision of June 8 to call the judges and bishops before the privy council to advise on the legality of a possible suspension of the Act, Privy Council Register, Public Record Office, PC 2/56, fol. 6. If correct, this theory would place the date extremely close to May 19, or at least before Charles went to meet his bride. Bosher's view, *Restoration Settlement*, pp. 257–258, that Bennet advised against lenity does not seem justified if one considers the conditional style of the letter and Bennet's position at court.

[44] Thomas Bates to Viscount Massereen, n.d., B.L., Carte MSS 31, fol. 328. This letter was written about June 2, perhaps as late as June 8, rather than on June 16 as Bosher implied. Bosher's error arose from the fact that the letter was endorsed on June 16, the date of its arrival in Dublin. Bosher also mistranscribed the horrible signature as Pares; *Restoration Settlement*, p. 258, note 2.

[45] Letter of Intelligence to Sir Edward Nicholas from the Public Record Office, SP 29/56, fol. 6, as quoted by Bosher, *Restoration Settlement*, p. 258.

[46] Privy Council Register, Public Record Office, PC 2/56, fol. 6; Hyde, *Life* 2: pp. 303–304; Bishop George Morley to Earl of Clarendon, September 3, 1662, B.L., Clar. MSS 77, fol. 339. Bosher, *Restoration Settlement*, p. 269, confused Clarendon's account with the Whitehall meeting of August 28, and was unaware of the June 10 conference.

[47] Letter to John Thornton, n.d., B.L., Rawlinson Letters 109, fol. 87. The signature and date have been torn away, but the reference to the ejectments places the date after August 24. The general points of this letter are confirmed by Baxter, *Reliquiae Baxterianae*, Pt. II: pp. 429–430.

[48] Rugge, "Mercurius Politicus Redivius," B.M., Add. MSS 10,117, foll. 42–45; Hyde (Clarendon) in his *Life* 2: p. 299, omitted his role, and shifted the responsibility to Albemarle.

[49] Rugge, "Mercurius Politicus Redivius," B.M., Add. MSS 10,117, foll. 42–45; *Mercurius Publicus*, No. 35, p. 579, *Oliver Heywood's Life of John Angier*, p. 127; Martindale, *Life of Adam Martindale*, p. 167; Pepys, *Diary* 2: p. 306; Francis Chandler, "Diary," B.M., Add. MSS 24,485, fol. 22; Henry Newcombe, *The Diary of the Rev. Henry Newcombe from September 30, 1661, to September 29, 1663*, ed. Thomas Heywood (Manchester, 1849), p. 118.

[50] Dr. William Denton to Sir Ralph Verney, August 27, 1662, H.M.C., *Seventh Report, Appendix, Part I*, p. 484; Martindale, *Life of Adam Martindale*, p. 167.

[51] *Mercurius Publicus*, No. 35, p. 579; Daniel O'Neill to Duke of Ormonde, September 2, 1662, B.L., Carte MSS 32, foll. 3–4;

The court was thus forced to abandon any hope for immediate relaxation of the Act of Uniformity, but it accepted full enforcement grudgingly and with apprehension. Only York, Nicholas, and Bennet supported uniformity. Bennet may have had tongue in cheek when he explained his opposition to the proposed indulgence by stating that it would "certainly have disobliged [the Anglican party] and not gaine the other party which had been an unhappy midle to have affected." [52] Clarendon's opinion was that the unmitigated enforcement of the Act would "add more fewell to the matter that was before combustible enough. But wee are in, and must now proceede with steddynesse." [53] On this occasion the lord chancellor found himself allied with Countess Castlemaine who next to Clarendon was "the fiercest solicitor" for a prerogative dispensation of the Act and who quarreled with her royal lover for submitting to Sheldon.[54]

When the Act was enforced on August 24, 1662, most of the nonconformists retired quietly. The authority on the ejections has stated that 936 parish clergymen and 35 from academic and scholastic positions, or a total of 971, more than half of whom were Presbyterians, were affected by the Act.[55] Henry Newcomen and his Lancashire friends, who petitioned the king on August 28, resolved on September 5 "to sticke close to the publicke ordinances & not to separate" from the Church of England,[56] which seems to have been the general policy of the Presbyterians for the next year. Even the worried Nicholas voiced surprise and relief at the peaceful exit of the Presbyterians.[57]

Although a period of quiet followed the ejections, Charles II issued a Declaration of Indulgence on December 26, 1662, which has proved a mystery to historians. The most common explanation for the Declaration has been that it arose from a struggle for power between Bennet and Clarendon, that it was fashioned by Bennet, and that it was opposed by Clarendon.[58]

It is the opinion of this writer that each of these suppositions is incorrect in varying degrees.

What of the struggle for power theory? No real struggle occurred between Bennet and Clarendon prior to the Declaration. Entirely too much emphasis has been placed on a minor dispute early in September between the two men about the post office. What began as a true report that Bennet would soon replace the aged Nicholas as secretary of state grew into an unfounded rumor that a cabal headed by Bennet intended to take over the government at the expense of Clarendon, Southampton, Manchester, and Morice,[59] but Clarendon predicted Nicholas's retirement two weeks before it occurred. "I need not," he wrote on September 30, "tell you who is to succeed, their beinge but one man can be thought of." [60] While the gossip raged, Clarendon went unconcernedly about his legal visitation at Windsor.[61] On October 25, ten days after Bennet assumed office, the chancellor very carefully explained that "whatever other people discourse, my credit [is not] at all diminished with the King." [62] At no time prior to the Declaration did Clarendon complain of a loss of influence or power.

When and by whom was the Declaration of Indulgence conceived? Since it was a logical continuation of the basic principle pursued by Clarendon since 1642 and by Charles II since 1649, William Hooke, a Congregational minister with excellent court connections, was probably correct in thinking that the Declaration was "3 months forming up." [63] The earliest reference to the Declaration, however, is contained in Bennet's letter of December 16 to Ormonde. After complaining about the discontented dissenters, Bennet expressed a hope that "something for his Majestys security against them" would be prepared by the time the Cavalier Parliament assembled for its third session on February 18, 1663.[64] But why should Bennet rather than Clarendon

Bishop Gilbert Sheldon to Earl of Clarendon, August 30, 1662, B.L., Clar. MSS 77, foll. 319–320; Sir Edward Nicholas to Duke of Ormonde, August 30, 1662, B.L., Carte MSS 47, foll. 359–360.

[52] Sir Henry Bennet to Duke of Ormonde, September 9, 1662, B.L., Carte MSS 221, fol. 9.

[53] Earl of Clarendon to Duke of Ormonde, September 1, 1662, B.L., Carte MSS 47, foll. 3–4.

[54] Daniel O'Neill to Duke of Ormonde, September 2, 1662, ibid., 32, foll. 3–4.

[55] Matthews, Calamy Revised, pp. xii–xiv; the events of St. Bartholomew's Day are adequately treated in Stoughton, History of Religion 3: pp. 261–290.

[56] Newcombe, Diary, pp. 115, 119.

[57] Sir Edward Nicholas to Duke of Ormonde, September 13, 1662, B.L., Carte MSS 47, foll. 365–366.

[58] These views are advanced by Bosher, Restoration Settlement, p. 270; Lister, Clarendon 2: pp. 197, 211–212; Ogg, England in the Reign of Charles II, 1: p. 204; John Lingard, The History of England, from the first invasion by the Romans to the Accession of William and Mary in 1688 (10 v., Boston, 1883) 9: pp. 88–89; Ranke, History of England 3: p. 403; and Feiling, History of the Tory Party, pp. 116, 130; and are based

largely on Clarendon's Life 2: pp. 468–476, which on careful analysis does not seem applicable to 1662 or is badly garbled.

[59] Daniel O'Neill to Duke of Ormonde, September 13, 1662, B.L., Carte MSS 32, foll. 25–26; Daniel O'Neill to Duke of Ormonde, October 11, 1662, ibid., foll. 67–68; Daniel O'Neill to Duke of Ormonde, October 18, 1662, ibid., foll. 82–83; Sir Edward Nicholas to Duke of Ormonde, October 7, 1662, ibid., 47, foll. 371–372; Bishop John Hacket to Bishop Gilbert Sheldon, October 13, 1662, B.L., Tanner MSS 48, fol. 58; Comte d'Estrades to Louis XIV, October 9/19, 1662, Baschet Transcripts, Public Record Office, 31/3. As might be expected, these reports ranged from the possible to the ridiculous, and some of the rumors were undoubtedly started by Clarendon's enemies.

[60] Earl of Clarendon to Duke of Ormonde, September 30, 1662, B.L., Carte MSS 217, fol. 467.

[61] Daniel O'Neill to Duke of Ormonde, October 11, 1662, ibid., 32, foll. 67–68.

[62] Earl of Clarendon to Duke of Ormonde, October 25, 1662, ibid., 47, foll. 12–13. He was even more emphatic in a letter of November 1, Lister, Clarendon 3: pp. 228–229.

[63] William Hooke to John Davenport, March 5, 1663, Massachusetts Historical Society, The Mather Papers (Boston, 1868), p. 207.

[64] Sir Henry Bennet to Duke of Ormonde, December 16, 1662, B.L., Carte MSS 46, foll. 21–22.

inform Ormonde about this important policy matter? The answer is simple, but absent from every known account of the Declaration. From December 4 until March 13, 1663, the state of Clarendon's health ranged from total incapacitation to slight mobility. Between December 13 and January 17 the chancellor, by his own admission, could barely scrawl his name on legal dockets. As late as February 21 he remained confined to his chair and unable "to stirr." Not until March 17 did Clarendon resume his regular duties, but he was still complaining of partial disability on June 6.[65] Obviously, a man so indisposed could give little personal assistance or opposition to any program, but the lord chancellor's absence from business would naturally lead to speculation that he was either in disfavor or in opposition to the king's policies.

With his friend, adviser, and chancellor ill, Charles II turned to Bennet as the most likely instrument to execute a policy which Clarendon had approved and prosecuted since 1642. If rumors had not developed that Clarendon opposed the Declaration, posterity would know far less about the authorship of the document. Neither Bennet nor Clarendon discussed the matter in their correspondence with their mutual friend Ormonde until January 13 and 31 respectively. Despite the chancellor's confinement, Bennet personally conferred with him at least twice before submitting the document to the privy council. According to Bennet,

my lord Chancellor had it distinctly read twice to him, periode by periode, and *not only approved it but applauded the contents of it and assured mee it was entirely according to his minde. Your Grace may judge by this, how falsely it is suggested that his Lordship was not privy to it.*[66]

When Clarendon wrote Ormonde two weeks later public resentment toward the Declaration had become pronounced, but he did not contradict the essential points made by Bennet. He did assert, correctly it seems, that he was not consulted prior to Bennet's first visit. But consultation on a policy already adopted in June and August was hardly necessary. Clarendon made "many objections against severall parts" of the original draft and questioned its "seasonablenesse," but his approval of the principles was attested by his own silence. Bennet later returned with an amended draft which "hee thought would answere all [Clarendon's] objections" and with the king's decision to publish it then rather than later as Clarendon apparently suggested. Clarendon said he told Bennet that

by that time hee had writ as many declarations as I had done hee would find they are a very ticklish commodity and that the first care is to see that it shall doe no hurt.

Bristol, Ashley, and Bennet he thought responsible for the conception and execution of the project.[67] As for Clarendon's objecting to the Declaration, it seems very strange that of the nine letters written to Ormonde by Clarendon and his son between December 13 and March 7 only that of January 31 made any direct reference to the Declaration, and this one exception, as well as that of Bennet, failed to indicate any basic disagreement with the expressed policy.

The foregoing conclusion is well substantiated by the king's continued confidence in Clarendon. Contact and consultation between the two men naturally slackened during the most serious of Clarendon's seizures of gout, but at no point prior to March 12, when Clarendon went to the lords, did the king fail to seek the advice of his chancellor. Bennet consulted twice with Clarendon on the Declaration, and Charles was a frequent visitor at Worcester House. Early in February, for example, Charles, York, and Clarendon discussed the Irish situation at great length, and Clarendon was made responsible for sending instructions to Ormonde.[68] The king spent the afternoon of February 21 privately closeted with Clarendon,[69] returning at least once prior to February 28.[70] The committee on foreign affairs met at least once at Worcester House,[71] and after parliament met on February 18 and until March 12, when Clarendon returned to Whitehall, "frequent consultations," with the king present, were held in Clarendon's house.[72] Therefore, there is no reason to assume that Clarendon had been, or was being, cast aside; nor is there any evidence that he ever expressed any strong objection to the Declaration or the implementing bill.

The Declaration, and perhaps the implementing bill, was not carried by a small clique as most writers have assumed. On December 26 it was presented to the privy council. Present were Charles II, York, Albemarle, Manchester, Berkshire, Carlisle, Lauderdale, Hatton, Hollis, Ashley, Sir William Compton, Sir George Carteret, Sir William Morice, Sir Henry Bennet, and Sir Edward Nicholas,[73] and only Lauderdale

[65] M. Battailler to M. Lionne, December 4/14, 1662, Baschet Transcripts, Public Record Office, 31/3; Earl of Clarendon to Duke of Ormonde, January 13, 1663, B.L., Carte MSS 47, foll. 20–21; Viscount Cornbury to Duke of Ormonde, January 24, 1663, *ibid.,* foll. 22–23; Earl of Clarendon to Duke of Ormonde, January 24, 1663, *ibid.,* foll. 24–25; Viscount Cornbury to Duke of Ormonde, February 21, 1663, *ibid.,* foll. 30–31; Earl of Clarendon to Duke of Ormonde, June 6, 1663, *ibid.,* fol. 52.
[66] Sir Henry Bennet to Duke of Ormonde, January 13, 1663, B.L., Carte MSS 221, foll. 19–20; italics added.
[67] Earl of Clarendon to Duke of Ormonde, January 31, 1663, B.L., Carte MSS 47, foll. 34–35.
[68] Earl of Clarendon to Duke of Ormonde, February 7, 1663, Lister, *Clarendon* 3: pp. 234–238.
[69] Viscount Cornbury to Duke of Ormonde, February 21, 1663, B.L., Carte MSS 47, foll. 30–31.
[70] Earl of Clarendon to Duke of Ormonde, February 28, 1663, Lister, *Clarendon* 3: pp. 239–243.
[71] Sir Henry Bennet to Sir Richard Fanshaw, March 6, 1663, H.M.C., *Heathcote MSS,* p. 65.
[72] Pietro Ricardo Neostad to Alvise Sagredo, March 5/15 and March 12/22, 1663, *Calendar of State Papers, Venetian* 33: pp. 232, 237.
[73] Privy Council Register, Public Record Office, PC 2/56, fol. 261.

spoke against the measure.[74]   Oddly enough, Robartes, an alleged promoter of the plan,[75] was not even present; Nicholas, a member of the Clarendon faction, was not only present but apparently approved the Declaration.

The Declaration was really not a declaration of indulgence. Religion was only one of the subjects discussed, and no indulgence was specifically declared. The Declaration merely stated the king's views on religious persecution and his hope that some act would be passed in the forthcoming session to recognize his prerogative power to dispense with the Act of Uniformity and to alleviate the condition of Roman Catholics.[76]

When published on December 30, the Declaration failed to receive the acclaim anticipated. Even Bennet admitted that the thing

> which choques most people in it is the favourable mention of Roman Catholiques and the saying is much better then the doing it in the darke which by doing soe is reproach and scandal upon his Majesty which limited and qualified as it is in the Declaration will I hope bee noe longer accounted soe.[77]

Sheldon, never consulted on the matter, did not fear what he first learned of the Declaration,[78] but soon warned the king that he would "set up that most damnable and heretical doctrine of the Church of Rome, whore of Babylon." Sheldon made no direct reference to Protestant dissent, though it is possible that he included the nonconformists in his general condemnation of toleration.[79]

Reaction from the nonconformists varied. Neither Presbyterian nor Congregational ministers were consulted prior to December 26.[80] According to Richard Baxter, Charles II mistakenly assumed that all nonconformists would approve legalizing, if not extending, that liberty already granted to the Roman Catholics clandestinely. The Presbyterians flatly refused, however, to condone popery by supporting a measure which offered some freedom to Roman Catholics. Philip Nye, one of the Congregationalists consulted by the king

after issuing the Declaration, went to Baxter on January 2 and begged him to send thanks to the king. Baxter refused. Nye and his kind thereafter held Baxter and the Presbyterians responsible for the failure of the indulgence plan.[81] Several of the Presbyterians were summoned before the king, but they were never persuaded to support the Declaration. According to one report, a number of Presbyterian members of parliament deliberately avoided parliament until Charles dropped his plan.[82] As for the Congregationalists, they embraced the Declaration wholeheartedly.[83]

Despite the cool reception to the Declaration, the king decided to carry his plan to parliament. With Clarendon still confined to Worcester House, Charles II had to bear the burden of stating his case. In a short speech he informed parliament of his motives and announced his legislative wishes. In general, Charles asked for little more than Clarendon had advocated in the previous session.[84]

Three days later the commons voted to consider the Declaration and the king's speech on February 25.[85] Probably with a view to influencing the lower house, a bill to bestow a dispensing power on the king was read in the lords on February 23.[86] Undaunted by the upper house's action, the commons voted 269 to 30 to debate both the Declaration and the king's speech and then voted *Nemine contradicente* to render thanks for every section of the Declaration and speech except those parts touching on indulgence. The pro-indulgence faction, with Sir Richard Temple and Sir John Talbot as tellers, lost a vote to adjourn the debate by 161 to 119, and no division followed on the resolution against indulgence.[87] A committee headed by Sir Heneage Finch brought in a stiff address on February 27, which was made even stronger by amendments from the floor. The commons denied the king's claim to a prerogative power in religious matters; they also declared that indulgence would "establish Schism by a law," would increase "Sects and Sectaries," would lead to disturbance rather than quiet, and might "end in Popery." This message to the king, according to the *Journals*, passed without a division, which seems strange indeed in view of the strength displayed by the opposition only two days previously.[88] Charles II immediately insisted that there was some misunderstand-

[74] William Hooke to John Davenport, March 5, 1663, *The Mather Papers*, p. 207.

[75] Lister, *Clarendon* 2: p. 204, without giving any authority, maintained that Robartes attended the council when the question was debated.

[76] Printed with slight omissions in *English Historical Documents, 1660–1714*, ed. Andrew Browning (London, 1953), pp. 371–374.

[77] Sir Henry Bennet to Duke of Ormonde, December 30, 1662, B.L., Carte MSS 211, foll. 15–16.

[78] Bishop Gilbert Sheldon to Bishop John Cosin, December 26, 1662, *The Correspondence of John Cosin,* ed. George Ornsby (2 v., Surtees Society, 1869–1872) 2: pp. 101–102, in which he expressed more concern about a possible attack on the Church of England because of its wealth than on the Act of Uniformity.

[79] Bishop Gilbert Sheldon to Charles II, [January, 1663], Osmund Airy, "Notes on the Reign of Charles II," *British Quarterly Review* 77: pp. 332–333.

[80] William Hooke to John Davenport, March 5, 1663, *The Mather Papers,* p. 207.

[81] Baxter, *Reliquiae Baxterianae*, Pt. II: pp. 429–430.

[82] Pietro Ricardo Neostad to Alvise Sagredo, January 22/ February 1, 1663, *Calendar of State Papers, Venetian* 33: p. 229; William Hooke to John Davenport, March 5, 1663, *The Mather Papers,* p. 207. Charles ordered Calamy released from prison and apparently offered the Presbyterians benefices if they would support him.

[83] *Ibid.;* "A M[emorandum] of what yᵉ Independᵗ Ministers sayd to yᵉ Kinge, February 27, 1663," B.M., Sloane MSS 4107, foll. 16–20; Baxter, *Reliquiae Baxterianae*, Pt. II: pp. 429–430.

[84] Cobbett, *Parliamentary History of England* 4: pp. 258–260.

[85] *Commons Journals* 8: p. 438.

[86] *Lords Journals* 11: p. 482.

[87] *Commons Journals* 8: p. 440.

[88] *Ibid.*, pp. 442–443.

ing and implied that he would further explain his position when the address had been properly studied.[89]

Two days after the commons began considering the Declaration on February 21, the court opened an offensive in the upper house by submitting a proposal to grant the king's wishes. Accounts of this measure contain more fiction than fact. Briefly stated, the conventional story maintains that the measure was introduced by Robartes, that it was never committed, and that it was defeated because of Clarendon's opposition.[90] York, not Robartes, introduced the measure.[91] It was not short as Clarendon insisted. Phrases and provisions were lifted bodily from Clarendon's dispensation proviso of the previous session. It contained a specific prohibition against licenses for Roman Catholics and provided for the sanctity of the Book of Common Prayer and the Thirty-nine Articles by requiring use of the first and subscription to the latter before an archbishop or bishop. The implied toleration, as opposed to limited indulgence, was the major difference between this and Clarendon's proviso, and even this can be read into the Clarendon measure. At first the proposal contained a clause for authority to dispense with any statute on religion, but at the recommendation of the grand committee the lords restricted the measure to the Act of Uniformity of 1662.[92]

According to Clarendon, the proposed measure was never committed, but this is grossly false. It received a first reading on February 23, and a second reading and committal to a committee of the whole two days later. On February 27, with Manchester as chairman, the committee debated the title and preface, and the following day it ordered the attorney general to bring in a list of all acts and oaths connected with religion on March 5. Debate was adjourned on March 6 until March 12. Clarendon had not been present during the early proceedings, but he attended on March 12 and 13 when the proposal was discussed in a grand committee and sent to a subcommittee on the thirteenth.[93] No further mention of the matter occurs in the *Journals*.

The adjournment from March 6 to 12 and the appearance of Clarendon at the resumption of debate appear to be more than coincidence. First of all, the campaign in the commons had already failed. Part of this failure must be attributed to the Presbyterian members who shied from a general toleration and part to the normal reaction of staunch Anglicans to anything less than uniformity and conformity. However, "two of the greatest Proctors the Bishops had in the House

of Commons fell in with the Court Party."[94] Daniel O'Neill, Ormonde's contact with Clarendon and his agent in London, insisted that the lower house was "fond" of the Declaration until Bristol engaged Sir Richard Temple to manage the house for the king.[95] Bennet brought Coventry and Churchill over from Ireland, apparently with Clarendon's assent,[96] for the same purpose, and the commons bitterly resented this interference with their freedom of action. In the words of O'Neill, "all the honest party" joined together against the court and the undertakers.[97] Sir Philip Warwick, secretary of the treasury and a Southampton follower, implied the same thing when he wrote his brother-in-law on April 12.[98]

A second reason to believe that the adjournment in the lords and Clarendon's return to duty were more than coincidence comes from the activities of the king and the Roman Catholic party. Charles expressed considerable apprehension when he told the Congregational ministers on February 27 that "I shall at least keepe off the severity of persecution and hard proceedings if not at present give you your full liberty,"[99] and this was exactly what Clarendon did after his return. By March 5, the Queen Mother, Bristol, and others of the Roman Catholic party decided that further efforts in behalf of a legal indulgence would only result in vigorous persecution of themselves and their friends. Preferring to retain existing privileges rather than gamble for new ones, they advised the king to retire with as much honor as possible. At that time, however, Charles was refusing to retreat.[100] He soon found it necessary to drop his indulgence plan.

Clarendon's sudden appearance in the lords on March 12 came at the request of the king. Clarendon told the lords that the king, though still opposed to severity, desired parliament to proceed "as might seem best to them" and that the king would support and execute whatever parliament advised.[101] According to Comminges, the French ambassador, the chancellor's real mission was to secure a month's postponement of the measure introduced by York so that a satisfactory and honorable retreat could be arranged and revenue se-

[89] *Ibid.*, p. 451.
[90] See the works cited in footnote 58 of this chapter.
[91] William Hooke to John Davenport, March 5, 1663, *The Mather Papers*, p. 208.
[92] Printed in W. D. Christie, *Shaftesbury* 1: Appendix, pp. lxxix–xi; the version in H.M.C., *Seventh Report, Appendix, Part I*, pp. 167–168, summarizes the preamble and omits the closing sentences.
[93] *Lords Journals* 11: pp. 482–492.
[94] William Hooke to John Davenport, March 5, 1663, *The Mather Papers*, p. 207.
[95] Daniel O'Neill to Duke of Ormonde, June 20, 1663, B.L., Carte MSS 32, fol. 597.
[96] Sir Henry Bennet to Duke of Ormonde, January 13, 1663, *ibid.*, 221, foll. 19–20.
[97] Daniel O'Neill to Duke of Ormonde, June 20, 1663, *ibid.*, 32, fol. 597.
[98] Sir Philip Warwick to Sir Richard Fanshaw, April 12, 1663, H.M.C., *Heathcote MSS*, pp. 77–78.
[99] "King's Address to the Congregational Ministers, February 27, 1663," B.M., Add. MSS 4164, fol. 114.
[100] William Hooke to John Davenport, March 5, 1663, *The Mather Papers*, p. 207; the Roman Catholics began deserting the king about February 28, William Coventry to Duke of Ormonde, February 28, 1663, B.L., Carte MSS 47, fol. 397.
[101] Pietro Ricardo Neostad to Alvise Sagredo, March 19/29, 1663, *Calendar of State Papers, Venetian* 33: p. 238.

cured.[102] At least once, and perhaps twice, Clarendon spoke against the lower house's bill and proclamation against Jesuits and other priests,[103] and, in line with his master's promise to the Congregationalists, he prevented any action in the lords on the first Conventicle Bill. Moreover, Clarendon probably sponsored the attempt by the lords to liberalize the assent and consent provisions of the Act of Uniformity.[104]

The conclusive evidence on Clarendon's alleged opposition to the Declaration of Indulgence and the dispensation bill is contained in a document which he prepared as the king's reply to the lower house's address of February 27. Clarendon's document has immense importance because it gives the court's religious policy and interpretation of the constitution and because it clarifies Clarendon's position with regard to the Declaration of Indulgence and to York's bill.

What might be called the preamble paid the customary honors and respects due a parliament. It also expressed surprise that the commons should approve every section of the Declaration except those touching on religion. After weighing the advice of the commons against the pre- and post-Restoration counsel and conditions past and present, Clarendon defended the Declaration "as one of the best mediums that did occure for the settlement of this divided kingdome." Indulgence, he declared, was consistent with the "King's owne principles & inclinations, which alwayes dispose hym, especially in matters of Religion," to a policy of leniency.

Clarendon next proceeded to an explanation of the Declaration. The king would have it understood that he never intended a "generall Indulgence to all who may pretend to scruples in conforminge to the Religion Established"; he offered indulgence only to men of peaceable principles and of "true tenderness of conscience, which is not hard to be discerned from its counterfeit" by the king. Nor did Charles desire toleration to be made a right. Instead, he preferred that dissenters be granted only such conditional liberty as might be considered desirable and necessary. Dispensation on this basis would not give the nonconformists any "encouragement to continue their unconformity" but would eventually return them to the Anglican fold. Moreover, the king considered himself bound by the Declaration of Breda and by considerations for the public security to grant the liberties outlined in his Declaration of Indulgence. As for the argument that the promises made at Breda were not binding, Clarendon stated categorically that the king considered them obligatory and expressed the opinion that the entire kingdom was under a similar obligation.

Another section of Clarendon's paper dealt with the constitutional principles involved. Although Charles recognized at Breda that he did not possess sufficient power to accomplish all that he wished for nonconformists, he did not think himself without some prerogative over religious matters. In Clarendon's words, Charles knew "what power his royal predecessors have exercised in all Ages by virtue of their supreme authority in Ecclesiastical Affairs," and under this interpretation of the constitution had issued his Declaration Concerning Ecclesiastical Affairs of October 25, 1660. This, of course, implied that the Declaration Concerning Ecclesiastical Affairs should constitute a precedent. Since no one had questioned the dispensation of 1660, the king doubted whether the commons proposed to deny him rights which "former times have looked upon as inseparably annexed to the Crowne." Nor did he

conceive that the passing of the late Act of Uniformity did neither disenable hym from making good his promise, or abridge hym in the exercise of any power he had before, for then as well for his word sake, as to preserve the rights of the Crowne, he had been necessitated not to passe that Act.

On the contrary, the Act of Uniformity was considered a prerequisite to indulgence, which could not precede the definition and the establishment of the thing from which exemption was to be granted.

Having answered the general objections of the commons, Clarendon turned to the more detailed points. He denied that it would be unwise for parliament to amend or to provide for indulgence from the Act of Uniformity. He asserted that Charles, and perhaps parliament, had underestimated the number of nonconformists. As for the charge of creating schism by law, Clarendon cited the statute of 13 Elizabeth as proof that previous parliaments had not considered that religious differences permitted through legal dispensation constituted schism. The question was not whether dissent could be stamped out or even contained; the real problem was keeping the dissenting groups from combining against the Established Church and perhaps the civil government. Persecution would never exterminate dissent. On the contrary, "an indispensible execution of the Lawes upon them all alike [would] unite them . . . in an opposition to what is setled." Annex the moderate dissenters to the Church of England and the government by indulgence and there would be no combination by nonconformists for general toleration or for a second religious establishment. Clarendon urged relaxation of the penal laws against Roman Catholics, but he denied that the Declaration intended to grant them liberty of worship or eligibility for office. If the commons persisted in their attitude, the king would be forced to seek a larger revenue in order to provide for the forces which would be required to enforce the Act of Uniformity.[105]

[102] Christie, *Shaftesbury* 1: pp. 267–268.
[103] William Denton to Sir Henry Verney, March 26, 1663, H.M.C., *Seventh Report, Appendix, Part I*, p. 484; Pietro Ricardo Neostad to Alvise Sagredo, April 2/12, 1663, *Calendar of State Papers, Venetian* 33: p. 241.
[104] *Lords Journals* 11: pp. 573, 577.
[105] [Earl of Clarendon], "Touching Liberty of Conscience," B.M., Sloane MSS 4107, foll. 260–264. The title given here is

In summary, Clarendon so far agreed with the Declaration of Indulgence and the implementing bill that he drafted, some time between February 27 and March 12, a message defending both, for he recognized the inevitable consequnces of the Act of Uniformity. Unless the various laws against dissent, whether Protestant or Roman Catholic, were executed moderately, the government would be forced into the uncooperating arms of an Anglican Church party. Neither king nor chancellor relished the thought of working with the thrifty, anti-court squires. Employed sharply, the Act of Uniformity would result only in a perpetuation, and perhaps an extension, of the Civil War factionalism; modified properly, and with sufficient curbs on Laudianism, it might lead eventually to the pre-Laudian Church of England in which Puritan and solid Anglican lived in communion with each other. Behind all this façade of public policy and public security was, however, a fervent desire to preserve intact all remaining instances of monarchical prerogative. This basic motivation, tempered only by considerations of political necessity, was explicit or implicit, in the Declaration of Breda, in the Declaration Concerning Ecclesiastical Affairs, in the king's proviso of 1662, in the Declaration of Indulgence, and in York's bill of 1663.

Clarendon may have objected to certain features of the Declaration of Indulgence and even to the persons employed by the king, but he was not the cause for the Declaration's failure. In fact, he continued to work toward the fulfillment of the policy expressed in the Declaration throughout 1663 at least. On August 11, 1663, Anglesey discussed religious policy with Clarendon and found him favoring moderation. The court was then considering a measure to extend "such liberty as may be safe to men of peaceable spirits, though they differ in judgment." [106] It was probably in 1663 that Clarendon set William Prynne to work on the task of displaying to public view the extent of the king's authority in religious matters,[107] and it was in 1663, rather than 1660, that Clarendon published his own defense of "a Limited Toleration." [108]

---

from a near contemporaneous endorsement. The document is a smooth draft with numerous interlineations and alterations and is completely in the hand of Clarendon. How the paper became separated from the other Clarendon manuscripts is a mystery, but the paucity of important manuscripts for this period in the Bodleian Library suggests that many of the chancellor's post-1660 manuscripts were intentionally removed from the main collection by Clarendon or some other person.

[106] Earl of Anglesey to Duke of Ormonde, August 11, 1663, H.M.C., *Calendar of the Manuscripts of the Marquess of Ormonde, New Series* (8 v., London, 1902–1920) **3**: p. 71.

[107] William Prynne, *An Exact Chronological Vindication and Historical Demonstration of Our . . . King's Supreme Ecclesiastical Jurisdiction . . .* (4 v., London, 1665–1670) **2**, "Epistle Dedicatory" to Clarendon.

[108] [Edward Hyde, Earl of Clarendon], *Second Thoughts; or the Case of Limited Toleration, stated according to the present Exigence of Affairs in Church and State* [London, 1663]. This work is dated 1660 or 1663 by libraries, but its content suggests 1663 as its date of publication.

Support for such schemes was not readily forthcoming, and in the face of contrary pressures the court soon lost heart for the struggle. The Presbyterian leadership retreated from any proposal which might benefit the Catholics. The events of 1663 drove the leading Catholics, with the exception of Bristol, into inactivity. By frustrating the hopes of the Presbyterians for inclusion within a broadened Church of England, the hopes of the Independents for toleration, and the policy of king and chancellor the Anglican House of Commons and the Laudian clergy helped to narrow the base of both the church and the monarchy.

VIII. SUMMARY

The brief success and power which the Presbyterians had enjoyed from 1643 to 1648 ended with Colonel Pride's Purge of the Long Parliament in December, 1648. Classis by classis the Presbyterian system collapsed, discouraged by the Cromwellian government and its policy of toleration for nearly every religious faction, and disliked even by some Puritan laymen for the tyranny of its clergy. By virtue of their heavy concentration in the army and government, the Independents effectively denied the Presbyterians the support of the civil power which was so essential to the establishment and maintenance of a national church.

The disappearance of the Presbyterian classical organizations meant the decay of practically all ecclesiastical discipline and government and of intercommunication among the parishes. Aware at last of their inability to enforce uniformity by rigid Presbyterianism, and prizing order in the church before any particular polity, many Presbyterians strove to compromise their differences with the Independents and Anglicans on nonessential principles and practices in the interest of a comprehensive and ordered religious system. They hoped for legislative adoption of any settlement which the various parties might agree upon, but they were willing to accept voluntary enforcement by the clergy. Their plans were opposed by the strict separatists among the Independents, by the rigid Presbyterians, and by the Laudian Anglicans. Toward the close of the Cromwellian period, the proposals for unification seemed on the verge of widespread adoption on the local, and perhaps on the national, level, but the alliance between the leading Independents and the army council in 1659 terminated all Presbyterian hopes of reaching an understanding with the total separatists.

From the time of Charles I's discussion with the Presbyterians at the Isle of Wight in 1648 and from Richard Baxter's conference with Archbishop Usher in 1654, Presbyterian discussions with the Low Church or moderate Anglicans indicated that the essential differences between the Presbyterians and Anglicans on matters of government might be resolved on the basis of Usher's plan to replace episcopacy by synodical government or by some less potent type of episcopacy.

Baxter and Usher came to essential agreement on ecclesiastical polity in thirty minutes. By 1659, the idea of modified episcopacy had gained many supporters among the Presbyterians and the moderate Anglicans, and the heavy Anglican participation in the voluntary county associations encouraged the Presbyterians to feel that the moderate Anglicans would willingly join in opposing the Laudians. The Presbyterians after 1659 felt they had more in common with the moderate Anglicans than with the Independents. It was not surprising, then, that the moderate Presbyterians in 1660 proposed the adoption of Usher's plan as the constitution of the Church of England.

In the realm of politics the Cromwellian period was marked by an increasing acceptance of Oliver and Richard by the Presbyterians. Although the Royalists had expected support from the Presbyterians after the execution of Charles I, the Presbyterians were predominantly apathetic to Charles II until May, 1659. They were passively obedient to Cromwell until 1654, but thereafter they gave the government increasing support. Oliver's growing conservatism, the stability of his government, and his gradual adoption of a more historic constitutional basis for his government were important factors in winning him Presbyterian adherents. Merchants and lawyers of necessity worked with Cromwell almost from the execution of Charles I. Presbyterian acceptance of Richard Cromwell exceeded that accorded his father. Baxter, Bowles, Reynolds, and others of the Presbyterian clergy paid open allegiance to Richard. Although there were Presbyterians among the opposition, Richard's support in the parliament of 1659 came largely from the Presbyterian ranks.

The events of April and May, 1659, forced the Presbyterians to seek a substitute for a government which they refused to accept. The army council dictated the dissolution of Richard's parliament in April and the protector's abdication in May. The army council and the Independents substituted the Rump Parliament for the Protectorate and returned to their Good Old Cause of republicanism and toleration. Many Presbyterians immediately rose in revolt in combination with the Royalists in August. Although successful in suppressing the Presbyterian-Royalist insurrection, the army council and Rump Parliament could not agree on constructive programs, and Lambert dissolved the Rump in October, by which time the Presbyterian clergy and laymen almost universally had broken with the Independents.

Lambert's seizure of power further united the Presbyterians and Royalists and brought General Monck into England with his Scottish forces. Many Presbyterian politicians were so eager to escape from the oppressive rule of Lambert and his army that they willingly discarded many of their political demands of the Civil War in exchange for royal assurances as to their personal safety and property. The most active of the Presbyterians were the nearly two hundred survivors of the Long Parliament who hoped to be the instruments of Charles's return. They competed with the Royalists and the Rumpers for Monck's support.

As Monck marched southward from Scotland he was harangued along the way by groups of Presbyterians bearing petitions and declarations favoring the restoration of the Long Parliament or the election of a new parliament. Lord Fairfax and the Yorkshire Presbyterians gave Monck their assurance of support. Monck reacted by summoning James Sharp to work with the Presbyterian clergy, and William Morice to organize the secluded members of the Long Parliament. On February 21, 1660, Monck allied himself with the secluded Presbyterians by protecting their entry into the House of Commons. Once in power, the Presbyterian politicians displayed considerable eagerness to see Charles II back in England. They proved more secular than their clerical friends and more anxious than Monck to recall the king. If Monck had not interfered the Long Parliament probably would have restored the king without calling the Convention Parliament. It might have provided for no qualifications for election to the Convention Parliament. At Monck's insistence, however, the Presbyterians agreed to dissolve the Long Parliament and to leave the future settlement to a parliament elected under restrictions calculated to disqualify many Royalists.

Between March 16, when the Long Parliament dissolved itself, and April 25, when the Convention Parliament assembled, important negotiations were carried on between the key politicians in power and the king. Hyde had already indicated the king's willingness to negotiate a treaty with the Long Parliament and had proposed the Uxbridge treaty as the basis for negotiations. When the Long Parliament dissolved, Hyde's proposal was automatically dropped. Monck, probably with the approval of the leading Presbyterians, suggested that the king grant toleration and amnesty, confirm land sales, and pay the military and naval forces. Six days later, on March 25, the Presbyterian London council urged essentially the same terms. A Presbyterian cabal composed of aspiring politicians negotiated for the king's acceptance of the Isle of Wight treaty, but the cabal's efforts were defeated through countless personal alliances between Presbyterian laymen, including the leading members of the council of state, and the king and by the general fear of republicanism and military and mob rule.

By April 25, an unconditional restoration of monarchy was almost assured, and the membership of the Convention Parliament insured that any terms imposed on the king would be mild. Before the Convention met a large number of the Presbyterians had agreed with the Royalist agents to accept the king's Declaration of Breda as the basis for his return. The entry of the young peers into the upper house frustrated Manchester's cabal, and the heavy Anglican and Royalist membership in the lower house prevented any conditions from being forced upon the king. There is definite evidence that Hyde, Charles, Monck, the king's agents, and the Presbyterian Royalists favored the enactment of bills on lands, religion, indemnity, and other questions, but the young Royalists joined with the embittered country squires to block all legislation prior to the king's return on May 29. After the king's return the Anglican Royalist party in the lower house of the Convention Parliament grew from a position of equality with the Presbyterians and Independents to one of superiority.

Faced with the inevitability of a Stuart Restoration and the probable return of episcopacy, the leading Presbyterian clergy gradually, and in some cases reluctantly, accepted modified episcopacy as the only likely substitute for Laudianism. The London clergy had seen their petition for Presbyterianism rejected by the Long Parliament and their lay support, even in London, steadily decline. Under the guiding hands of James Sharp and the Earl of Lauderdale from February 13 and later of Manchester, Broghill, Annesley, and Dr. George Morley, the leading Presbyterian clergy worked for inclusion in a modified Anglican Church. When they decided to send a delegation to Charles II on May 4, the Presbyterian clergy surrendered any hope of abolishing episcopacy and of totally reforming the doctrine and worship of Queen Elizabeth's Church of England. This decision also meant the division of the Presbyterian clergy into two major camps. Crofton was typical of the unbending group; Baxter of the compromisers.

From his return, the king and his government struggled for the adoption and implementation of the indulgence policy stated in the Declaration of Breda. There is no evidence that the court opposed the doctrinal portion of the parliamentary bill on religion, but the king undoubtedly objected to any interference with his personal control of the religious settlement. Step by step, Charles II and Hyde led the Presbyterians and Anglicans to discuss their differences. The bishops, who were predominantly Laudian, resisted the Presbyterians and the king at every point. Under pressure from the king both parties finally accepted the provisions of the king's Declaration Concerning Ecclesiastical Affairs of October 25, 1660, as a means of retaining the Presbyterians within the Established Church. Although the king had hoped to include the Independents and perhaps the Catholics in his Declaration, he had achieved his main objective of establishing his prerogative and of gaining time. The failure of the bill to convert the Declaration into law aroused the fears of the Presbyterians of their eventual defeat and the hopes of the Laudians for a final settlement more to their liking.

Hardly had the ink dried on the Declaration Concerning Ecclesiastical Affairs before it was under direct fire from its opponents. Despite the Declaration and an Act for Settling Ministers in their livings, several hundred ministers were ejected in 1660 and 1661. The Anglican Cavalier Parliament of 1661 and the Anglican Convocation immediately attacked the king's policy and the Presbyterians. The failure of the Savoy Conference on the Book of Common Prayer adversely affected the king's policy and the hopes of the Presbyterians for a comprehensive Church of England. Charles rescued the Presbyterians from the angry jaws of the Cavalier Commons in 1661 by adjourning parliament, but he was not so fortunate in 1662. After initial defeats in the upper house Charles and Clarendon succeeded in securing the adoption of a proviso to enable the king to retain nonconformists in the Established Church through dispensation or indulgence, but only after exerting all the court's influence on the bishops and the lay peers. The king's policy was thoroughly defeated by the House of Commons, who forced the king to accept the Act of Uniformity which called for its rigid execution against all who failed to conform.

From the passage of the Act of Uniformity on May 19, 1662, Charles II and Clarendon, with the support of the Presbyterians and others, endeavored to evade the act by various means. Opponents to Clarendon also presented plans for alleviating the conditions imposed by the Act of Uniformity. The court first tried a plan of suspending the Act for three months but retreated in the face of opposition from the bishops and the lawyers. The government next turned to a scheme for issuing individual letters of indulgence to the Presbyterian clergy, but it was defeated by the opposition of Bishop Sheldon. By St. Bartholomew's Day, August 24, 1662, approximately 1,800 nonconforming clergy had been ejected from their livings, of whom perhaps more than a thousand were Presbyterians.

Although the Presbyterians had supported his efforts to evade the Act of Uniformity by general suspension and by letters of dispensation, the king's Declaration of Indulgence of December 26, 1662, was opposed by the Presbyterians. Drafted by Sir Henry Bennet, amended by Clarendon, and approved by the privy council, the Declaration was too favorable to the Roman Catholics for the Presbyterians, who rejected the pleas of the king and the Independents to support it. Deserted by the Presbyterians and Catholics, resisted by the bishops, and denounced by the Anglican squires, Charles II had Clarendon kill the bill to implement his Declaration by sending it to a subcommittee of the House of Lords.

In the final analysis, the Presbyterians lost at the Stuart Restoration through their disunity, their numerical weakness, their indecision, their lack of a positive and consistent policy, and their unwillingness to support Charles II and Clarendon at the risk of gains for Catholics.

BIBLIOGRAPHY

PRIMARY MATERIALS

Manuscripts

Bodleian Library, University of Oxford
Carte Manuscripts
Clarendon Manuscripts
Rawlinson Manuscripts
Salway Deposit
Tanner Manuscripts
British Museum, London
Additional Manuscripts
Egerton Manuscripts
Harleian Manuscripts
Lansdowne Manuscripts
Sloane Manuscripts
Stowe Manuscripts
Dr. Williams' Library, London
Baxter Manuscripts, Letters
Baxter Manuscripts, Treatises and Papers
Doreen, Lady Brabourne, London
Sir Edward Dering's Diary
Public Record Office, London
Baschet Transcripts
Privy Council Register

Published Autobiographies, Diaries, Documents, and Letters

AIRY, OSMUND (ed.). 1884–1885. *The Lauderdale Papers* (3 v., London).

AXON, ERNEST (ed.). 1937. *Oliver Heywood's Life of John Angier of Denton* . . . (Manchester).

BAILLIE, ROBERT. 1841–1842. *The Letters and Journals of Robert Baillie.* . . . Edited by David Laing (3 v., Edinburgh).

BAKER, SIR RICHARD. 1655. *A Chronicle of the Kings of England* . . . . With a continuation by Edward Phillips (London).

BARWICK, PETER. 1724. *The Life of the Reverend Dr. John Barwick, D. D.* . . . (London).

BAXTER, RICHARD. 1696. *Reliquiae Baxterianae* . . . . Edited by Matthew Sylvester (London).

BERWICK, EDWARD (ed.). 1819. *The Rawdon Papers* . . . (London).

BIRCH, THOMAS (ed.). 1762. *A Collection of the State Papers of John Thurloe* . . . (7 v., London).

BRAMSTON, SIR JOHN. 1845. *The Autobiography of Sir John Bramston* . . . . Edited by P. Braybrooke (London).

BROWN, RAWDON, and ALLEN B. HINDS (eds.). 1864–1940. *Calendar of State Papers, Venetian* (38 v., London).

BROWN, T. 1702. *Miscellanea Aulica* . . . (London).

BROWNING, ANDREW (ed.). 1953. *English Historical Documents, 1660–1714* (London).

BURNET, GILBERT. 1833. *Bishop Burnet's History of His Own Time* . . . . Edited by M. J. Routh (2nd ed., 6 v., Oxford).

CARTE, THOMAS (ed.). 1739. *A Collection of Original Letters and Papers* . . . . *Found among the Duke of Ormonde's Papers* (2 v., London).

COATE, MARY (ed.). 1945. *The Letter-Book of John Viscount Mordaunt, 1658–1660* (London).

COBBETT, WILLIAM. 1806–1820. *Parliamentary History of England* (36 v., London).

FIRTH, C. H. (ed.). 1891–1894. *The Clarke Papers* (4 v., London).

—— 1895. "A Letter from Lord Saye and Sele to Lord Wharton, 29 December 1657." *English Historical Review* **10**: pp. 106–107.

GARDINER, SAMUEL R. (ed.). 1893. "Draft by Sir Richard Hyde of a Declaration to be Issued by Charles II in 1649." *English Historical Review* **8**: pp. 304–305.

—— 1958. *The Constitutional Documents of the Puritan Revolution, 1625–1660* (3rd ed., Oxford).

GREEN, MARY ANNE EVERETT (ed.). 1861–1886. *Calendar of State Papers, Domestic Series, 1654–1662* (8 v., London).

GROSART, ALEXANDER B. (ed.). 1872–1875. *The Complete Works in Verse and Prose of Andrew Marvell, M. P.* (4 v., London).

HEYWOOD, OLIVER. 1881–1883. *The Rev. Oliver Heywood, B. A., 1630–1702; His Autobiography, Diaries, Anecdote and Event Books.* Edited by J. Horsfall Turner (4 v., Brighouse and Bingley).

HISTORICAL MANUSCRIPTS COMMISSION. 1872. *Third Report* (London).

—— 1876. *Fifth Report* (London).

—— 1878. *Seventh Report* (London).

—— 1887. *Tenth Report* (London).

—— 1890. *The Manuscripts of S. H. Le Fleming* . . . (London).

—— 1894. *Fourteenth Report, Appendix, Part II, The Manuscripts of His Grace the Duke of Portland* (4 v., London).

—— 1899. *The Manuscripts of J. M. Heathcote* . . . (London).

—— 1899–1926. *Report on the Manuscripts of the Duke of Buccleuch and Queensberry* . . . (3 v., London).

—— 1899. *Report on the Manuscripts of F. W. Leyborne-Popham* . . . (London).

—— 1902–1920. *Calendar of the Manuscripts of the Marquess of Ormonde, New Series* (8 v., London).

—— 1907. *Calendar of the Manuscripts of the Marquis of Bath* . . . (2 v., London).

—— 1928–1947. *Report on the Manuscripts of the late Reginald Rawdon Hastings* (4 v., London).

HOUSE OF COMMONS. *Journals of the House of Commons.*

HOUSE OF LORDS. *Journals of the House of Lords.*

HYDE, EDWARD, Earl of Clarendon. 1759. *The Life of Edward Earl of Clarendon* . . . (3 v., Oxford).

—— 1888. *The History of the Rebellion and Civil Wars in England begun in the Year 1641.* Edited by W. Dunn Macray (6 v., Oxford).

JACKSON, CHARLES (ed.). 1877. "The Life of Master John Shaw." *Yorkshire Diaries and Autobiographies in the Seventeenth and Eighteenth Centuries* (London).

JOHNSTON, SIR ARCHIBALD. 1940. *Diary of Sir Archibald Johnston of Wariston, 1655–1660.* Edited by James D. Ogilvie (Edinburgh).

JOSSELIN, RALPH. 1908. *The Diary of the Rev. Ralph Josselin, 1616–1683.* Edited by E. Hockliffe (London).

LUDLOW, EDMUND. 1894. *The Memoirs of Edmund Ludlow* . . . . Edited by C. H. Firth (2 v., Oxford).

MACRAY, W. D. (ed.). 1896. *Notes Which Passed at Meetings of the Privy Council Between Charles II and the Earl of Clarendon, 1660–1667* . . . (London).

MARTINDALE, ADAM. 1845. *The Life of Adam Martindale, written by Himself.* Edited by Richard Parkinson (Manchester).

MASSACHUSETTS HISTORICAL SOCIETY. 1868. *The Mather Papers* (Boston).

NEWCOMBE, HENRY. 1849. *The Diary of the Rev. Henry Newcombe* . . . . Edited by Thomas Heywood (Manchester).

—— 1852. *The Autobiography of Henry Newcombe . . . .* Edited by Richard Parkinson (2 v., Manchester).

OGLE, O., W. H. BLISS, W. D. MACRAY, and F. J. ROUTLEDGE (eds.). 1869–1932. *Calendar of the Clarendon State Papers . . .* (4 v., Oxford).

ORNSBY, GEORGE (ed.). 1869–1872. *The Correspondence of John Cosin, D. D., Lord Bishop of Durham . . .* (2 v., London).

PEPYS, SAMUEL. 1923. *The Diary of Samuel Pepys.* Edited by Henry B. Wheatley (8 v., London).

POWICKE, FREDERICK J. (ed.). 1922. "Eleven Letters of John Second Earl of Lauderdale (and first Duke), 1616–1682, to the Rev. Richard Baxter (1615–1691)." *Bulletin of the John Rylands Library* 7: pp. 73–105.

—— 1931. "Some Unpublished Correspondence of the Rev. Richard Baxter and the Rev. John Eliot, 'The Apostle to the American Indians,' 1656–1682." *Bulletin of the John Rylands Library* 15: pp. 138–176, 442–466.

RUTT, JOHN TOWILL (ed.). 1828. *Diary of Thomas Burton . . .* (4 v., London).

SCHLATTER, RICHARD (ed.). 1957. *Richard Baxter and Puritan Politics* (New Brunswick, N. J.).

SCROPE, R., and T. MONKHOUSE (eds.). 1767–1786. *State Papers Collected by Edward, Earl of Clarendon* (3 v., Oxford).

SHAW, WILLIAM A. (ed.). 1890–1891. *Minutes of the Manchester Presbyterian Classis* (3 v., Manchester).

SKINNER, THOMAS. 1724. *Life of General Monck, late Duke of Albemarle.* Edited by W. Webster (Dublin).

TOWNSHEND, HENRY. 1915–1920. *Diary of Henry Townshend of Elmley Lovett, 1640–1663.* Edited by J. W. Willis Bund (2 v., Worcester).

TREVELYAN, SIR WALTER CALVERLEY, and SIR CHARLES EDWARD TREVELYAN (eds.). 1872. *The Trevelyan Papers* (London).

WARNER, SIR GEORGE F. (ed.). 1920. *The Nicholas Papers . . .* (4 v., London).

WHITELOCK, BULSTRODE. 1853. *Memorials of English Affairs* (4 v., Oxford).

WILLIAMS, J. B. (ed.). 1835. *Memorials of . . . Sir Matthew Hale . . .* (London).

Books, Broadsides, and Pamphlets, 1643–1679

[ANNESLEY, ARTHUR ?]. 1659. *England's Confusion: Or a True and Impartial Relation of the late Traverses of State in England . . .* (London).

ANONYMOUS. 1651. *Mr. Love's Case* (London).

—— 1654. *The Copy of a Letter sent out of Wiltshire to a Gentleman in London . . .* (London).

—— 1659. *The Censures of the Church Revived . . .* (London).

—— 1659. *An Express from the Knights and Gentlemen now engaged with Sir George Booth . . .* (n. p.).

—— 1659. *A Faithfull Searching Home Word . . .* (n.p.).

—— 1659. *An Invocation to the Officers of the Army . . . in a Letter Presented to them on Wednesday 20 April 1659* (London).

—— 1659. *Twelve Seasonable Quaeries Proposed to all True Zealous Protestants and English Free-men . . .* (n. p.).

—— 1660. *The Anatomy of Dr. Gauden's Idolized Non-sence and Blasphemy, in his Pretended Analysis . . .* (London).

—— 1660. *Certain Considerations . . . Presented to the Freeholders . . . to Regulate their Elections . . .* (London).

—— 1660. *Complaints Concerning Corruptions and Grievances in Church-Government* (n. p.).

—— 1660. *Council Humbly Propounded for the speedy Settlement of these long Disturbed Nations . . .* (London).

—— 1660. *A Declaration of the Nobility and Gentry that adhered to the late King, now residing in and about the City of London* (London).

—— 1660. *A Declaration of the Presbiterians; Concerning his Maiesties Royal Person, And the Government of the Church of England . . .* (London).

—— 1660. *Englands Directions for Members Elections* (n. p.).

—— 1660. *Expedients for Publique Peace. Shewing the Necessity of a National Union . . .* (n. p.).

—— 1660. *An Extract of a Letter from York, dated the 31. of Decemb. 1659. concerning the Lord Fairfax's Raising that County in Arms . . .* (London).

—— 1660. *A Form of Prayer with Thanksgiving to be used on 28 June 1660 for his Majesty's Happy Return* (London).

—— 1660. *A Happy Handfull, Or Green Hopes in the Blade; in order to a Harvest, of the Several Shires, humbly Petitioning, or heartily Declaring for Peace* (London).

—— 1660. *A second Seasonable Speech made by an Honourable Member of the House of Commons, demonstrating the Necessity of the Kings Restauration by this present Parliament* (London).

—— 1660. *Things Just and Necessary, which the Parliament Must do if ever they would Prosper* (n. p.).

—— 1660. *The Army's Declaration: Being a True Alarum in Answer to a False and Fiery one . . .* (n. p.).

BAXTER, RICHARD. 1653. *Christian Concord . . .* (London).

[——] 1653. *The Worcester-Shire Petition . . . Defended . . .* (London).

—— 1655. *Humble Advice . . .* (London).

—— 1658. *Confirmation and Restauration . . .* (London).

—— 1658. *The Judgement and Advice of the Assembly of the Associated Ministers of Worcester-Shire . . .* (London).

—— 1659. *Five Disputations of Church-Government, and Worship* (London).

—— 1659. *A Holy Commonwealth . . .* (London).

—— 1659. *A Key for Catholicks . . .* (London).

—— 1660. *Catholick Unity: Or the only way to bring us all to be of one Religion* (London).

—— 1660. *The True Catholick, and Catholick Church Described . . .* (London).

BERNARD, NICHOLAS. 1656. *The Reduction of Episcopacy unto the Form of Synodical Government by Dr. James Ussher* (London).

—— [1660]. *A Letter of Dr. Bernards to a Friend of His at Court* [London].

BOLDE, THOMAS. 1660. *Rhetorick Restrained . . .* (London).

BOOTH, SIR GEORGE. 1659. *A Letter from Sir George Booth to a friend of his . . .* (n. p.).

BRISTOL, APPRENTICES. 1660. *A Letter of the Apprentices of the City of Bristol to the Honourable City of London . . .* (London).

BURGESS, CORNELIUS. 1649. *A Vindication of the Ministers of the Gospel, in and about London . . .* (London).

[——]. 1660. *Reasons Shewing the Necessity of Reformation . . .* (London).

CASE, THOMAS. 1658. *Eliah's Abatement: Or, Corruption in the Saints . . .* (London).

CAWDRY, DANIEL. 1658. *The Account Audited and Discounted . . .* (London).

CHAMBERS, HUMPHREY, and others. 1654. *An Apology for the Ministers of the County of Wilts . . .* (London).

CLARKE, SAMUEL. 1659. *Golden Apples . . .* (London).

COLLINGS, JOHN. 1651. *Vindiciae Ministerii Evangelici . . .* (London).

CORNELIUS, PETER. 1659. *The Way to the Peace and Settlement of these Nations . . .* (London).

CORNISH GENTRY 1660. *To the Right Worshipful our Worthy Patriots of our County of Cornwall, Assembled at Truroe the 27th of December, Anno., 1659 . . .* (n. p.).

CROFTON, ZACHARY. 1660. *. . . The Fastning of St. Peters Fetters . . .* (London).

—— 1660. *Faelix scelus, Querela piorum, et Auscultatio Divina . . .* (London).

—— 1661. *Berith Anti-Baal, Or, Zach. Croftons Appearance before the Prelate-Justice of Peace* . . . (London).

—— 1661. *A Serious Review of Presbyters Reordination* . . . (London).

CUMBERLAND AND WESTMORLAND ASSOCIATION. 1656. *The Agreement of the Associated Ministers and Churches of the Counties of Cumberland and Westmorland* (London).

D., I. 1660. *The History of His Sacred Majesty Charles the II* . . . (London).

DEVONSHIRE GENTRY. 1660. *A Letter from Exeter, Advertizing the State of Affairs there* . . . (London).

DOUCH, JOHN. 1660. *Englands Jubilee* . . . (London).

DURY, JOHN. 1648. *A Peace-Maker without Partiality and Hypocrisie. Or the Gospel-way to make up the present breaches of Brotherhood, and heale the divisions* . . . (London).

FAIRFAX, THOMAS LORD. 1660. *The Declaration of Thomas, Lord Fairfax, and the rest of the Lords, Knights, Esquires, Citizens, Ministers and Freeholders of the County and City of York* (London).

FIRMIN, GILES. 1659. *Tythes Vindicated from Anti-Christianisme and Oppression* . . . (London).

—— 1660. *Presbyterical Ordination Vindicated* . . . (London).

—— 1661. *The Liturgical Considerator Considered* . . . (London).

GAILHARD, JOHN. 1660. *The Controversy between Episcopacy and Presbytery Stated and Discussed* (London).

GAUDEN, JOHN. 1660. *. . . The Loosing of St. Peters Bonds* . . . (London).

—— 1660. *. . . Slight Healers of Publick Hurts Set forth in a Sermon Preached in St. Pauls Church, London* . . . (London).

—— 1660. *A Sermon Preached . . . at the Funeral of . . . Dr. Brownrig late Lord Bishop of Exeter* . . . (London).

—— 1661. *Considerations Touching the Liturgy of the Church of England* . . . (London).

[GEE, EDWARD] 1650. *A Plea for Non-Scribers* . . . (n. p.).

[HARRINGTON, JAMES] 1659. *A Proposition in order to the Proposing of a Commonwealth or Democracie* (n. p.).

[HAY, JAMES] 1655. *Collonel James Hays Speech to the Parliament upon the Debate concerning Toleration* . . . (n. p.).

HUDSON, SAMUEL. 1658. *A Vindication of the Essence and Unity of the Church-Catholick Visible* . . . (London).

[HYDE, EDWARD, Earl of Clarendon]. [1663]. *Second Thoughts; or the Case of Limited Toleration, stated according to the present Exigence of Affairs in Church and State* [London].

KEME, SAMUEL. 1660. *King Solomon's Infallible Expedient for Three Kingdoms Settlement* . . . (London).

L., S. 1659. *A Letter to the Right Honorable the Lord Lambert* . . . (n. p.).

LAWRENCE, GEORGE. 1658. *Peplum Olivarii* . . . (London).

L'ESTRANGE, R. S. 1660. *A Necessary and Seasonable Caution, concerning Elections* (n. p.).

—— 1666. *L'Estrange His Apology* . . . (London).

[LONDON PROVINCIAL ASSEMBLY]. 1648. *A Testimony to the Truth of Jesus Christ, and to Our Solemn League and Covenant* . . . (London).

[——] 1649. *A Serious and Faithfull Representation of the Judgements of Ministers of the Gospel within the Province of London* . . . (London).

[——] 1650. *A Vindication of the Presbyteriall-Government, and Ministry* . . . (London).

[——] 1654. *Jus Divinum Ministerii Evangelici* . . . (London).

[——] 1654. *Jus Divinum Regiminis Ecclesiastici* . . . (London).

LOVE, CHRISTOPHER. 1651. *A Cleare and Necessary Vindication of . . . Christopher Love* . . . (London).

MARSHALL, STEPHEN. 1653. *A Sermon Preached . . . on Easter Monday April 1652* . . . (London).

MEADE, MATTHEW. 1660. *Spiritual Wisdom improved against Temptation* . . . (London).

MONCK, GEORGE. 1660. *A Letter from his Excellencie the Lord General Monck and the Officers under his Command to the Parliament, in the Name of Themselves, and the Souldiers under Them* (London).

—— 1660. *A Letter of General George Monck's, dated at Leicester 23 Jan. and directed unto Mr. Rolle* . . . (London).

—— 1660. *The Lord General Monck His Speech Delivered by Him in the Parliament on Munday, Feb. 6. 1659* (London).

—— 1660. *The Speech and Declaration of His Excellency the Lord General Monck delivered at White-hall upon Tuesday the 21. of February 1659* . . . (London).

MOSSOM, ROBERT. 1660. *An Apology in the behalf of the Sequestred Clergy; Presented to the High Court of Parliament* (London).

MOULIN, LEWIS DU. 1659. *Proposals and Reasons* . . . (London).

OWEN, JOHN. 1656. *God's Work in Founding Zion* . . . . *A Sermon preached* . . . (Oxford).

POOLE, MATTHEW. 1660. *Evangelical Worship is Spiritual Worship* . . . (London).

PRYNNE, WILLIAM. 1643. *The Soveraigne Power of Parliaments and Kingdoms* . . . (London).

[——] 1657. *King Richard the Third Revived* . . . (London).

[——] 1659. *An Answer to a Proposition in order to the proposing of a Commonwealth or Democracy* (London).

[——] 1659. *A Brief Narrative* . . . (London).

—— 1659. *The Re-publicans and others spurious Good Old Cause, briefly and truly Anatomized* . . . (n. p.).

P[RYNNE], W[ILLIAM]. 1659. *Six Important Quaeres, Propounded to the Re-sitting Rump of the Long Parliament* . . . (n. p.).

—— 1659. *Ten Considerable Quaeries concerning Tithes* . . . (London).

—— 1659. *A True and perfect Narrative* . . . (n. p.).

[——] 1659. *The true Good Old Cause rightly stated, and the False un-cased* (n. p.).

—— 1660. *The Case of the old Secured, Secluded, and Excluded Members, Briefly and truly Stated* . . . (London).

[——] 1660. *Seasonable and Healing Instructions Humbly Tendered* . . . (n. p.).

[——] 1660. *Seven Additional Quaeres in behalf of the secluded Members* . . . (n. p.).

—— 1660. *The Unbishoping of Timothy and Titus, and of the Angel of the Church of Ephesus* (2nd ed., London).

—— 1665–1670. *An Exact Chronological Vindication and Historical Demonstration of Our . . . King's Supreme Ecclesiastical Jurisdiction* . . . (London).

[REYNOLDS, EDWARD]. 1650. *The Humble Proposals of Sundry Learned and Pious Divines within this Kingdome* . . . (London).

—— 1657. *The Peace of Jerusalem; a Sermon preached in the Parliament-House* . . . (London).

—— 1659. *The Brand Pluck'd out of the Fire* . . . (London).

—— 1659. *The Misery of a Deserted People* . . . (London).

—— 1660. *The Author and Subject of Healing in the Church* . . . (London).

—— 1660. *Divine Efficacy without Humane Power* . . . (London).

—— 1660. *The Wall & Glory of Jerusalem* . . . (London).

—— 1678–1679. *The Works of the Right Reverend Father in God, Edward Reynolds, D. D., Late Lord Bishop of Norwich* (2 pts., London).

REYNOLDS, EDWARD, and others. 1660. *A Seasonable Exhortation of Sundry Ministers in London to the People of their Respective Congregations* (London).

SUDBURY, JOHN. 1660. *A Sermon Preached at the Consecration of . . . Gilbert Lord Bishop of London* . . . (London).

T., D. 1659. *Irenicum; Or, An Essay Towards a Brotherly Peace & Union, Between those of the Congregational and Presbyterian Way* . . . . *by Disciplus de Tempore Junior* [pseud.] (London).

TOMBES, JOHN. 1660. *A Supplement to the Serious considera-tion of the Oath of the Kings Supremacy* (London).

TREV[OR], J[OHN]. 1660. *The fair Dealer: Or, a Modest Answer to the Sober Letter of His Excellency, the Lord General Monck . . .* (London).

VINES, RICHARD. 1656. *Obedience to Magistrates, Both Su-preme and Subordinate . . .* (London).

WALKER, CLEMENT. 1661. *The Compleat History of Independ-ency* (London).

WICKINS, WILLIAM. 1660. *The Kingdom's Remembrancer . . .* (London).

[WORCESTERSHIRE]. 1652. *The Humble Petition of Many Thousands, Gentlemen, Freeholders, and Others, of the County of Worcester . . .* (London).

YORKSHIRE GENTRY. 1660. *A Letter and Declaration of the Nobility and Gentry of the County of York, to His Excellency the Lord Generall Monck* (London).

YOUNGER, WILLIAM. 1660. *A Brief View of the late troubles and confusions in England . . .* (London).

Contemporary News Journals

The Faithfull Scout, 1659, No. 4.
The Loyall Scout, 1659, Nos. 13, 14, 15, 16.
Mercurius Politicus, 1658, No. 443; 1660, No. 603.
Mercurius Publicus, 1660, No. 22; 1662, No. 35.
The Publick Intelligencer, 1658, No. 147; 1659, No. 188; 1660, No. 214.
The Weekly Intelligencer, 1659, Nos. 13, 23.
The Weekly Post, 1659, Nos. 13, 14.

SECONDARY MATERIALS

Books

BOSHER, ROBERT S. 1951. *The Making of the Restoration Settlement: The Influence of the Laudians, 1649–1662* (West-minster).

BROWN, LOUISE FARGO. 1933. *The First Earl of Shaftesbury* (New York and London).

CARTE, THOMAS. 1735–1736. *An History of the Life of James Duke of Ormonde, from his Birth in 1610, to his Death in 1688* (3 v., London).

CHRISTIE, W. D. 1871. *A Life of Anthony Ashley Cooper, First Earl of Shaftesbury, 1621–1683* (2 v., London and New York).

COATE, MARY. 1933. *Cornwall in the Great Civil War and Interregnum, 1642–1660: A Social and Political Study* (Ox-ford).

DAVIES, GODFREY. 1949. *The Early Stuarts, 1603–1660* (Ox-ford).

—— 1955. *The Restoration of Charles II, 1658–1660* (San Marino).

ECHARD, LAURENCE. 1707–1718. *The History of England* (3 v., London).

FEILING, KEITH. 1924. *A History of the Tory Party, 1640–1714* (Oxford).

FIRTH, CHARLES HARDING. 1909. *The Last Years of the Pro-tectorate, 1656–1658* (2 v., London and New York).

GARDINER, SAMUEL RAWSON. 1901. *History of the Great Civil War, 1642–1649* (4 v., New York).

—— 1905. *History of the Commonwealth and Protectorate, 1649–1656* (4 v., London).

GUIZOT, M. 1866. *Monk: Or the Fall of the Republic and the Restoration of the Monarchy in England, in 1660.* Translated by Andrew R. Scoble (London).

HARRIS, F. R. 1912. *The Life of Edward Montagu, K. G., First Earl of Sandwich, 1625–1672* (2 v., London).

KIRBY, ETHYN WILLIAMS. 1931. *William Prynne: A Study in Puritanism* (Cambridge, Mass.).

LINGARD, JOHN. 1883. *The History of England, from the First Invasion by the Romans to the Accession of William and Mary in 1688* (10 v., Boston).

LISTER, T. H. 1837–1838. *Life and Administration of Edward, First Earl of Clarendon* (3 v., London).

MASSON, DAVID. 1859–1894. *The Life of John Milton* (7 v., London).

MATTHEWS, A. G. 1934. *Calamy Revised, Being a Revision of Edmund Calamy's Account of the Ministers and Others Ejected and Silenced, 1660–1662* (Oxford).

OGG, DAVID. 1934. *England in the Reign of Charles II* (2 v., Oxford).

POWICKE, FREDERICK J. 1924. *A Life of the Reverend Richard Baxter, 1615–1691* (London).

RANKE, LEOPOLD VON. 1875. *A History of England Principally in the Seventeenth Centry* (6 v., Oxford).

ROUTLEDGE, F. J. 1953. *England and the Treaty of the Pyre-nees* (Liverpool).

SHAW, WILLIAM A. 1900. *A History of the English Church during the Civil Wars and under the Commonwealth, 1640–1660* (2 v., London).

STOUGHTON, JOHN. 1881. *History of Religion in England from the Opening of the Long Parliament to 1850* (8 v., London).

WODROW, ROBERT. 1722. *The History of the Sufferings of the Church of Scotland, from the Restauration to the Revolution* (2 v., Edinburgh).

Articles

ABBOTT, WILBUR C. 1906. "The Long Parliament of Charles II." *English Historical Review* 21: pp. 21–56, 254–285.

—— 1909. "English Conspiracy and Dissent, 1660–1674." *American Historical Review* 14: pp. 503–528, 696–722.

AIRY, OSMUND. 1886. "Notes on the Reign of Charles II." *British Quarterly Review* 77: pp. 332–333.

BROWN, LOUISE FARGO. 1907. "The Religious Factors in the Convention Parliament." *English Historical Review* 22: pp. 51–63.

—— 1941. "The Reconcilers and the Restoration, 1660–1662." *Essays in Modern English History in Honor of Wilbur Cortez Abbott* (Cambridge, Mass.).

COATE, MARY. 1918. "William Morice and the Restoration of Charles II." *English Historical Review* 33: pp. 367–377.

COLLIGAN, J. HAY. 1927. "The Provincial Meeting of Cumber-land and Westmorland." *Congregational Historical Society Transactions* 4: pp. 159–168.

DAVIES, GODFREY. 1935. "The Army and the Downfall of Richard Cromwell." *Huntington Library Bulletin* 7: pp. 131–167.

—— 1948. "The Election of Richard Cromwell's Parliament, 1658–1659." *English Historical Review* 43: pp. 488–501.

—— 1952. "The General Election of 1660." *Huntington Li-brary Quarterly* 15: pp. 211–235.

DODD, J. A. 1895. "Troubles in a City Parish under the Pro-tectorate." *English Historical Review* 10: pp. 41–54.

HEXTER, J. H. 1938. "The Problem of the Presbyterian Inde-pendents." *American Historical Review* 44: pp. 29–49.

MUSKERJEE, H. N. 1934. "Election for the Convention and Cavalier Parliaments." *Notes and Queries* 166: pp. 398–403, 417–421.

ROBBINS, CAROLINE. 1951. "Seymour Bowman, Esq., M. P., Diarist of the Convention, 1660." *Notes and Queries* 183: pp. 56–59.

THIRSK, JOAN. 1954. "The Restoration Land Settlement." *Journal of Modern History* 26: pp. 315–328.

MEMOIRS

OF THE

AMERICAN PHILOSOPHICAL SOCIETY

———

TRANSACTIONS

OF THE

AMERICAN PHILOSOPHICAL SOCIETY